LAND OF BLUE SHADOWS

MOUNTAIN LIFE IN VERSE & VIEW

GEORGE ELLISON

Artwork by Elizabeth Ellison | Photography by Quintin Ellison

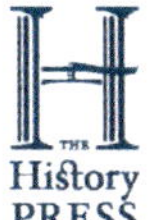

Published by The History Press
An imprint of Arcadia Publishing
Charleston, SC
www.historypress.com

First published 2025

Manufactured in the United States

ISBN 9781467157971

Library of Congress Control Number: 2025933729

To George Robert Ellison Jr., wordsmith, naturalist, football player, teacher, partner and father. This is the book that we promised you.

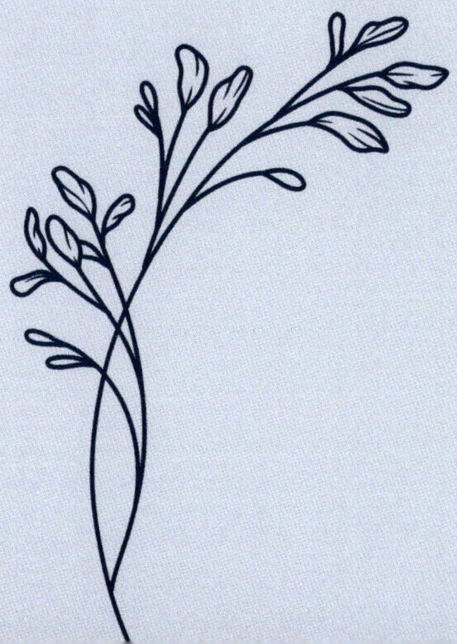

CONTENTS

PREFACE

A local tourism official once told me that she has given up explaining to would-be visitors that because nature is unpredictable, she cannot predict when "peak color" will occur in the mountains. Worn down by years of insistence, she now randomly picks a day in October, declares it peak color and tells the leaf lookers to pack up and come then.

It's understandable why visitors flock here each fall. Autumn is indeed a wonderful time in the mountains of North Carolina, and it is in mid-October—at peak color—that I'm writing this.

Who does not welcome the mix of crisp nights and summer-like, still-languid days touched with a hint of briskness; the honking of Canada geese as they fly overhead in their tight "V" bomber formations; the leaves, forever falling and twirling their way to the ground, sometimes dallied by a brief breeze, then dropped again to tumble to earth; those vibrant colors—yellow, different greens and both muted and bright reds, all splashed across the mountainsides seemingly willy-nilly, but in actuality, in perfect, one-of-a-kind and never-to-be-repeated patterns.

I believe autumn is best, however, when you also experience the other three seasons. It pays to be in the mountains for all four—not just year after year, but decade after decade and, if you are lucky, generation after generation.

An Appalachian spring in Western North Carolina features fresh green shoots and the annual search for ephemeral flowers. Summer moves in, bringing with it hot, humid weather and mountains cloaked in dense jungles of verdant green. In winter, once again you see the bones of the mountains: exposed ridge lines, switchbacks, small coves and large valleys.

If my father were still alive and writing this preface, he would, about now, devote a few paragraphs to describing the geography of this region. People who were enrolled in his workshops or have read his and my mother's books sometimes quote him to me, saying, "To know who you are, you need to know where you are."

So, where are we?

I lack my father's expertise. He quite possibly might have started with an explanation of plate tectonics and dinosaurs (the latter is an exaggeration, but the bit about plate tectonics is not). But I am me and not my father, so in my own words:

Big picture, this book is about the Southern Appalachians, which wend from Pennsylvania into Georgia.

Still smaller, this book is about the southern portion of this great mountain chain.

Smaller still, in this book my father, mother and I describe in our own ways—through poems, prose, photos and paintings—the mountains of North Carolina and, more specifically, one cove in Swain County that is bordered on three sides by Great Smoky Mountains National Park. In the cove is a creek, ramshackle barn, random fencing, a little house, an old horse and a German shorthaired pointer.

As a child I loved to read, and I loved to play in our woods. I'd walk home from the bus stop after school with my sister and brother and then often disappear on my own, eager to suss out what might have changed from the day before.

It could be a box turtle to pick up and examine. Is the underside of the shell curved? If so, you know it's a male. Maybe I'd spy a fence lizard, sunning on a rock and staring at me with tiny, beady, brownish eyes. Perhaps I'd flush a grouse, and then my heart would pound just as hard and fast as these birds' wings flap in panicked flight.

Without conscious effort, during those years in our cove and surrounding woods, I mentally mapped the property. Today, when walking the familiar trails, I still note childhood landmarks.

There is the small set of caves on the mountainside across the creek and above an old buckeye tree. I've never found the nerve to crawl inside those caves. Who knows what lurks in the dark and probably not-so-deep depths?

For years, you entered the cove through a sagging gate beside the buckeye tree. It served as a small family joke: We, too, lived in a gated community, just like those more well-heeled move-ins who reside behind password-controlled electronic entrances.

Alongside the road lies a dry pine ridge with interesting rock formations. Then, a path that slowly ascends into an adjoining hollow. Once, when I was twelve or so, my then eight-year-old brother and I set up camp in this hollow. We ran home at dusk, freaked out by the noise of the wind and creaking trees and scraping branches.

High above our cove tower two ridges. These are the boundary lines between us and the national park. On the other side of the cove, a third park boundary exists.

One time only do I remember meeting someone official on the trails. Two uniform-clad, assault rifle–toting men suddenly appeared one day, startling me as I walked the high ridge. I don't know what or who they were hunting—bear poachers, maybe, or wild ginseng thieves? I nodded, they nodded and we went our respective ways.

Because of the national park, my playground theoretically extended an additional 522,419 acres. I didn't explore much beyond our property's boundaries, however. There are cliff drop-offs from the ridges to Fontana Lake and, on the other side, a steep and perilous descent to Peachtree Creek.

"Our" creek, Lands Creek, and the land around it, provided enough space for endless adventures, both as a child and as an adult.

My parents and I, along with my siblings for some of those years, experienced the change of seasons on this land for more than five decades. While my mother and I continue to watch and marvel, my father is gone. He died in February 2023.

My father finished his poems before his death. He worked on them in one way or another for as many years as we have lived beside Lands Creek.

This book is perhaps less than it would have been if he'd been with us to the publishing end, but Mom and I have made our own sincere, honest efforts to make it just as good as we can. I think he would have liked the result.

—Quintin Ellison

Introduction

BETWEEN HERE AND THERE

George was the essence of "being present." Whether sitting at his kitchen table studying a dark-eyed junco foraging under his feeder or hiking the well-worn path on Lands Creek to show me a painted trillium, George was ***in*** the natural world. He could hear and see things most mere mortals could not. Yet George did not let us languish in our ignorance. He was a patient teacher who helped us see the natural world through his writing.

Nature infuses George's poetry, as does "all of the common/everyday little things/that can make of this/life a holy venture." In the opening poem in this collection, George urges us not to overlook the familiar, but instead to experience it in a new light. Does the poet have a persona, or is the "I" in the poems the George we know? The poetry feels intimate. He is "the surveyor/of the boundaries" in his scenes. He is the one sitting "on the porch with the dogs & watch[ing] the creek go by...while the same old thoughts arise then fade but keep on coming back again & again." He's sitting with me every time I visit Lands Creek and watch it "on its long journey to the Gulf of Mexico."

We were an unlikely pair—he, a writer and naturalist in North Carolina, and I, a librarian living in upstate New York. We shared a passion for Horace Kephart and for the Smokies; our book, *Back of Beyond: A Horace Kephart Biography*, won the Thomas Wolfe Memorial Literary Award. Our writing, like our storytelling, began to mesh, so much so that we had a hard time discerning who wrote which sentence. I learned a great deal from George—how to be a better writer, how to be more present in the woods. I am still wrestling with fern morphology, but I wonder if George wrote "Predisposition" to help me? "Fiddleheads unfurl from darkness/into predisposed patterns of leaves/called fronds, either simple or pinnate."

George was a storyteller. He didn't lecture or make declarations; he simply wove mesmerizing stories to deepen our understanding. This was true whether he was writing about Kephart's search for a "back of beyond" or patiently explaining pinnae to students in a workshop at Smoky Mountain Field School.

His poetry often resembled his stories. In "View from a Cemetery: A Fantasy," the poet presides over the scene, describing all he witnesses from his hilltop perch in the cemetery. We hear the train whistle and watch the tourists waving to their friends from the Great Smoky Mountains Railroad; we follow the flock of pigeons circling the bridge over the Tuckaseigee before landing atop the golden cupola of the courthouse. When the wind shifts, the poet gets lost in a reverie and takes us to Greece, where we meet some high priestesses at the oracle of Dodona who study the rustlings of the sacred oak tree and the flights of pigeons to inform their prophecies. Hold my hand and listen to the wind, the oracular poet invites us. "Whenever you are lonely and far from home/seek out a local burying ground with sunken graves & careworn markers," and listen to the murmur of the oak leaves. The last words the prophet of Bryson City shouts are, "STAY TRUE/TO THE/DREAMS OF/YOUR YOUTH."

The shriek of a blue jay rouses the poet from his trance. He looks down on Bryson City to find the excursion train "still bound on its journey to nowhere," the oak leaves silent and the pigeons tucked back under the bridge. The narrative poem, a love song to his adopted town, also reflects George's broad learning and wild imagination.

George died on February 19, 2023, while this collection, *Land of Blue Shadows*, was being assembled. Having been diagnosed years ago with Parkinson's disease, he never complained, even as the disease stole his agility and mobility. Although his explorations became more limited after he was forced to give up hiking and then driving, his world never contracted. George just went deeper and became more intimate with his binoculars, his hand lens and his inquisitive mind.

Both George and my husband died within one year, a double loss of two wonderful men. In the poem "Here & There," dedicated to the novelist David Joy, the last stanza offers some comfort about death to the poet and this reader:

> Light fills the void
> between here & there
> hovering over the living
> & the dead, which is, as
> you say, almost no distance at all.

—Janet McCue

POEMS
BY GEORGE ELLISON

Excerpt from Wordsworth's "Tintern Abbey"

And I have felt
A presence that disturbs me with the joy
Of elevated thoughts; a sense sublime
Of something far more deeply interfused,
Whose dwelling is the light of setting suns,
And the round ocean and the living air,
And the blue sky, and in the mind of man:
A motion and a spirit, that impels
All thinking things, all objects of all thought,
And rolls through all things. Therefore am I still
A lover of the meadows and the woods
And mountains; and of all that we behold
From this green earth; of all the mighty world
Of eye, and ear,—both what they half create,
And what perceive; well pleased to recognize
In nature and the language of the sense
The anchor of my purest thoughts, the nurse,
The guide, the guardian of my heart, and soul
Of all my moral being.

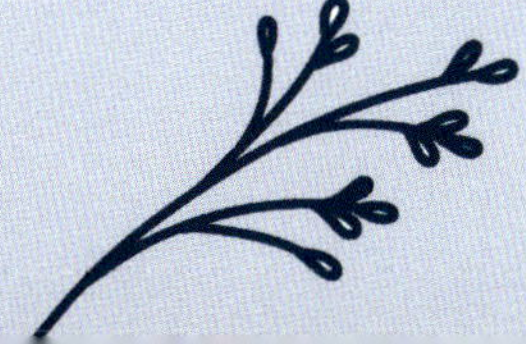

1.

HOLY VENTURES

I am the surveyor
of boundaries
that divide
dark & light
ridge & sky
past & present
dream & reality
here in the land
of stout-hearted
men & women.

Within those confines
familiar sights & sounds
should not be avoided:
old women & men
singing & dancing;
shining rivers & dark forests;
dragonflies & skinks;
toads & all of the everyday
little things that can make
of this life a holy
venture.

But should events
darken blue skies
(as they always will)
we can pass through
the gate with the
wrought-iron rose
& transcend the realm
of fallen angels.

That said mostly I just sit here on the porch
with the dogs & watch the creek go by on
its journey to the Gulf of Mexico while the
same old thoughts arise then fade but keep
on coming back again & again
like radio signals from afar
whispering my name.

2.

SHADOWS

The future might never
arrive & the present is hard
to grasp but the past is
always with us as a
presence in the marrow of
our bones, never seen
except as shadows lingering
in the corners of our eyes.

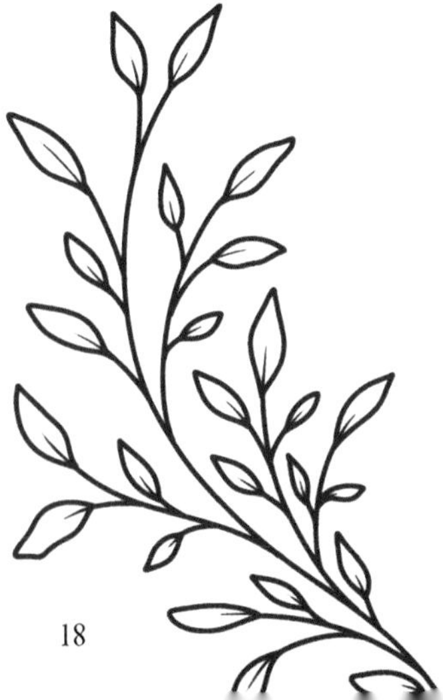

3.

SHIFTING DEPENDENCIES

The natural world is a web
of shifting dependencies.
All the strands are interrelated
to a greater or lesser degree.
But our comprehension of it
is fleeting & often unreliable.

This is because we, too, are a
part of things. Our perspectives
are limited...we are, as they say,
embedded...so that if we could
see the real world underlying the
veneer of everydayness it might
well differ in many ways from
what we had supposed.

4.

PREDISPOSITION

Fiddleheads unfurl from darkness
into predisposed patterns of leaves
called fronds, either simple or pinnate
or some variation thereof that
conform enough to be classified as
species, even though
a closer look reveals that no two
things are ever exactly alike...
nor should they be.

5.

INDIFFERENCE

Indifference provides the capacity to
hover above contradictions in the
manner of a kestrel riding an updraft
searching the ground far below for
movement knowing the perfect moment
to swoop is one that may never arise.

6.

IN THE BACK OF MY MIND

The cooler air cast a blanket of mist over the creek
that thinned to transparency as it skimmed lightly
over the grass in the meadow & dissolved in scrub
pine...a spectral visitation that I realized, too late,
was also forewarning.

In the blink of an eye clouds blotted sky.
Thunder rolled wave on wave as lightning
blazed downwardly in streaks that forked
then forked again, until the interconnected
tips exploded in fiery sequences & the
deluge reeked of fumes that lingered
in the stricken air for days.

Transfixed as if the lightning had pierced
fibrous marrow short-circuiting synapses,
I descended into the first of those steamy
un-mind-less-nesses wherein equilibrium
& memory are stymied & there can be
but errant return.

It was then that I began to view the world
anew from vistas in the back of my mind.

7.

CONSTELLATIONS

In a recurring dream that I find disquieting
I shuffle aimless along a misremembered
path that arcs upward beside a nameless
stream through a forest to a vista almost
always shrouded in mist, above which the
stars...when they can be seen...form
random patterns assigned meanings as if
they were cryptic messages from the dark
otherwise silent depths of the universe.

When awakened it is not difficult to return
with considerable relief to this green world
of shining rivers & bright tomorrows.

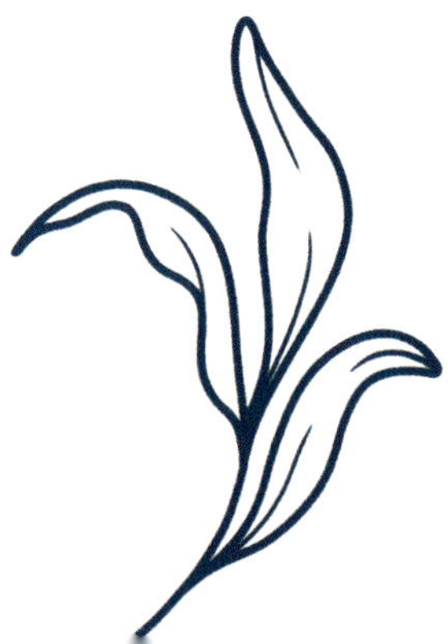

8.

VIEW FROM A CEMETERY: A FANTASY

By way of prelude the whistle of the
excursion train on the far side of the river
shrieked three times. From where I stood
in the graveyard on the knoll overlooking
Bryson City I could see passengers waving the
way travelers never do when
departing on a train that's going somewhere.

It was an eventful afternoon.
From my vantage point I watched a dog.
A hiker came out of Bojangles & gave him a biscuit.
He smiled the way dogs do as he watched her walk away.
Then he yawned wheeled counterclockwise as if chasing
his tail & lay down all curled up in the sun.

Twenty-six pigeons arose from under the
lower bridge where they roost & circled
the knoll on upwardly flexed wings the
way pigeons do before settling one-by-one
on the golden cupola atop the old
courthouse where the clock was for years
always reliably an hour ahead or an hour
behind depending on the season.

The blue-gray wind descended from high
country & skimmed over the Tuckaseigee
gathering moisture before passing through
the oak grove on the knoll where each tree
stood attentive with its branches outspread
over sunken graves that had settled &
silently intermingled generations ago.

Magnetized by water from the river the
oak leaves glowed as they had when the oracular
priestesses at Dodona first sang their prophesies
of the ever-after & a town official accused them
with madness & consorting with
priests with dirty feet.

The ladies readily acknowledged to being
habitually spellbound...which was
after all their job...but avoided the
part about the dirty feet.

They giggled & invited the official to a
party going on down in the basement of the
shrine. He declined but a blind poet readily
accepted & helped them finish a poem they had
been working on for many years.

Whenever you are lonely & far from home
seek out a local burying ground with sunken
graves & careworn markers over which tattered
oak leaves murmur so that if you listen carefully
you can hear the words they wrote while drinking
red wine with a poet somewhere long ago in a dusty corner
of ancient Greece:

You are awaiting the next vision?
Hold my hand & listen to the wind.
You are seeking the long way home?
If so you will travel across broad
water into lands where nothing will
be as it seems & you'll perish if you
fail to keep your wits about you &
practice indifference. Your journey
will be negated and your return
home will be empty unless you
always remember to:

STAY TRUE
TO THE DREAMS
OF YOUR YOUTH.

A blue jay's scream brought me back to earth.
I saw that the train was still bound on its journey
to nowhere...the pigeons had retired to their
roost under the bridge...the dog was sound asleep
by his wall...the oak leaves were silent & the clock
in the dome of the old courthouse overlooking town
says it's either going on or past time to go home.

9.

HERE & THERE

(In tribute to David Joy, author *Where All Light Tends to Go*)

You say it's a fierce white light
that fills the gaps & spaces
between here & there.

You say it shines down all around
illuminating the middle ground
between here & there.

Light fills the void
between here & there
hovering over the living
& the dead, which is, as
you say, almost no distance at all.

10.

UP ON EAGLE CREEK

Booted feet sought purchase in pebble
beds accumulated between the larger
boulders. Laurel limbs creaked as they
rubbed one against another in the
breeze that'd come up since I broke
camp in the dark to be home early.

Pausing midstream I watched an eddy
whirl like the blades on a windmill...
colors shifting from bluish gray to
pale green & back again.

Scanning the far side of the creek
my eyes returned to a vine-shrouded
overhang where he slowly emerged
in mind's eye.

Transfixed—as if in a waking
Dream—I placed my fingertips on
the surface of a boulder so as to
maintain my sense of equilibrium.

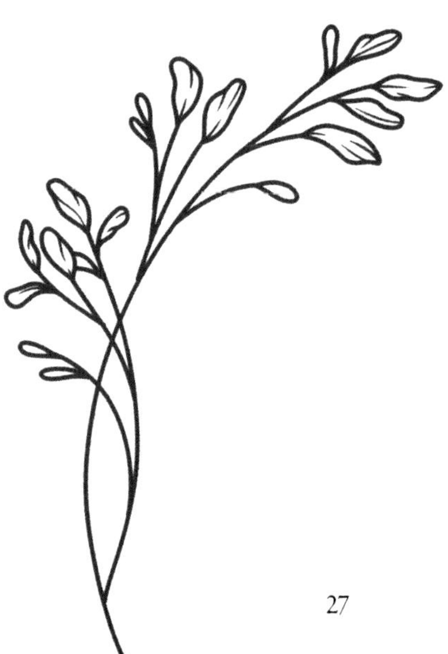

Suddenly without any apparent effort
he was moving with incalculable grace
...feet legs hips head synchronized as if
movement were music...to an opening on
the far bank. The sinuous dark-tipped tail
moved wand-like then froze in mid-air as
he stood perfectly still & perfectly quiet
so that everything...sky tree shrub rock
water...coalesced before it faded into the
forest shadows.

Water still whirled in the eddy.
Fingertips still rested
on stone. But there was an
empty place at the heart of
things now he was gone.

11.

EMPTINESS

From the Little Scaly over-
look above Blue Valley I often
watched in near trance as cloud
shadows drifted across the valley
floor & colors shift with each
change of light.

One evening with no other place to go
I sat with both legs dangling over the
void & watched the sun go down behind
the western horizon & the sky haze from
faded blue to yellow green before
congealing into a firm darkness
more purple than black.

The vast cauldron of stars overhead
& the sound of the wind in the twisted
branches of the dwarf white oaks on
the nearby rock dome were
heart-breaking.

In the well of my spine
the emptiness was strangely
compelling...one move &
I could be flying.

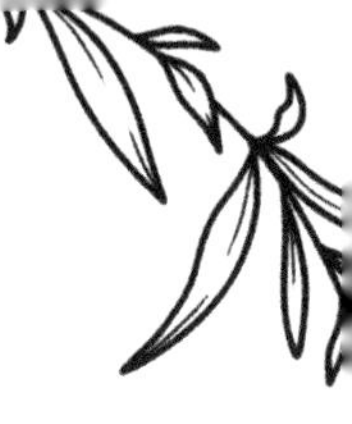

12.

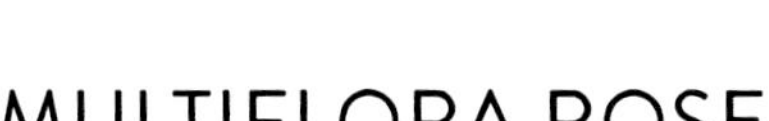

MULTIFLORA ROSE

Like a woman I once knew
your fragrance is always
in the air reminding me of
your thorn-laden tendrils
& belligerent ways. You
always come to stay even
when you aren't invited
& quickly wear out your
welcome but your fragrance
is always in the air & I will
remember you multiflora rose.

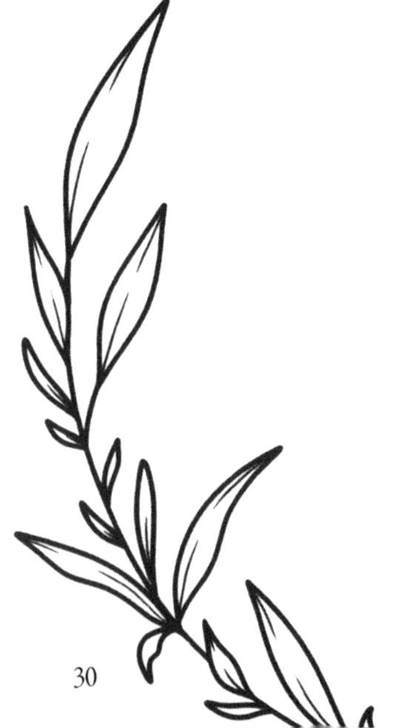

13.

SKY ISLANDS

On the eighth of April the air was radiant
as we ascended alongside the creek into a
basin carpeted with fringed phacelia and
spring beauty. But winter lingered along
the high divide. Twigs & buds overarching
the trail cast gray shadows on the ribbons
of bark unraveling from yellow birch trees.

Below the crest we made our way south across
boulder fields aggregated 18,000 years ago in
the folds of north-facing slopes when violent
freeze-thaw action prized huge stones from
high-elevation cliff faces that descended with
streams of muddy debris until they settled on
alluvial terraces or behind narrow gaps. No
glaciation this far south but cold enough year
round to create a stunted tree-line at 5,000 feet
above which hundreds of unnamed peaks
carpeted with lush icy layers of alpine
tundra drifted like sky islands.

The only sounds were the wind, the dry
rasp of boot soles seeking purchase on
stone & the insistent calls of a broad-
winged hawk just returned from wintering
grounds many miles away in Costa Rica.

Back on the divide we found the spur that led
through a rhododendron tunnel to the rock
bald named High Rocks where we stood
together once again naming all of the
mountains & all the rivers from east
to west for as far as we could see.

14.

WILL & FATE

"Fate finds its own way," the old man said to himself
as winter-worn & heart-troubled he arose into the
near light of an hour before dawn & located
the wooden bucket beside the sink.

He paused before lowering his gnarled hands into
the bone-cold water & lifting them to his face
so as to massage the bare skin around his eyes
& claw at the knotted tangles in his beard.

"Fate finds its own way," said the old man again
as if to himself or anyone else who might be
listening even though he knew of no one
now alive who might bother to do so.

"But I will continue to arise before the
dawning of each day," he said as he began
to clap & slide his gnarled feet back & forth
over the rough-hewn floor before launching
himself into the air where he remained
suspended arms akimbo for moments
before alighting with awkward grace.

"Fate will come on the appointed day,"
said the old man. "Until then
I will go where I go & do
what I do & dance
as if I were a
ballerina."

15.

GAUNT PHANTOMS: A TIMBER WOLF CHRONOLOGY

1643

Fast as the ground is slow
the iron gray wolves moved
silently in unison over the snow
casting dark shadows with each
bound their yellow eyes radiating
a degree of almost casual intent
as they closed the distance
between here & there.

–GE

1752

"We then passed into a faraway country
seldom visited since the day of Creation.
We have climbed on our hands & knees
dragging loads taken off of our trembling
horses so they wouldn't fall backwards.
Wolves sing all around before first light
such music as was never before heard."

–Diary of Moravian Augustus Spangenberg

1890

Rifle cradled in arm the old soldier turned bounty
hunter moved through the laurel...gaunt phantom
in a dream 'til he spotted the dull glint of dead eyes.
Clutching the creature by scruff of neck he deftly
separated scalp from bone with knife & tied it to
his waistband from which six wolf scalps worth
$5 each now swung back & forth in time with
his stride as Quill Rose marched home again.

–GE

1929

"Went to...Mount Le Conte with my dog Cumberland Jack and built a cabin....Only company we had was a grizzled old timber wolf hoping for food he couldn't no longer hunt....In January 1929 we went back not expecting to see the wolf but there he was watching as best he could... probably one of the last if not the last of his kind."

–Paul Adams, Mount Le Conte *(1969)*

16.

WRETCHED SEDGE: TAXONOMIC VERSE

Wretched Sedge (*Carex miser,* Buckley, 1843; *C. misera,* Small, 1903); endemic to 13 counties in the Blue Ridge (TN, GA, NC); clumps of narrow pale-green grass-like leaves up to 16 inches droop forlornly from crevices in shaded seepage cliffs underlain by dry pale-brownish hair-like tussocks of older leaves resembling the headpiece of a Cherokee woman in mourning & of a certain disposition might have deemed suitable to mark the occasion as she danced & whirled around the funeral pyre bare feet hovering above the indifferent soil & forlorn leaves masking her dull cold eyes.

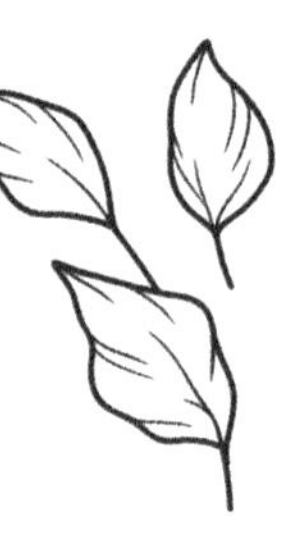

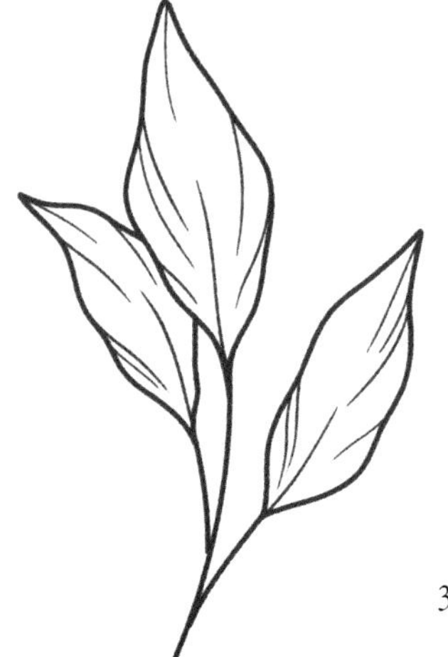

17.

DESCENDING LEVELS

Shadows linger
as yet another golden
autumn day is ending.
Leaves swirl counter-
clockwise in gravity-
resistant spirals before
settling one-by-one.
each in its own place
on the surface of the
darkening stream.

But the bright-colored minnows
you'd hoped to see darting here-
&-there just above the pebbles
that line the creek bed—as they
did when you were a boy—can
no longer be seen except
in imagination.

18.

SUSPECT TERRAIN

Stratigraphies for some
terrains are known but
most are uncharted &
thereby "suspect" like
the uncertain terrain
sensed but not seen
that lies within
each of us:

buckling & eroding
slipping & sliding
thrusting & folding
always fault-ridden.

[Composed, in part, from intimations in Norma Tilden's "Stratigraphies: Writing a Suspect Terrain," *Biography* 25 (Winter 2002).]

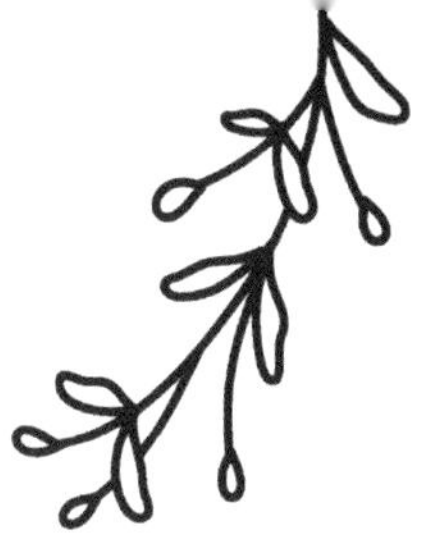

19.

SPRING—BRANCH—CREEK—RIVER

spray cliffs...always wet
sphagnum...emerald green
sundews...ruby red

~

From below the high divide water issuing
from vertical rock gathers itself &
becomes a branch darting here & there...
lingering in ornate asides...shining in
sunlight & darkening in rain...moving on...
gravity flowing...seeking confluence as
a prong or a fork...left or right or middle...
doesn't matter so long as it becomes
a creek pursuing its own syntax despite
enjambments...along the way
to a river that flows into a gulf that
becomes an ocean.

~

Under leaden skies dead
leaves in an eddy this side
of the creek swirl just above
water-rounded stones that
stare upward with blind
expectation awaiting
a bright ray of light
that never arrives.

~

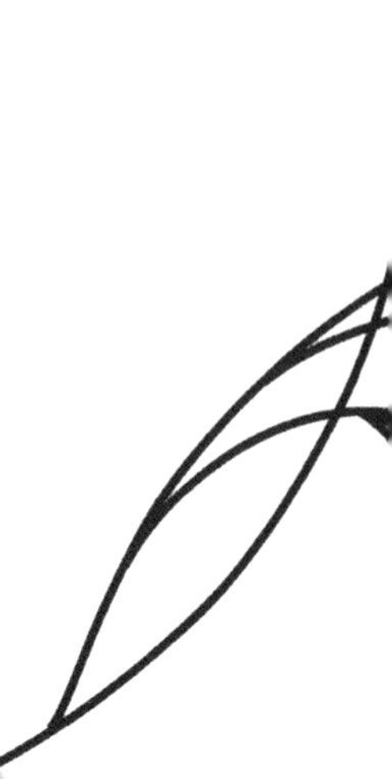

After torrential rain has fallen for days on end moving water voices its displeasure in a low-pitched constant growl. Farther down you hear the disquieting clatter of stone being forcefully transported downstream. And if conditions are favorable—so that abrasive material is free to move & the current is sufficient to churn around—an original inequality in the stream bed becomes deeper & more or less circular in shape until the negative space we call a pothole is formed.

~

Pale sky
bare branches
crosshatched
shadows &
reflections
rock rim
worn wafer-
thin water
falling lacey
patterns
grayish white
spectral ions
invisibly
dissolving
again &
again the
same
yet changed
dissolving
whorls of
white lace.

~

June 20, 2013...Mid-morning...Southwestern Virginia.
(In Tribute to Tim Spira)

From a ledge I watch as you move sure-
footedly from rock to rock seeking the right
angle in the right light in the right frame of mind
to capture on film the innate disposition of yet
another waterfall.

Ghostly patterns dissolve & then reappear as the
tapestry of water descends into the dark circle of its
plunge pool from which current spirals first clockwise
then counterclockwise from bank to bank until a
sluice carved in stone by water eons ago suddenly
diverts fallen water on its way again.

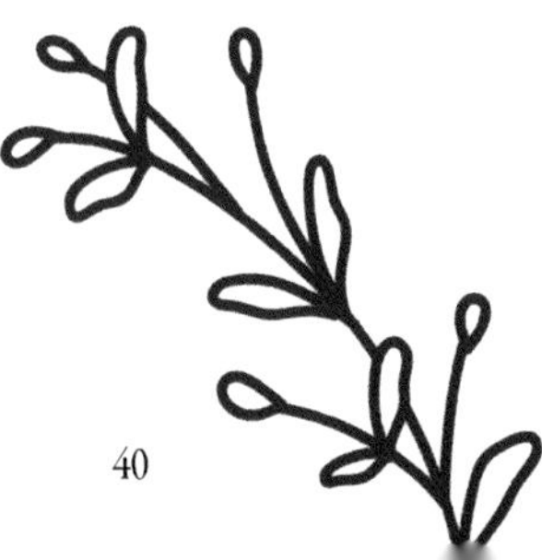

20.

"SEND IN THE CLOWNS"

Where are the clowns?
There ought to be clowns.

Send in the clowns.
Don't bother, they're here.

—Stephen Sondheim, "Send in the Clowns" (1973)

When everything that could go wrong
did go wrong & you need to get away
from it all, arise into the morning light
& go alone into the high backcountry
to watch ravens glide & tumble &
dive with such joy they'll
make you smile again.

Be patient...listen to the wind,
Just as you are about to give up
there'll be guttural "cronk! cronk! cronk!"
calls up above your head & suddenly the
ravens will be there ready as ever to stage
a performance that'll bedazzle your eyes.
Steady as an arrow on outstretched wings
they'll ride updrafts a thousand feet above
ground from which vantage point a series
of loop-the-loops, barrel rolls & somer-
saults can be launched. And by adjusting
wing tilt they are able to execute power
dives in which males & females spiral

in tandem only a few inches apart
until at the last instant before
striking earth they
pull out of it.

The avian circus will conclude as
swiftly as it commenced...one moment
the sky will be alive with ravens...the next
it will be perfectly silent as if nothing ever
had & never would take place there.

21.

GHOSTLY VISION

I looked up & saw the ghostly vision of a
white horse standing on the flank of a near
ridge looking down at me. I say ghostly not
because he was white but because in that
moment he seemed to be the apotheosis of
all the horses I'd ever seen or dreamt or
would ever see or dream. Framed by the
dark opening where a trail emerges from the
forest & descends into the valley the
creature was positioned so I could see the
ears on antennae-like alert & the moist
darkly-shrouded eyes embedded in the
downward-sloping expressionless face. His
nostrils flared silently & suddenly he was
gone hooves thudding on the bare ground
like drum-beats fading in the distance.

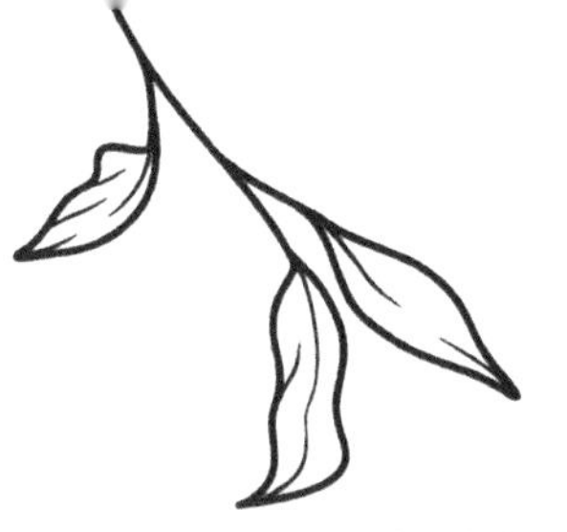

22.

GONE AWAY ON THE LAST TRAIN

I remember the first time ever I saw her.
It was summertime & just about to rain.
She was wearing a pretty red dress &
standing all alone by the garden wall.

I saw her walk down the avenue &
pause at the gate. I saw her go
down by the river & listen to the
water flowing to the sea.

Someone told me that she was
looking for a new place in a far-
away land. He said she was
scheduled to leave that very
night on the last train.

When she arrived at the station
I was standing in the shadows.
When she sat down by the
window I saw her for the very
last time.

But I just came to hear the whistle.
I just came to see that fiery engine
roll out of the station & pass over
the river into the darkened land.

I just came to say goodbye but I
never said hello & now she's
gone away on the last train
headed all alone for her
next destination.

23.

JASMINE FOR CHRISTMAS: TAXONOMIC VERSE

It is an elegant vine composed of wiry reddish
slightly-angled stems that grow from ten to thirty
feet high by twining clockwise; leaves are opposite
smooth-edged lance-shaped short-stemmed & from
two to four inches long; flowers borne in auxiliary
clusters funnel-shaped five-lobed & about an inch
in length with stamens that extend either beyond the
styles (or exactly the opposite) so as to implement
cross-fertilization.

Jasmin...jasmina...jasmine...jasminium...jasmyn...
jassamine...jesmine...jessamine...call it what you will
Carolina jasmine (*Gelsemium sempervirens*) bloomed here
for the first time on Christmas day.

On trellises attached to the deck
cascades of shiny evergreen leaves
& yellow flowers looked just right
in the pale winter light.

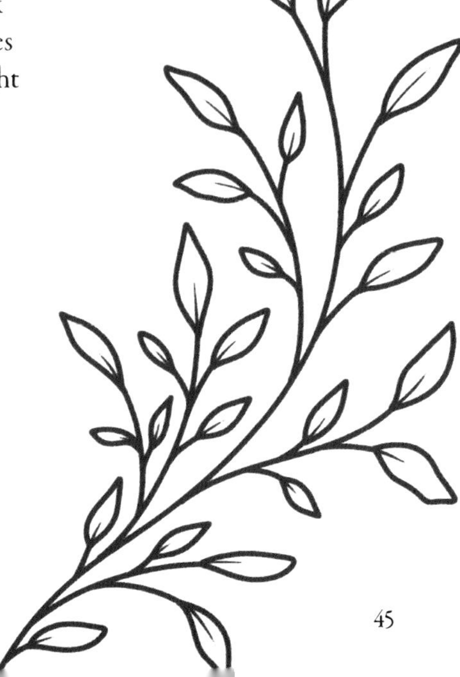

24.

NIGHT SOUNDS

The dogs bark into the night
air at nothing in particular
except one another...each
awaiting his turn to say "Here
I am...I still exist...this is
my ground."

A screech owl whinnies
from the depths of a hemlock...
her head swivels the yellow-
rimmed pupils slowly dilate
as if calibrated.

Under the back deck
buried up to his snout in
the debris a pickerel frog
snores every 240 seconds
awaiting an answer that
seldom comes.

From this high vista
inside my mind I can hear
each synapse crackle like a
dry twig in a campfire as the
system closes down.

Never-the-less
here I am again
awaiting my turn
to bark or snore
another message
that if you're on
my wavelength
you will
understand.

25.

A FAR LAND

EVELYN Z. SMYTH
(MAY 1, 1815–DECEMBER 3, 1909)

~

EVERY THING THAT COULD GO WRONG
DID & PURSUED ME OVER THE WATER INTO
A FAR LAND WHERE I NOW RESIDE IN DARK
DISCONTENT UNDER THIS COLD SLAB OF
NANTAHALA BLUE MARBLE.

26.

RHODODENDRON TUNNELS

Where ancient animal trails & footpaths
thread their way through rhododendron
thickets, overarching limbs form dimly lit
tunnels at either end of which there's the
proverbial light you say you've been
looking for.

The corridor narrows your space to the
here & now...debris crackles softly under
your feet...overhead waxy leaves float
motionless in the bluish-green almost
subterranean air.

As you pass from shade to light a bird
sings from somewhere in the dense tangle:
down-slurred notes followed by a musical
cascade that fades into silence.

Never looking back you move on but the image
of the calm open-ended passage resurfaces in
mind's eye wherever you might be when
the unseen bird sings & you descend all
over again below the surface of every-
day-ness into watchful intentness.

27.

DREAM ON

(In tribute to Miguel de Unamuno)

Dream on in mid-summer of embers
smoldering on the fireplace hearth
under a gray blanket of fallen ashes.

Dream on in mid-winter of leafy vines
suspended from outreaching branches
that cast blue shadows on the ground.

Dream on in summer of winter
nights when snowflakes are
secretly falling...deepening in
drifts of forgetfulness as yet
unseen outside your window.

Dream on in winter of summer nights when
the ghostly white petals of the mallows
enfold the dark eyes that have been
watching you all the day long.

Dream on in starlight or in daylight.
See how each snowflake falls with
certainty to the ground.

Greet the sleepy flowers as they
slowly unfurl in the shadows
with messages for you.

28.

POINTS OF LIGHT

Try to remember when we meet
& I have little or nothing to say that
doesn't mean I'm neither here nor there.
Look for the random points of light in the
shadows of my eyes. Listen to the rhythms
in these lines beating slowly just for you.

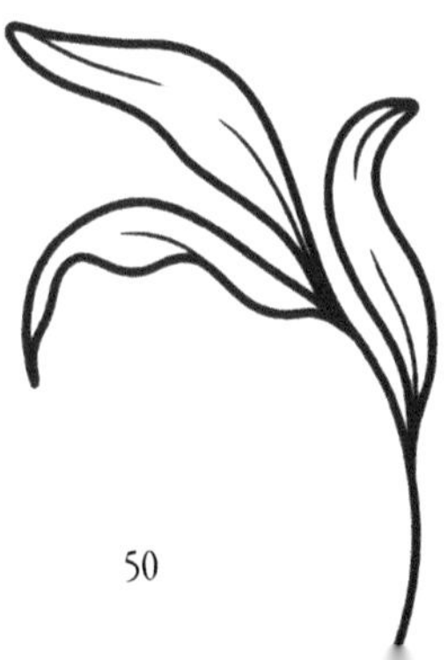

29.

THERE ARE GHOSTS IN THESE MOUNTAINS

Why, poor man, have you left the light of day
and come down to visit the dead in this sad place?
—The Odyssey, *Book XI*

I could summon the souls of fallen chestnut trees.
I could summon the souls of extirpated timber wolves.
I could summon the souls of Cherokees displaced.
I could summon the souls of black convicts buried in tunnels.
I could summon the souls of loggers crushed loading timber.
I could summon the souls of homes condemned by the park.
I could summon the souls of towns drowned by the TVA.
I could summon the souls of Cherokee boys hung in jails.
I could summon the souls of all these & they'd arise as if
the shade of Tiresias himself had summoned them!

But I am here today to summon the
ghosts of all the elegant mountains
slaughtered decapitated clearcut
asphalted burned raped pillaged &
debased...all for the sake of
a nice view & a round of golf.

I wish I could say
something other than "I am
so sorry we've done & are
still doing this to you...
I am so very sorry."

30.

A CONVENIENT SEASON

(Acts 24:25)

From the ridge above
the house a voice was
calling…singing in
her ears:

"Now is the time…
do come along."

"Not yet," she replied.
"Now is not a
convenient season to
go with you…I have
many things to do."

"Now is the only season,"
the voice replied. "Now is
the time…you must not
linger or you will be lost."

"I can find my way when
things must be left behind.
I have accounts to balance.
Very little will be lost."

"All will be lost…your journey
will be never ending & you will be
all alone in a barren land that seems
familiar but is never the same…
all because you lingered too
long waiting for a season
that will never arrive."

31.

A PRETTY SONG

From the cross vine
thicket beyond the old
outhouse the same bird
always sings the same
song over & over...
all I can tell you with
certainty is that it is a
pretty song sung in
language strange by
a bird I've never seen.

32.

MICA

"Mr. Carter come by a-riding
that big roan horse right up
to the door & without getting
down or even tipping his hat
said the side shaft was still
collapsed & he was plenty
sorry it was a-going to be
so long before next payday
but there was nothing he
could do cause like I knew
they always had to keep to
the schedule especially in
hard times like these but he
felt sure Joe's men would
pass the hat so as to get us
through like they always do.

"I told him we would pass
our own goddamn hat just
like we always had & if he
would just get that nag out of
my yard I'd be obliged.

"So after the service I want
you to walk over the ridge &
across the river to that new
mine up on Hunnicutt
Mountain & see if they got
the sort of work a young
man might be able to do...
maybe in a groundhog hole.*

"Like your father always said,
'The main thing we all need
to remember is that wherever
we wander there will always be
sunny days when 10 million flakes
of light will show us the way home.'"

**groundhog hole: a shallow surface mine.*

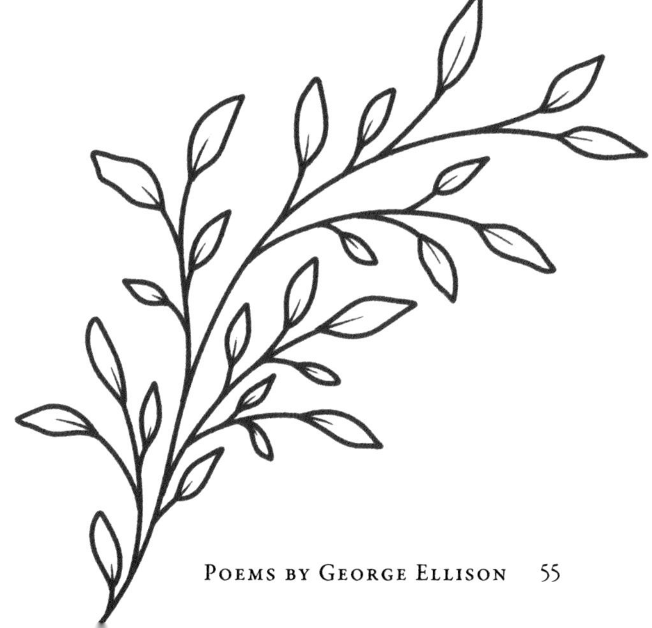

33.

DREAMING OF FIRE

Table mountain pine's place is high
on mountain ridges, where it looks
down on the soaring buzzards,
where the wildcat lives,
and the rattler suns
his coils.
—Donald Culross Peattie, A Natural History of Trees of Eastern and Central North America *(1940)*

Panthertown Valley lies sweltering
in the sunlight waiting for a soul-
cleansing fire that will arise from
the valley floor & sweep along the
crest burning bright as it passes
through vine-tangled scrub
reaching ever-upward for the
wind-gnarled pines seemingly
perched like dark birds of prey
on bare stone.

Should the spine-tipped cones be
ripe enough & the fire hot enough
& the stars aligned just right every
20 or so years the cones will open
& triangular light-brown seeds
will cover the scorched ground.

Sighs of relief will pass through
the valley as long-held tensions
are suddenly released by fire.

34.

SHADOWS OF REGRET: A SONNET

From inkling to inkling
I wander like an apparition
past the wrought-iron rose
looking for something that
may not exist within these
confines...a place where
the shadows of regret are
not cast over bare stone &
the light of remembrance
shines all around.

More often than not these days the tangle of
words flowing through my mind that could make
a poem come & go before I can grasp
& align them into some semblance of order.

35.

INVISIBLE SPIRIT

Wind is invisible
but we still see it
in ripples on water
in leaves on trees.

Spirit is invisible
but we still see it
in dancing shoes
in sudden smiles
in flashing eyes.

We make our way
each day from here
to there unknowingly
reliant upon inferences
of sight & sound.

36.

LANDS CREEK

The creek makes its own way
casting serpentine bends
that grasp worn stone
ever changing
never the same
taking its time
moving along
from where it's been
to where it's going.

37.

SARVIS WAS IN BLOOM: A STORY

She heard the cabin door
open & close followed by
the clatter of hooves fading
away over the frozen ground.
She also heard the dry whisper
of moccasins on the cabin floor.

Through the long winter around
dinner tables far from mountains
the rider polished his story about
savages & hand-to-hand combat.

Sarvis was in bloom when
the rider returned & reined
to a stop. Through a broken
window he saw what he
he had feared propped
upright on a table.

"Poised mutely attentive
for me to see," he thought
to himself as he rode away
with his wife's burnished
skull lashed securely with
rawhide through an eye-
socket to his saddle horn.

38.

SNAILS: A SONNET

Snails are wondrous creatures to behold!
They can't fly & they can't sing but like
the birds they are calcifiles addicted to
calcium for shell & egg construction.

Trending clockwise or counterclockwise
the shells of some species rival sea shells
in design & color. They make toads look
like speed demons but they don't stumble
& bumble through their Lilliputian world
of mosses, twigs & pebbles. They glide
like sailboats veering gracefully this way
& then that on tracks of sticky mucus
secreted where ever they go in order
to find their way home.

39.

WINTER SOUNDS

In winter sounds from afar seem nearby:
snatches of conversation from across a
wind-swept river become crystal clear...
hoof-struck stones ring in frozen air...
a dead tree on a far ridge crashes onto
the iron-cold ground & the echoing
silence that follows seems like sound.

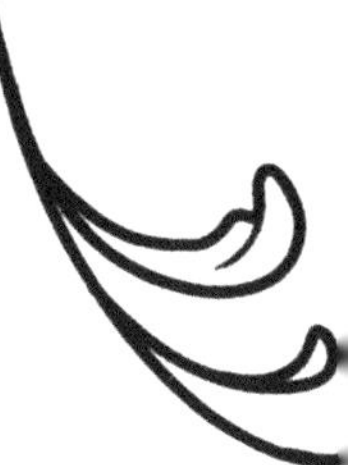

40.

ONE BELL RINGING IN THE WIND: A STORY

"You ask in your letter of the bird that nested beside
the cabin door before you went away," she wrote.
"The cabin burned in 1945. After moving to town
I listened to him sing on a vinyl record I found.
I still have the record but these days I don't
have anything to play it on. I do remember
how you always used to say before you
went away: 'Listen!...that bird sounds
just like one bell ringing in the wind.'
Those were pretty words but I knew
in my heart that I would never
see you or that bird again."

41.

<HAIKU>

In roadside tangles
misty white & wet with rain
wild plum blooms each spring.

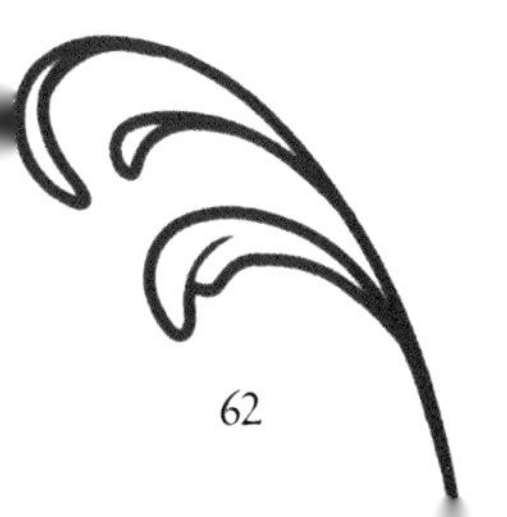

42.

ONE-BY-ONE

Poems flowed like jug wine
of a late summery afternoon
when the sky was heedlessly
blue & it was so easy to lie
there on the plaid blanket in
the long grassy meadow &
watch the flat daisies align
themselves with near-perfect
spacing the way the stars do
when one-by-one they fill
the empty sky with light.

43.

KATHRYN STRIPLING BYER (1944–2017)

Kay's gone now
flying with angels
over mountain tops
across wide rivers
to that far shore
where she patiently
waits for each & every
one of us to join her
when we can.

44.

RAIN CROW: A FABLE

The yellow-billed cuckoo has been given this name because of its tendency to call more frequently on cloudy days, although its reputation as a predictor of weather has never been demonstrated.

—Birds of North America Online

Recluse so secretive in leafy shadows
almost never seen…a wandering voice
seemingly almost anywhere or nowhere at
once…calling…calling…for rain.

Concealed in the foliage of a black cherry
tree a cuckoo eases from limb to limb with
restrained purpose. Arriving at his destination
he perches motionless…gold-rimmed eyes on
full alert…beside a tent caterpillar nest.
His mate calls for him with an inquiring
kolp from a nearby oak tree.

"She's just bored," he says to himself.
It's October & long ago she laid her
eggs in a thrush's nest. Last year she
deposited them in a catbird's nest.
She's equal opportunity when it
comes to egg distribution.

"'Next year,' she told me, 'I might raise
them myself…or maybe not…it's so
much easier this way.'"

Certain that the coast is clear he deftly extracts
caterpillars from their nest & ignoring the irritated
calls from his mate remains there until late after-
noon when he senses something in the pale light
slanting through the tree limbs that triggers an
inner beckoning not unlike the almost magnetic
force that passes through his body when he first
senses that it's time to move along down the
southwestward-tending Appalachian ridges to
the Mississippi coast...where he'll linger to
rest up for the journey on down the isthmus
to Costa Rica...a venture transacted in a
spellbound state via the stars & landforms
& inklings upon which survival depends.

He can't sing but the rain bird feels compelled
to recite a series of slowly-descending notes:

Kowlp Kowlp kowlp-kowlp-kolp-kolp

repeated with variations until the premonition
fades & the bird slips away with his mate.

~

Recluses so secretive in the leafy shadows
calling softly in the mid-distance until the
leaves on the ash tree across the creek
invert & flash pearl-gray undersides
in the rising wind & gnarled laurel
limbs creak as they yaw against
one another & suddenly you
hear the sound of rain falling
on tin one drop at a time
until after awhile it is a
steady downpour as
predicted.

45.

THE GOLDEN MOUSE: A FABLE

"I'm told you have come a long ways
...crossing seven mountains & seven rivers,"
said a woman who continued to braid the hair
of a girl who looked like her daughter.

"I need to ask why you bother to visit this
little village so far off the main-traveled way."

"Very well," she said after hearing his reply.
"Come with us...there's a small cove with
a spring halfway up the mountain. No need
to worry but try to place yourself in the right
frame of mind. Along the way say the names
of the mountains & rivers that you crossed."

Privet overgrown with greenbrier & multiflora
rose formed dense tangles that covered the forest
floor beneath a stand of hickory & oak crisscrossed
with strands of grapevine. From the treetops on the
ridge far above the hollow a scarlet tanager sang
a raspy robin-like song.

"Welcome to the realm of the golden mouse,"
said an old man as he emerged from woodland
shadows into the light near the spring. "The black-
winged firebird & the mouse that lives in the trees
are good friends. Few have seen him...most have
no idea that he even exists. But no one who has had
even a fleeting glimpse has ever denied he's one of
the most beautiful creatures on this earth."

The old man paused to listen to the tanager and began
to whistle an almost perfect imitation of the bird's song
that quickly lured him into full view.

"I never heard the golden mouse sing," said the old man.
"He can't be so easily fooled as his black-winged friend.
Look up above your head for a sun-struck patch of fur
or bright eyes watching...always watching...from a
cluster of rhododendron leaves or a platform of twigs
fastened with strips of bark. From those vantage points
he observes the world as it passes by with its seductive
glamour on display for all to see..."

"Glamour?" the visitor interrupted...but there was no
reply & the old man's voice continued as if he was talking
to himself, enjoying the opportunity to recite a favorite story:

"When startled he moves with arboreal grace," said the old man,
"using that long tail to maintain balance as he glides from vine to
vine...a circus performer dancing on a high wire. I've never seen
it for myself but there are those who swear he can fly just like the
black-winged firebird, which is why they're such good friends.
See if you can find him. That's why you came."

The visitor's eyes moved along each branch of each tree that rose
above the tangle of privet & greenbrier & honeysuckle until after
a long while he realized he was holding his breath and exhaled.

Dark eyes that seemed to be watching turned out to be mottled
patterns of bark & lichens. There was movement when a breeze
passed through the leaves. The insistent nasal *yank-yank-yank*
calls of a nuthatch broke his concentration. When he looked he
saw that the old man was no longer there. The woman smiled
but was silent until they were back in the village saying goodbye.

~

"Ustali is the old man's name," she said. "By glamour he meant the surface of things as they appear to be but aren't...like the inverse reflection of a face in a mirror. Those who can see the golden mouse can pierce the world of glamour & pass through its illusory surface into the heart of things. That's what the old people believe."

~

"If you can't see him just yet don't worry. Go home to your own people & stay true to the dreams of your youth. Each day recite the mountains & rivers of your homeland. Come back whenever you are ready & we'll try again. Like everything else it's just a matter of time. One day you will look up above your head & there he'll be... right where he always was...looking down at you."

PHOTOGRAPHY BY QUINTIN ELLISON

You stand, you wait; you walk, you look; something captures your attention. You raise the camera, push the button and make a record of what's in front of the lens.

Curator and critic John Szarkowski noted that the central task of photography is the act of choosing and eliminating.

Cameras are powerful tools for documenting the actual. A camera is a machine that can record daily details—minor or major, small or large, insignificant or profound.

It isn't important whether photography is art, craft or something in between. In two hundred years and counting, that debate has never been resolved and won't be because there is no definitive answer. The Henri Cartier-Bressons and the Josef Koudelkas, the Mary Ellen Marks and Alec Soths—isn't it praise enough to note they are great photographers?

In my own smaller way, the camera opened a pathway for me to seeing. I mean really seeing. When I moved from taking to making photographs, I suddenly noticed what should have been obvious but was not: The world is made up of pictures.

This amazing machine, the camera, allows me to cut out those pictures and place frames of my choosing around space and time.

I'd taken photographs on and off for twenty-eight years as a newspaper staff writer and, later, as an editor and manager. Although I'd enjoyed picture making, I largely viewed the camera as a means for decorating the page or illustrating writing, not as something of intrinsic value.

My thinking changed in July 2017 on a trip to Moab, Utah. I went there with a friend who wanted to enjoy a rafting trip. I stayed in town for the week, intent on continuing my research into ecologist and writer Edward Abbey, a former Moab and Western North Carolina resident.

In Moab, I interviewed a few people about Abbey. I found his former rental house, took some photographs...then took some photographs of other things, then drove into New Mexico, then Arizona and took photographs of still other things...and returned home in the throes of a passion.

I've yet to complete my writing project about Abbey. But I certainly have made a lot of photographs since that trip to Moab.

The images shared here are from 2017 to 2022. Almost all of the photographs are black-and-white, and almost all are in the documentary tradition.

My attention turned to wildlife photography after COVID in 2020 upended our lives. Taking photos of people in masks bored me. I thought to myself, "Well, birds don't wear masks." (Of course, some do—chickadees, cedar waxwings, blue jays—and there are other birds that wear masks, thinking through it, but that is part of how they actually look, not something donned to prevent contagion.)

Reviewing the images for this book and making the selections has rekindled my interest in documenting the world around me. Maybe now I will alternate bird and wildlife photography with photos of people and events.

And, just maybe, I'll finish that writing project on Edward Abbey.

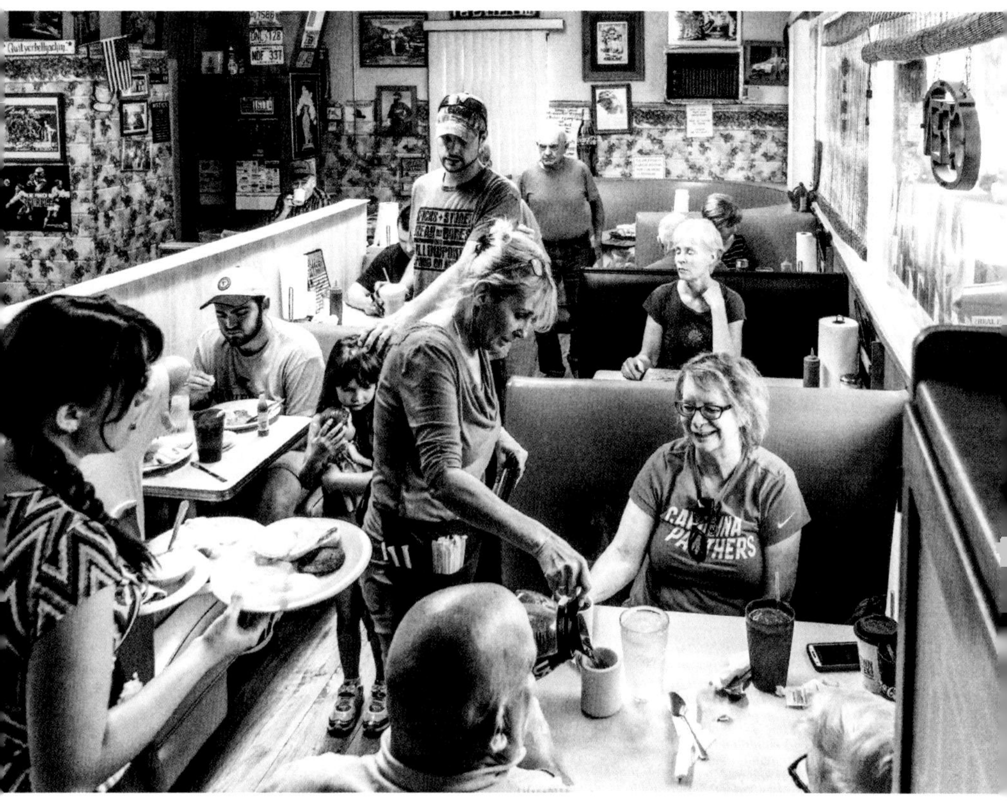

Locals have hung out for about ninety-five years in this small diner, the Coffee Shop, one generation giving way to the next. August 11, 2017, Sylva, North Carolina.

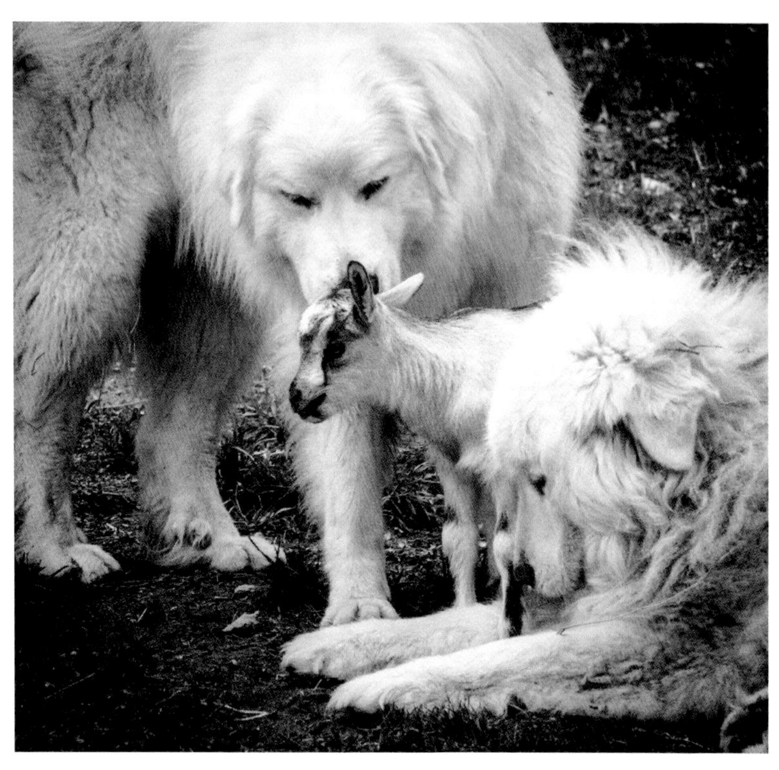

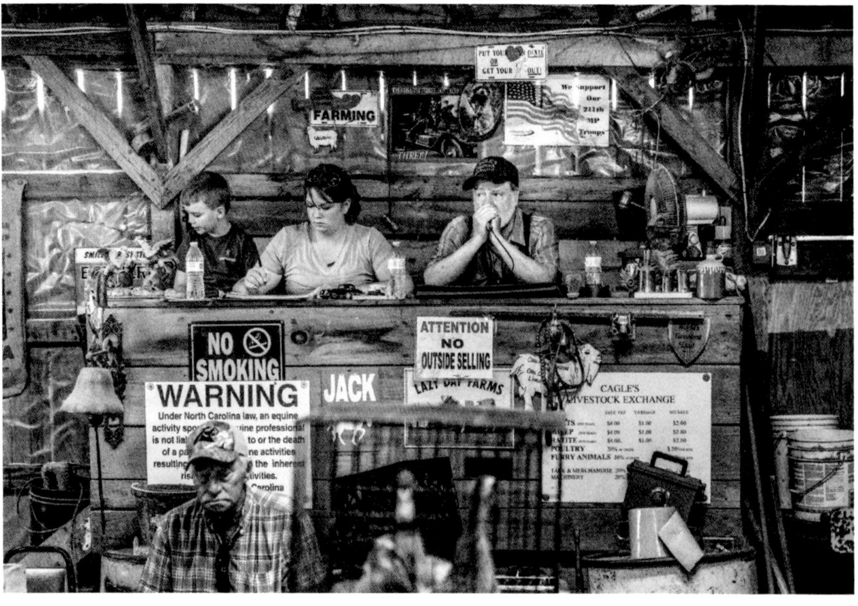
FARMING
NO SMOKING
ATTENTION
NO
OUTSIDE SELLING
WARNING
Under North Carolina law, an equine
JACK
LAZY DAY FARMS
CAGLE'S
LIVESTOCK EXCHANGE
POULTRY
FURRY ANIMALS

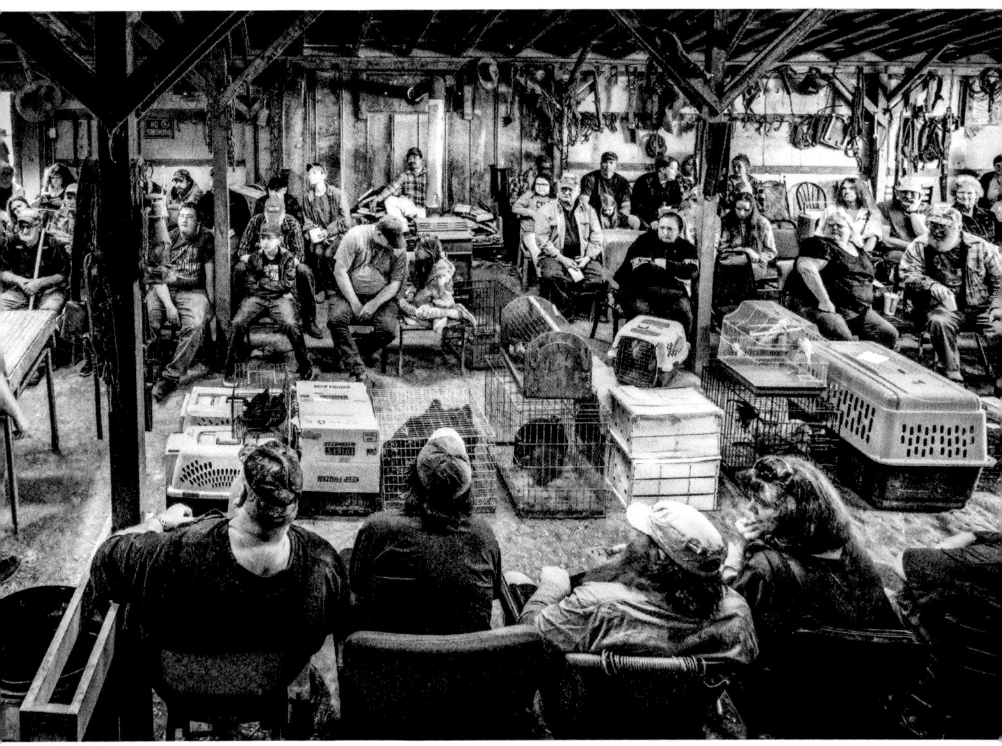

OPPOSITE, TOP Two Pyrenees dogs check out a baby goat, their newest responsibility in the goat yard. March 30, 2018, Haven Hollow Farm, Jackson County, North Carolina.

OPPOSITE, BOTTOM At Cagle's Livestock Exchange, auctioneer and owner Mike Cagle's patter mingles with the crows of roosters, quacking of ducks and chatter of the crowd. "These homer pigeons are as fat as little butterballs. Two dollars a bird? They will never be no cheaper. How 'bout $1.60...$1.70...$1.65?" May 25, 2019, Hyatt Creek Road, Haywood County, North Carolina.

ABOVE The crowd at Cagle's Livestock Exchange is a small sea of ball caps, blue jeans, steel-toed and rubber boots. April 14, 2018, Hyatt Creek Road, Haywood County, North Carolina.

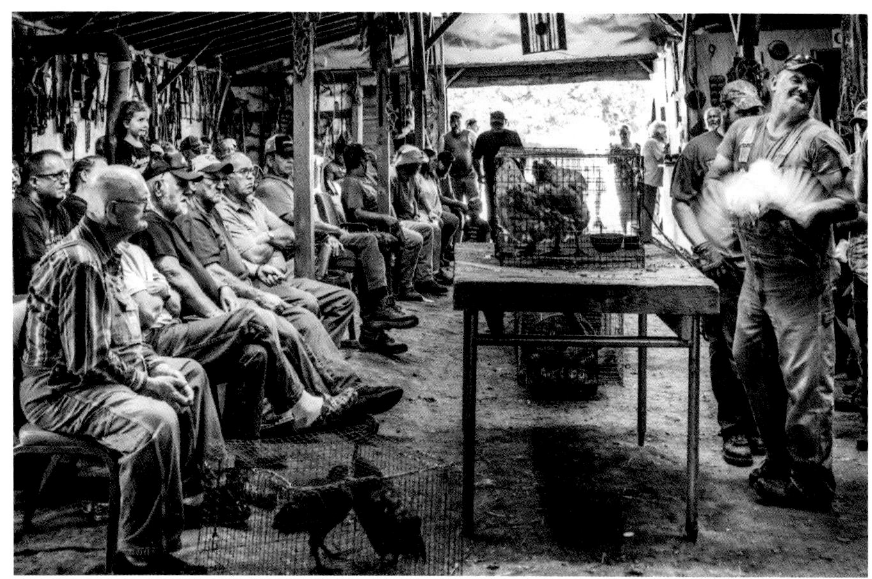

A worker at Cagle's Livestock Exchange struggles to control a chicken as the crowd watches. May 25, 2019, Hyatt Creek Road, Haywood County, North Carolina.

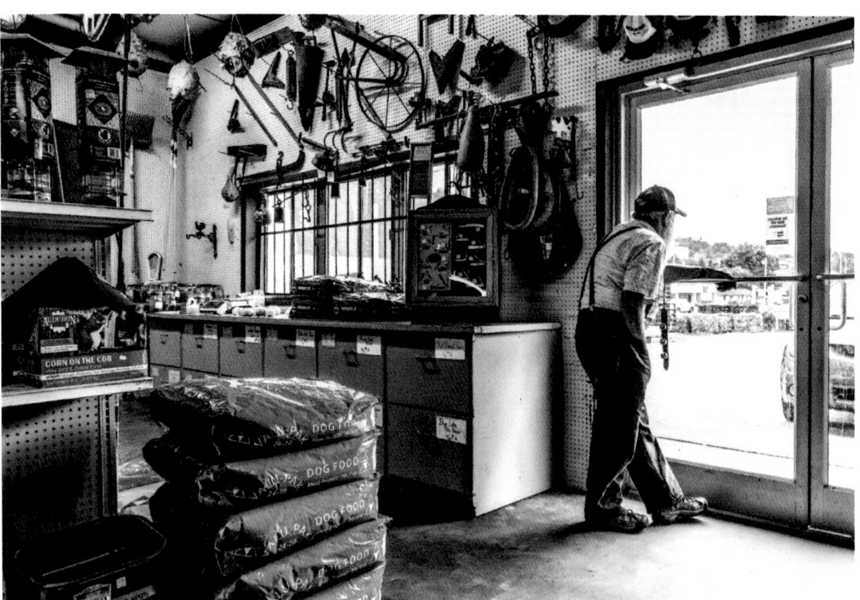

A store worker at Bryson Farm Supply watches the world pass by. The store opened in 1972 but has since closed. Sylva, North Carolina.

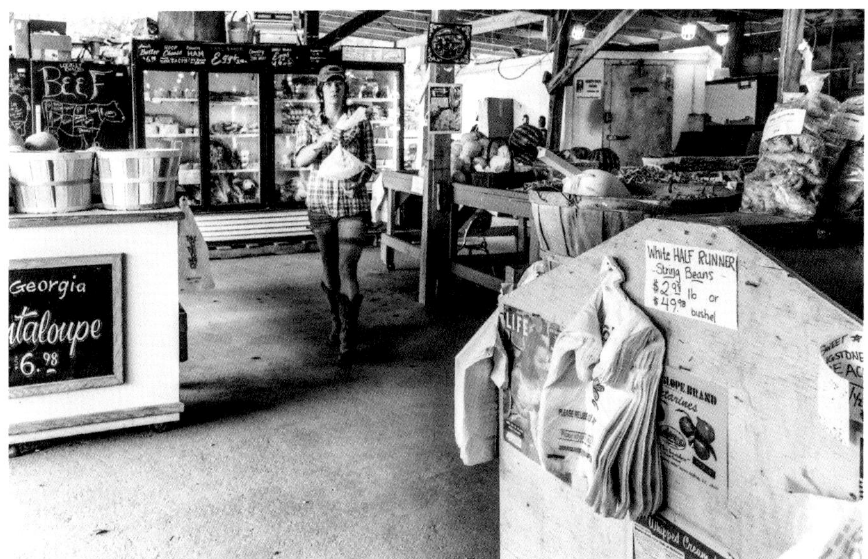

At Darnell Farms, the two-generation farming family produces about one hundred acres' worth of strawberries, pole beans, sweet corn, pumpkins, squash and a variety of tomatoes. June 12, 2019, Bryson City, North Carolina.

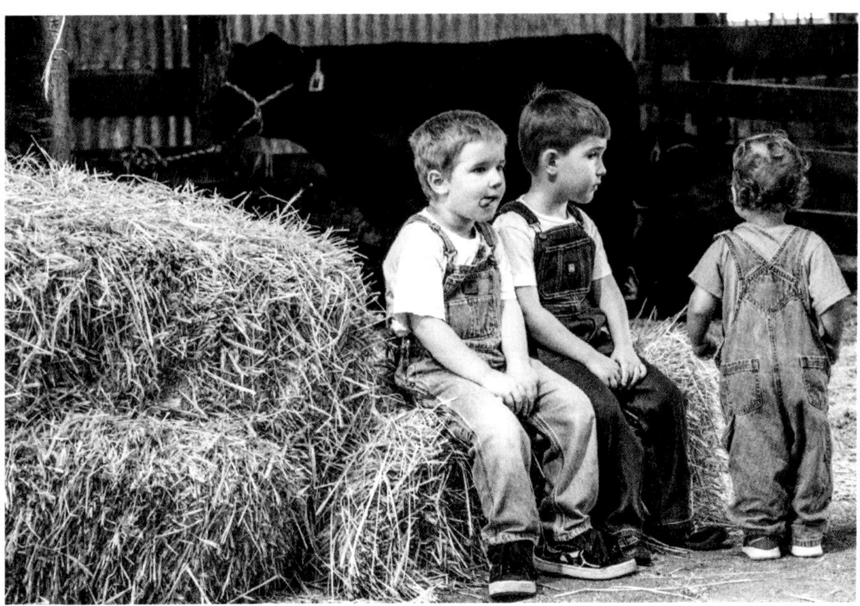

Three little boys in overalls at the Macon County Fair? No way I could resist taking this photo. Actually, there were four little boys in overalls, but I cropped out a portion of the image. The woman standing with the children toted a soft drink can, making it look as if I'd arranged product placement for Coca-Cola. September 13, 2018, Franklin, North Carolina.

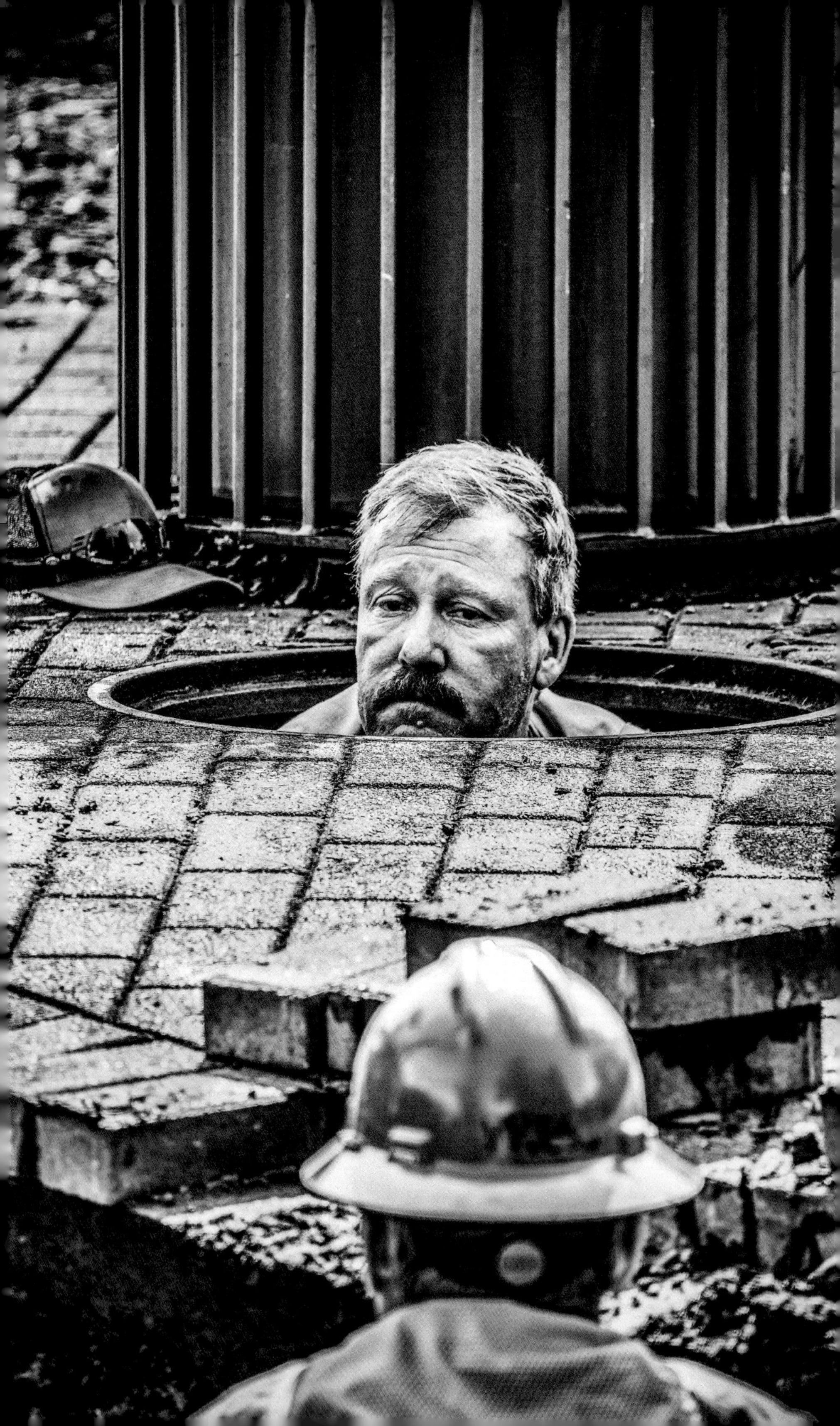

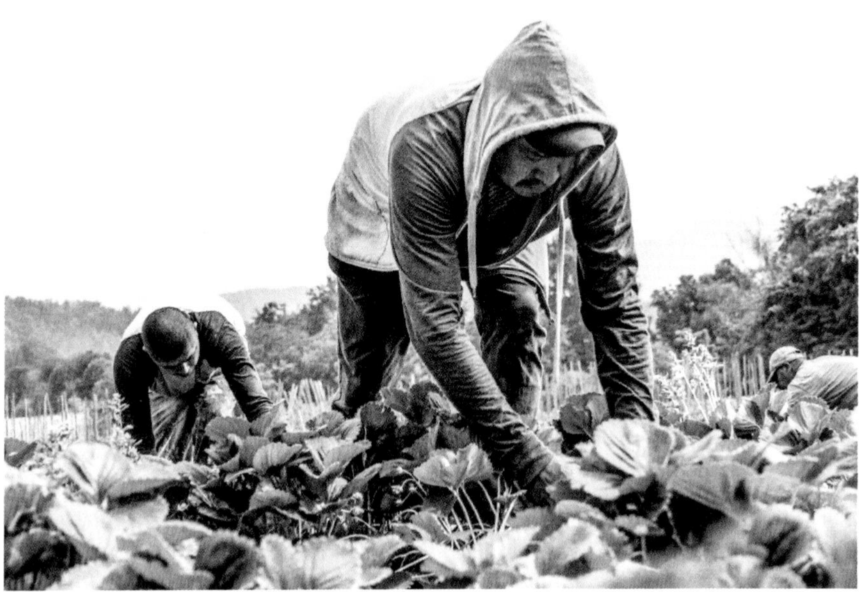

OPPOSITE Repairing water pipes, a worker for the local water and sewer authority emerges after going underground. July 11, 2019, Sylva, North Carolina.

ABOVE Migrant workers harvesting strawberries. The Darnell family has been wonderful about allowing me into their fields with my camera. This image is one of my favorites. I believe it documents a side of life in the mountains that often goes unseen. June 5, 2019, Bryson City, North Carolina.

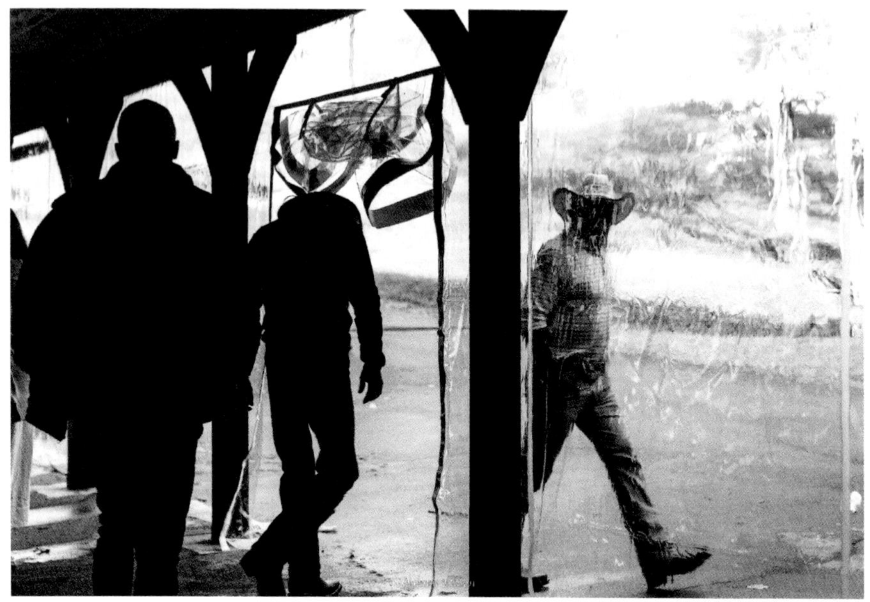

I like how the two men are in silhouette and the face of the main subject is in shadow. Sometimes less is more. October 30, 2021, Macon County, North Carolina.

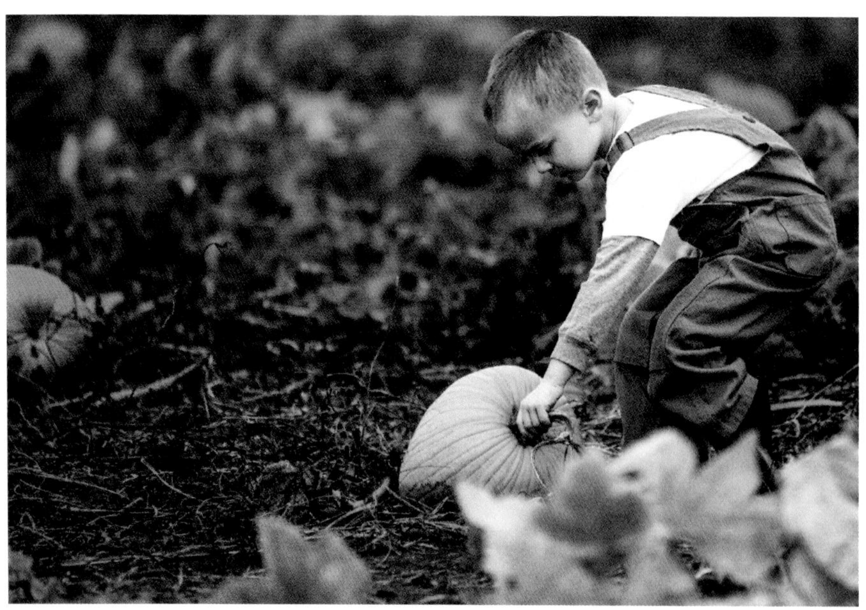

Boy selecting the biggest pumpkin that he can find in the field at Darnell Farms. October 21, 2019, Bryson City, North Carolina.

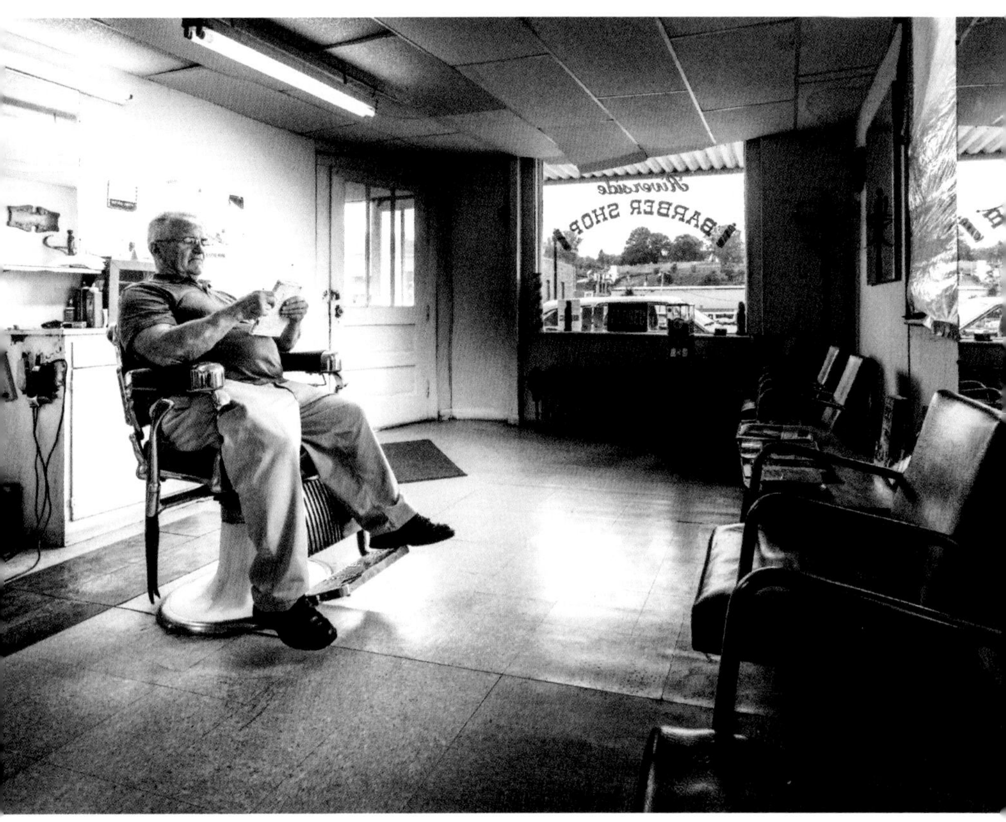

Buford Smith's barbershop has one chair that he uses for cutting hair, and in this photo, he's sitting in it. July 30, 2019, Bryson City, North Carolina.

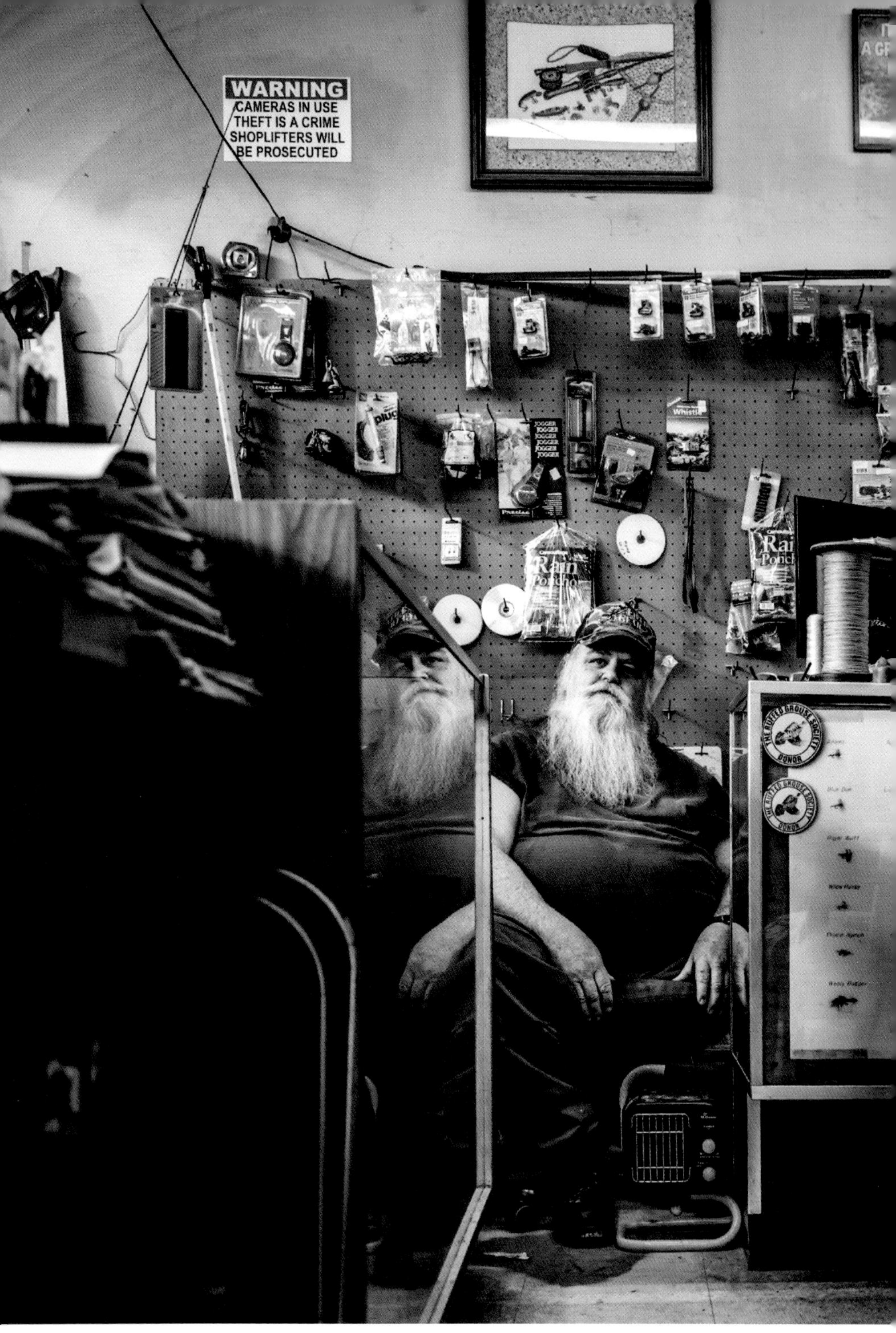

At Lester Sport & Variety, Kenneth Lester runs the front part of the shop, while in the back, his mother, Juanita, handles clothing alterations. December 12, 2018, Bryson City, North Carolina.

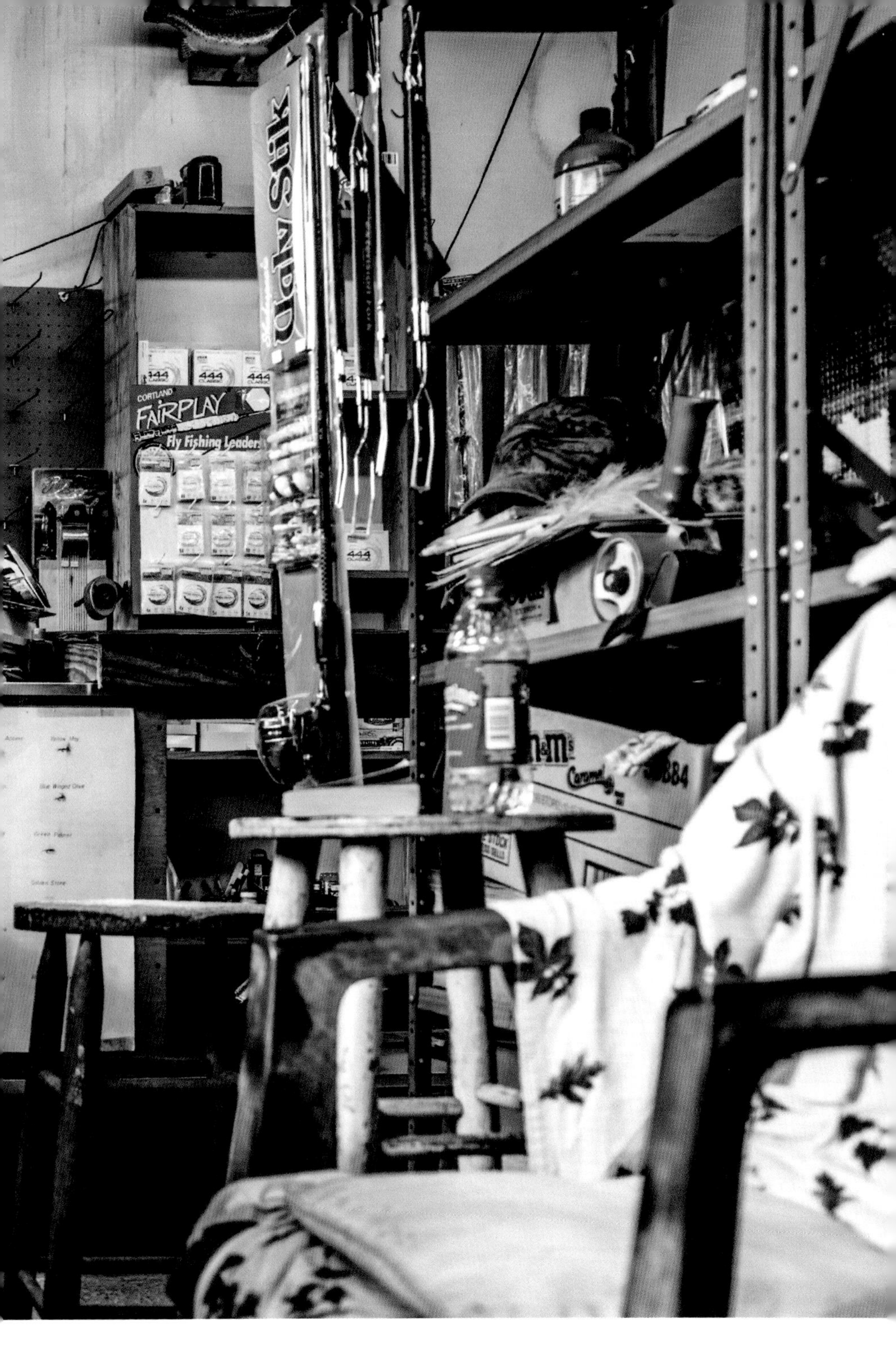
CORTLAND
FAIRPLAY
Fly Fishing Leaders
444
m&m's
Caramel

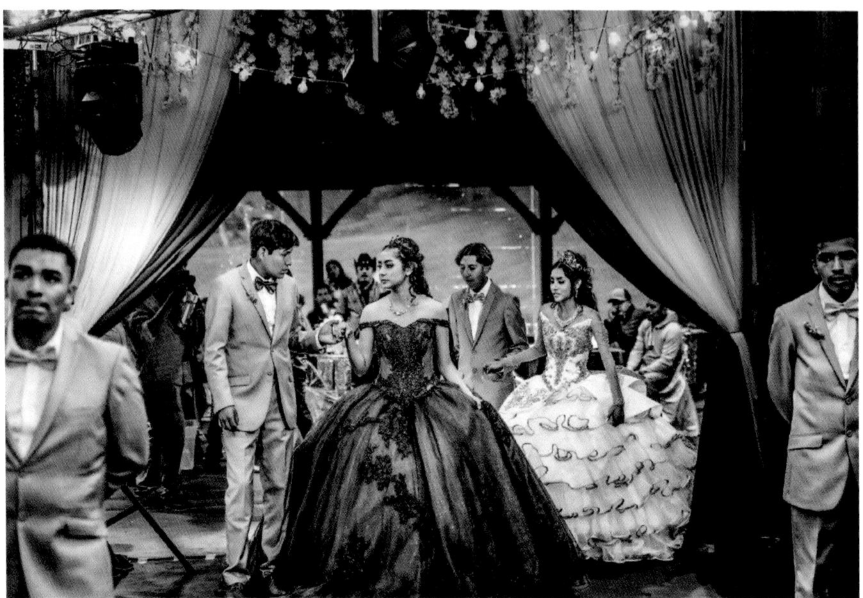

I'd never been to a quinceañera before, and now I can't wait to go to another. Sisters Stephanie and Haley celebrated their transitions from childhood to adulthood with an epic party. I was smitten with the fairy tale atmosphere, complete with ball gowns, tiaras and tuxedos. October 30, 2021, Macon County, North Carolina.

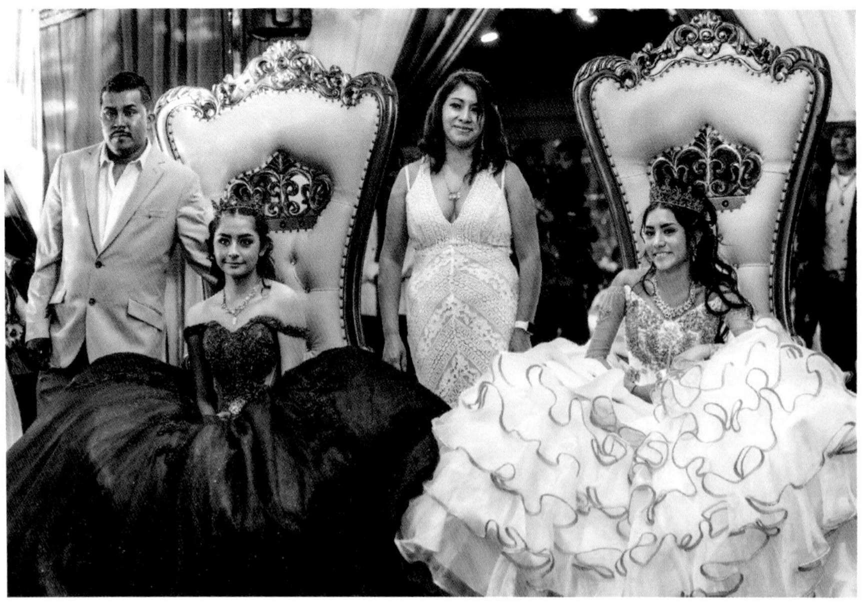

Antonio and Alma pose with their daughters for a family portrait at the quinceañera. October 30, 2021, Macon County, North Carolina.

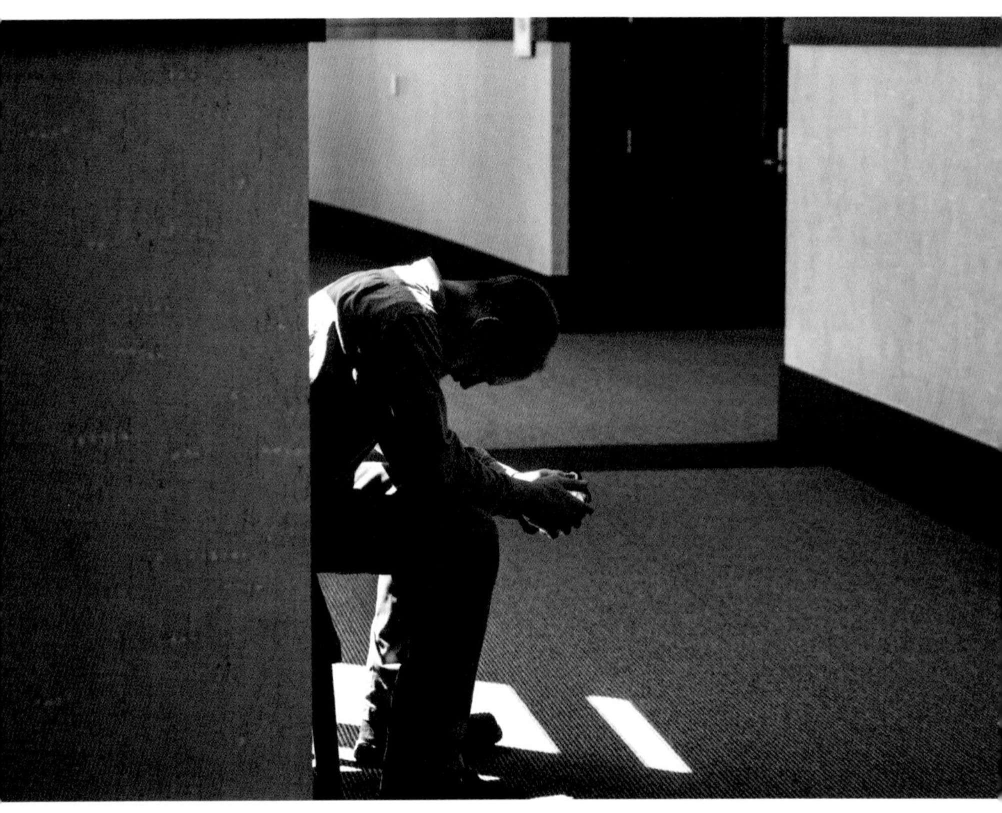

Outside the courtroom, this man awaited his turn in court. One of the perks of my current job with the District Attorney's Office is access—I'm in and out of courtrooms, camera in hand, with official blessings to make photographs. March 21, 2022, Haywood County Courthouse, North Carolina.

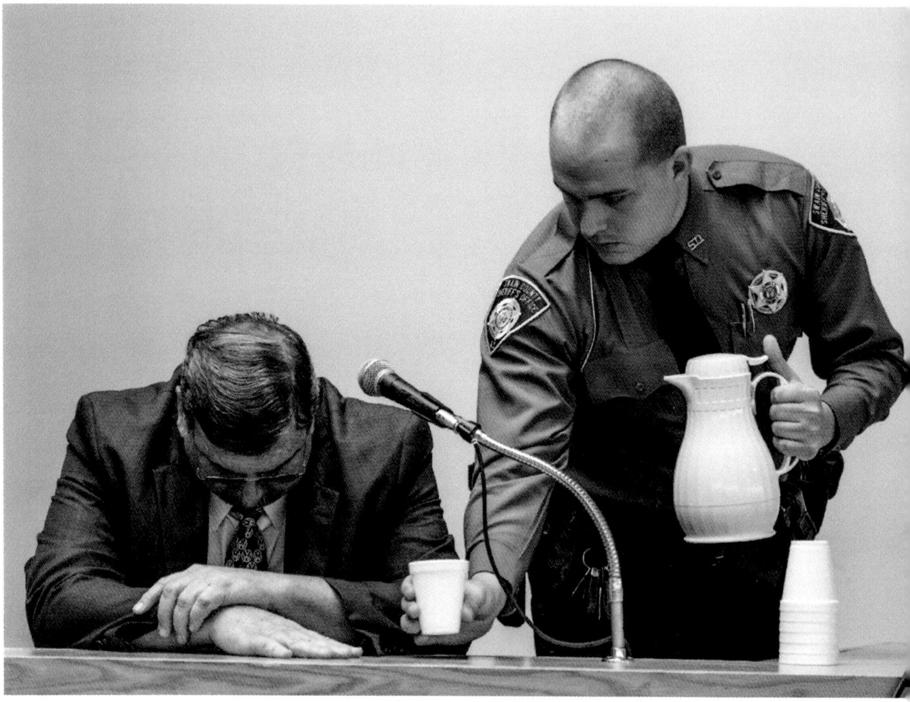

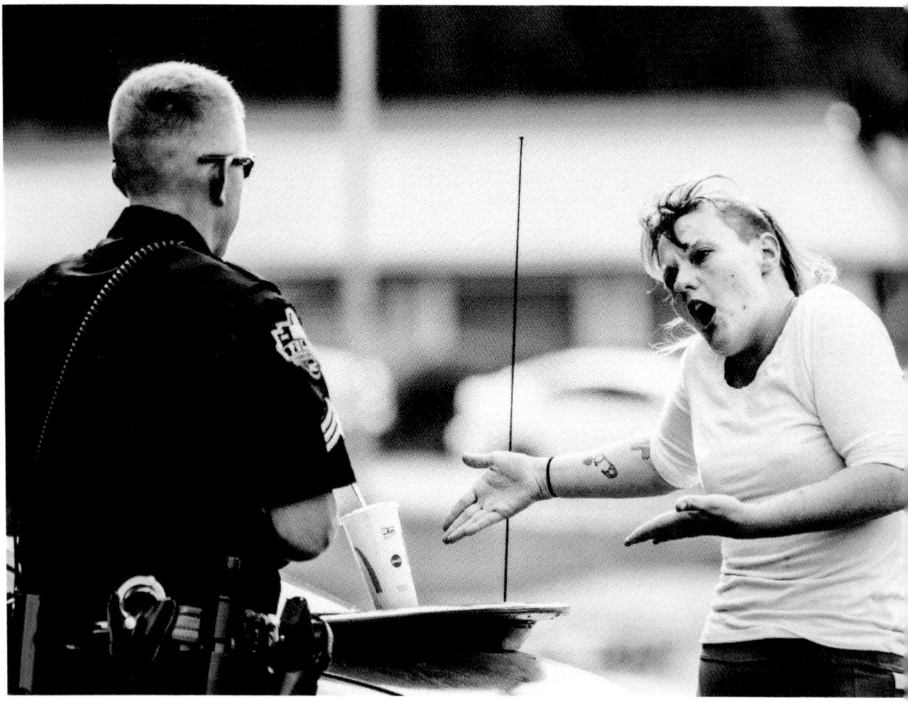

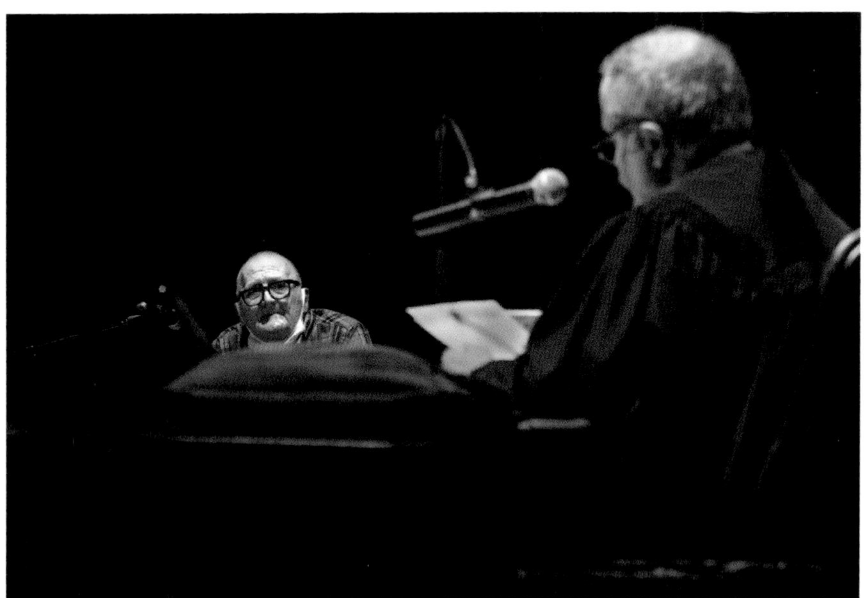

OPPOSITE, TOP You can see the concern etched on the face of the court bailiff as he offers the witness a cup of water. This man testified on behalf of his son, breaking down in tears on the witness stand. His son is now serving a prison sentence for fatally shooting his live-in girlfriend. August 14, 2019, Swain County Courthouse, North Carolina.

OPPOSITE, BOTTOM I have no idea what the woman is telling the officer. I suspect she is insisting that she didn't do whatever it is she's suspected of doing and probably did. July 16, 2020, Sylva, North Carolina.

ABOVE Senior Resident Superior Court Judge Bill Coward hands down a prison sentence following guilty pleas. Because of COVID and the need for safe distancing, Macon County rented court space in a large entertainment hall. This court proceeding was held then—you can see the obligatory mask hanging around the defendant's neck. October 12, 2021, Franklin, North Carolina.

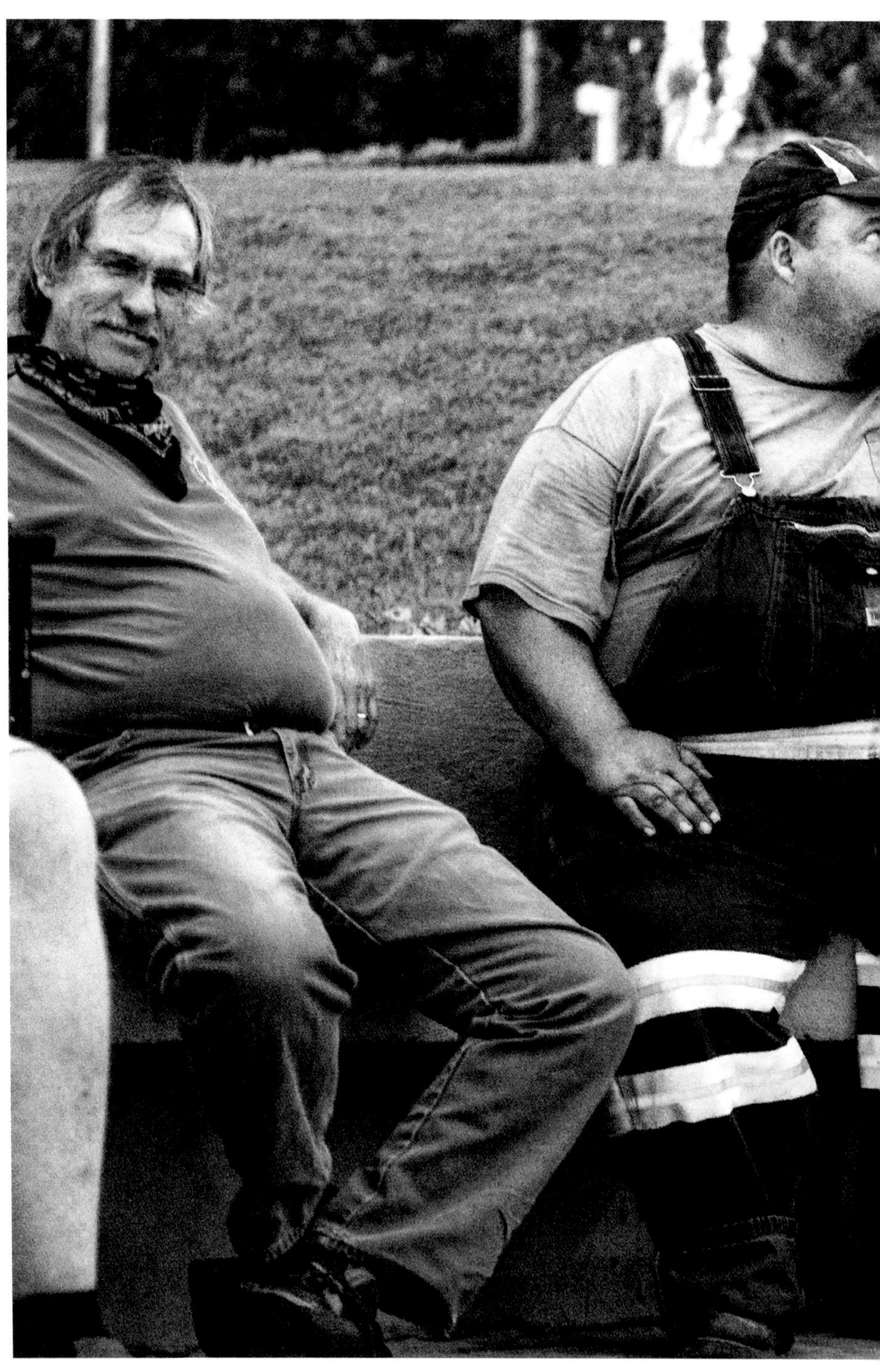

Small towns were not immune to the Black Lives Matter and other protests after they erupted across the nation. Jackson County became embroiled in an argument about its Confederate statue. These folks came out each night to sit near the monument, saying that they were there to guard it from being toppled or vandalized. August 4, 2020, Sylva, North Carolina.

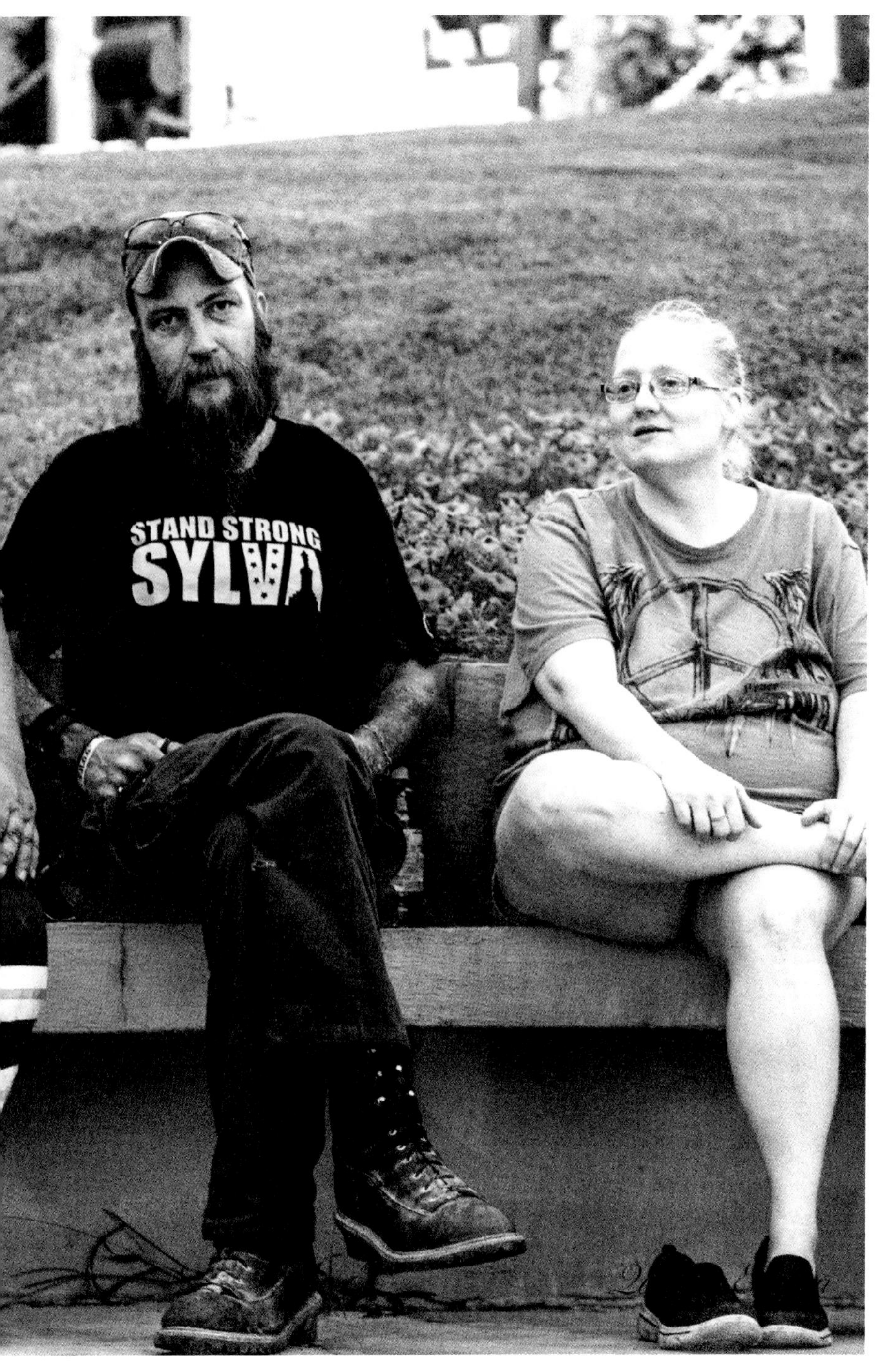
STAND STRONG
SYLVA

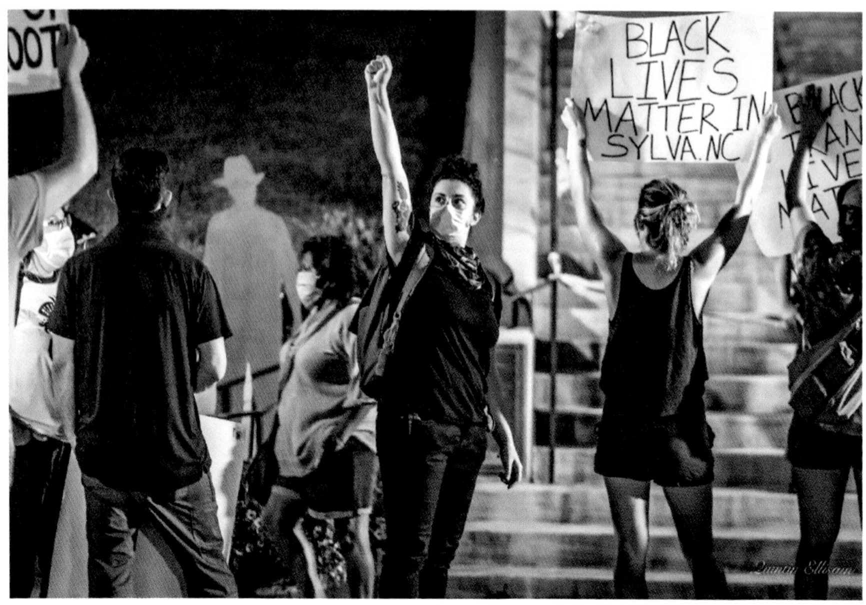

Black Lives Matter protest. A photo that speaks for itself. August 4, 2020, Sylva, North Carolina.

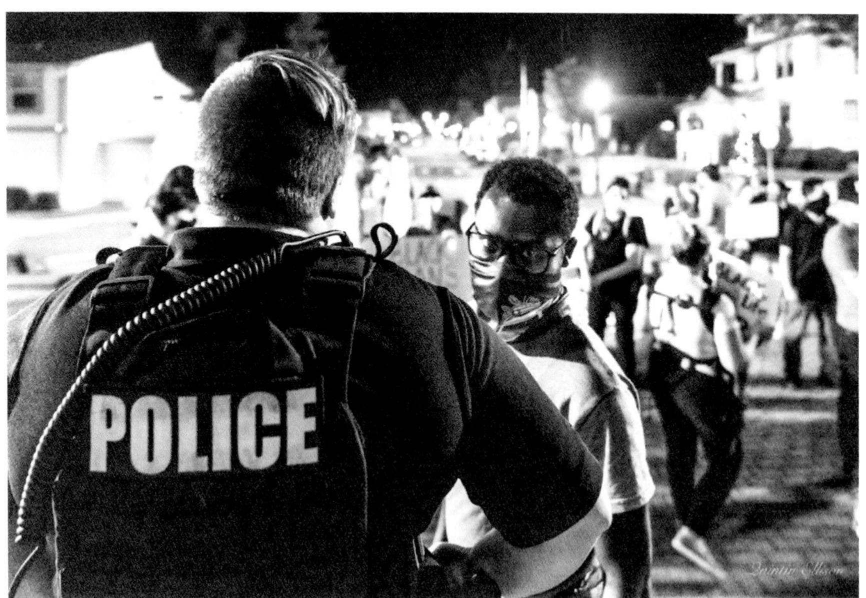

Despite the seemingly hostile gaze, this is actually a friend of mine who participated in protests. Police officers had positioned themselves between the protesters and counter protesters. I am on neutral ground. August 4, 2020, Sylva, North Carolina.

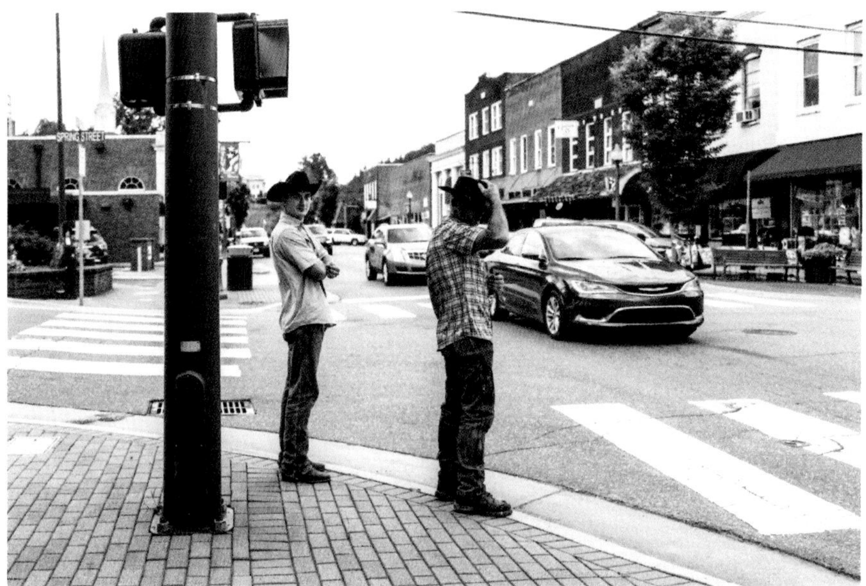

Corner of Spring and Main. Wandering around with camera in hand, I came across these two fellows. Later, someone told me that the man facing the camera is nicknamed "Coleslaw." I love those sorts of details. July 15, 2019, Sylva, North Carolina.

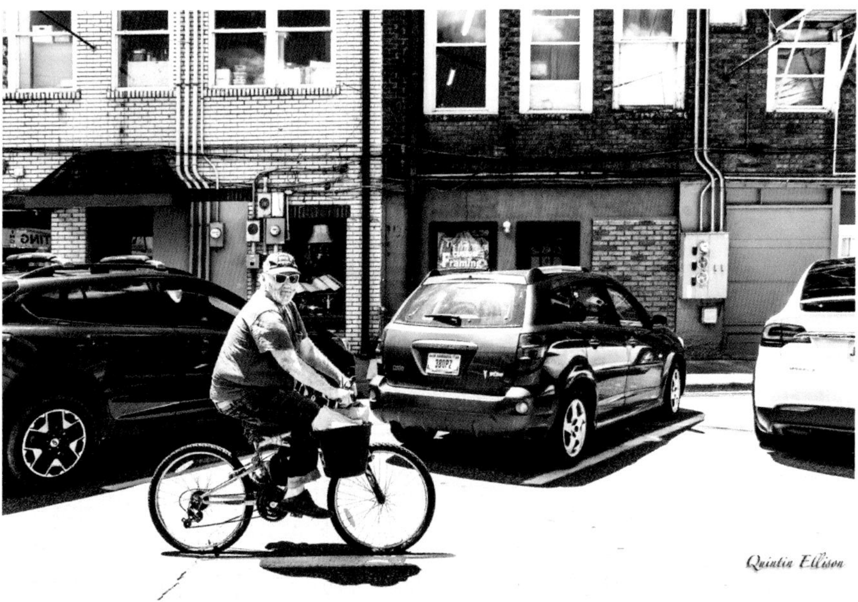

There is something just a little bit funky about Sylva when compared with neighboring small towns. You just never quite know what you will see. July 11, 2020, Sylva, North Carolina.

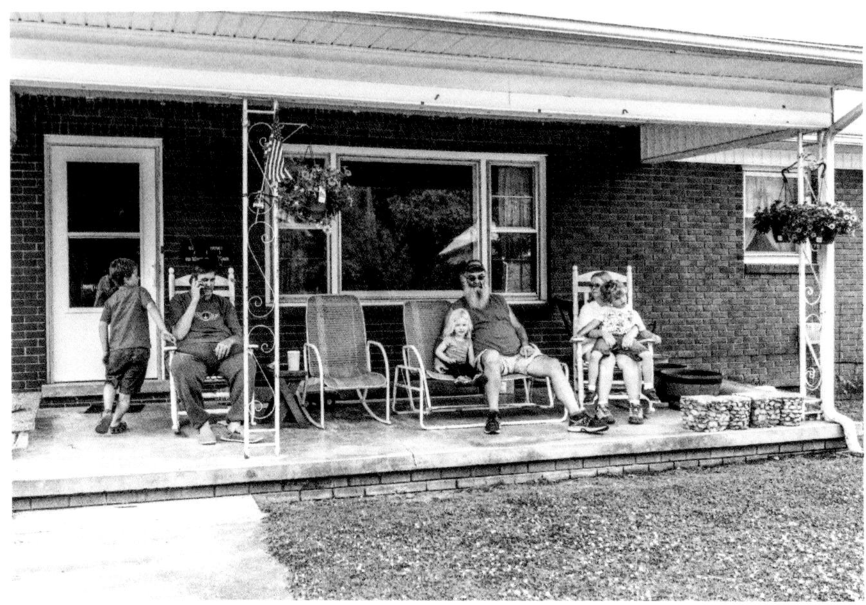

ABOVE I love to walk around small residential communities and watch families or neighbors interacting. June 7, 2019, Hazelwood, North Carolina.

OPPOSITE, TOP Upward of 14 million people per year visit Great Smoky Mountains National Park, and they are loving it to death. When I was a child, you could walk to Clingmans Dome and encounter only a handful of people. Now the trail, at least in warm weather, is heavily congested. I find it unsettling. September 22, 2020, near the North Carolina–Tennessee state line.

OPPOSITE, BOTTOM I try to keep a camera near me at all times, including in the car. You never know when something interesting might occur. I first noticed the woman's fingernails, and then I saw the man's reflection in the car mirror. December 31, 2020, Murphy, North Carolina.

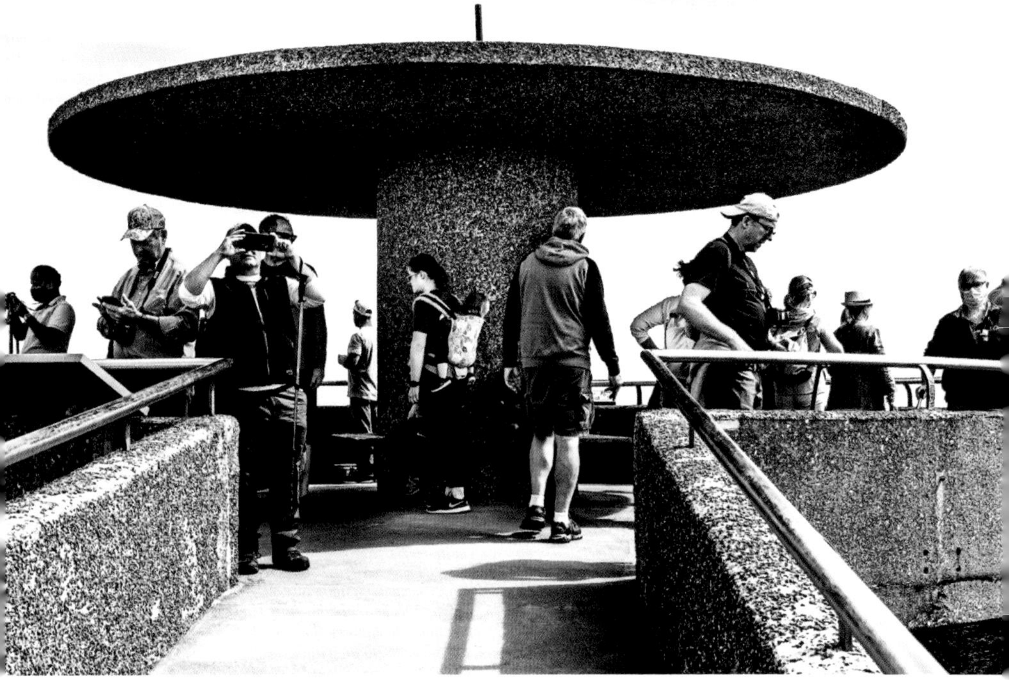

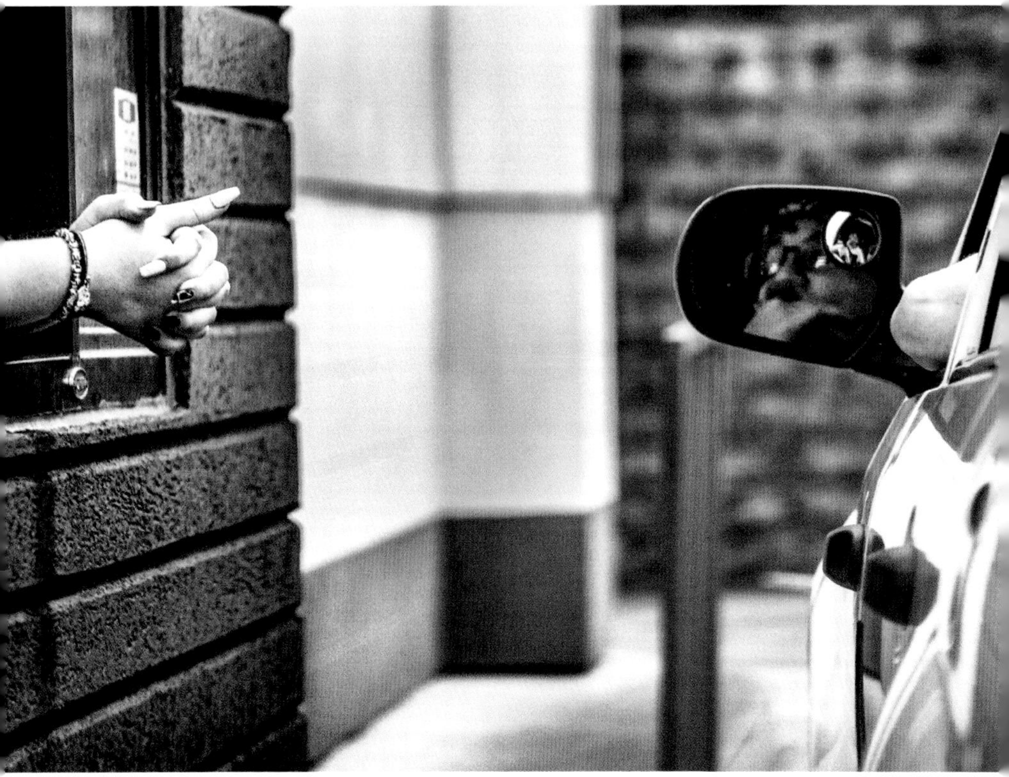

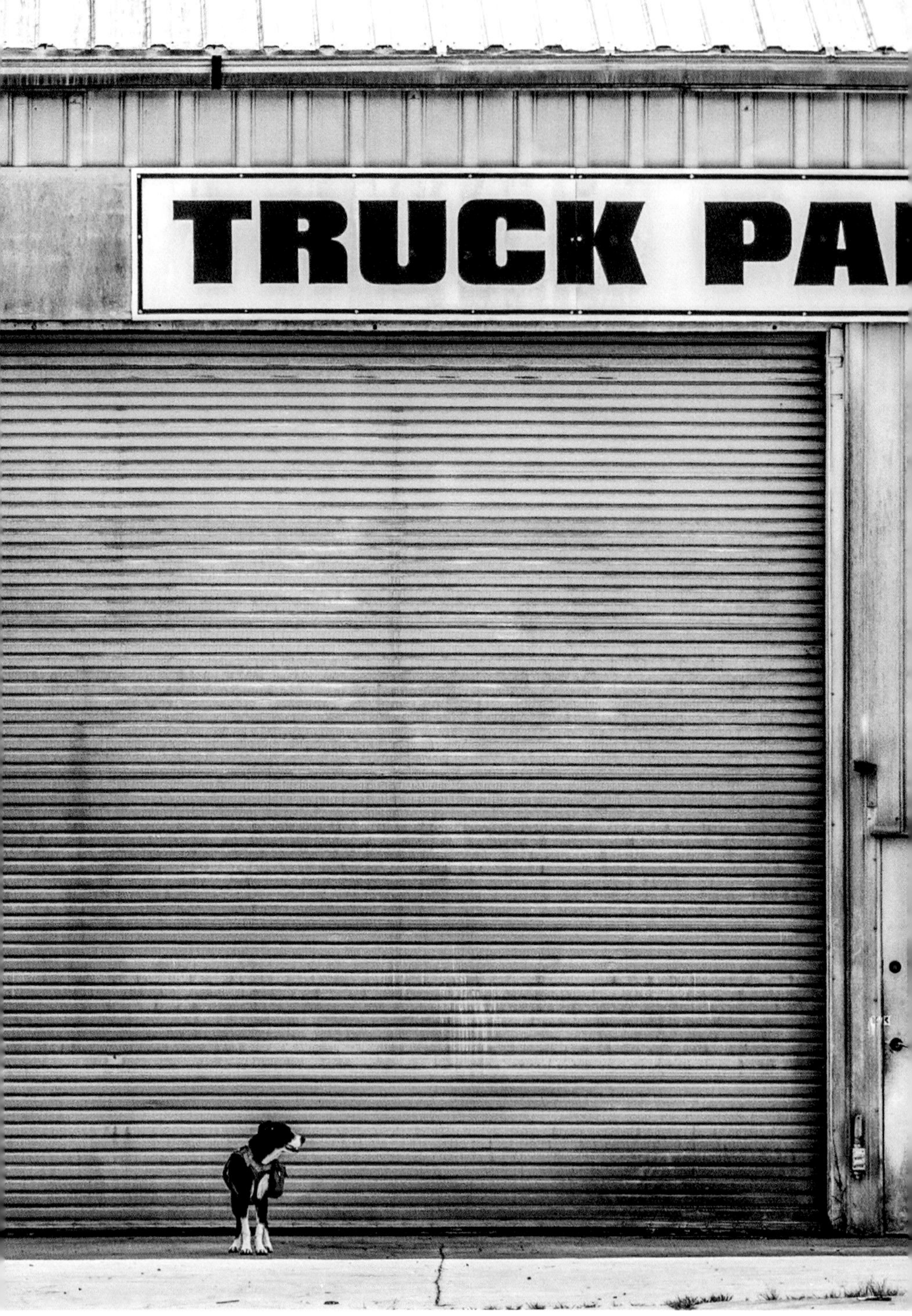

Frequently you take photos and are left to invent the stories that might go with them. Does the dog belon
to the man? Is the man angry with the dog? I have no idea. July 20, 2020, Franklin, North Carolina.

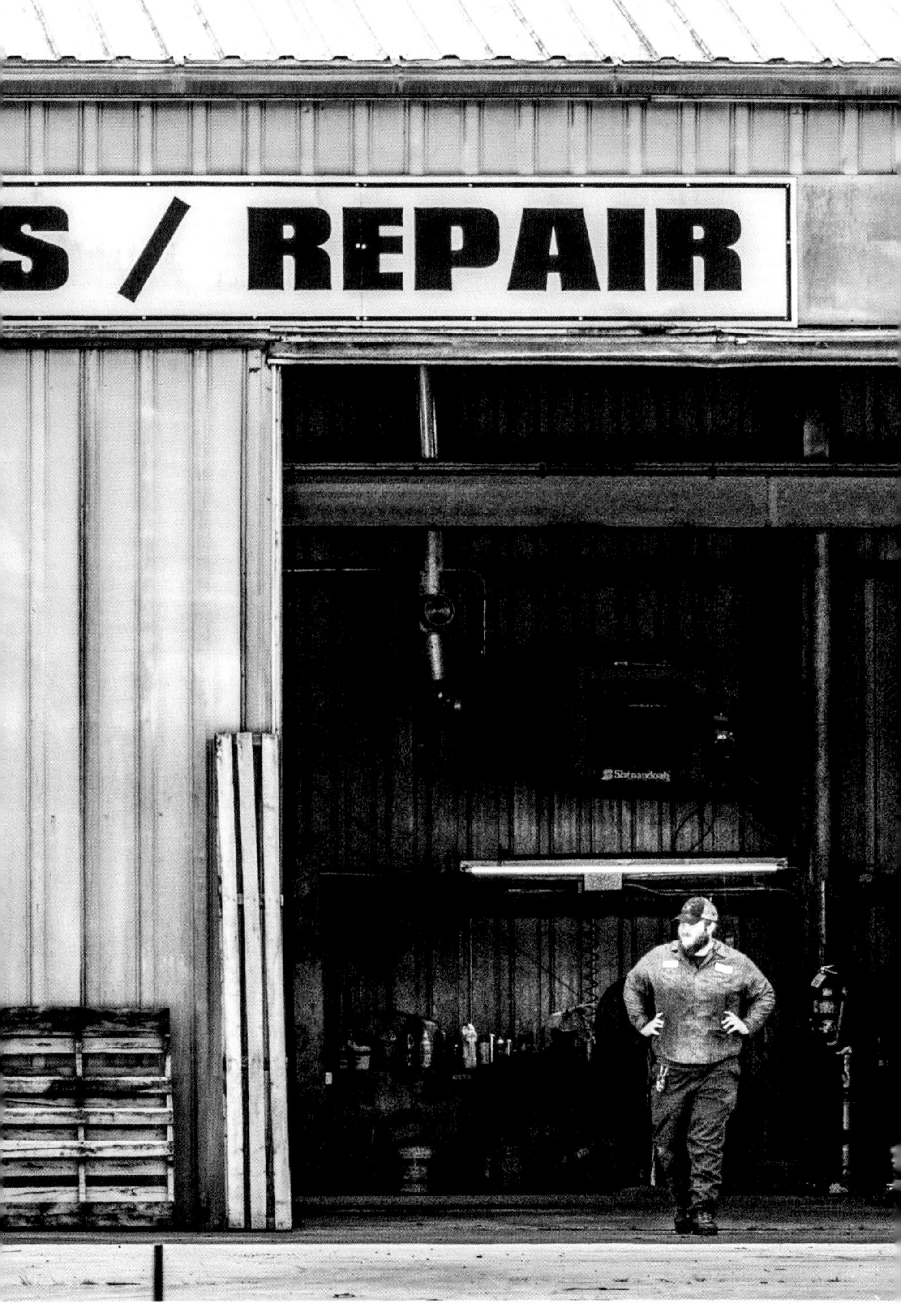

Photography by Quintin Ellison

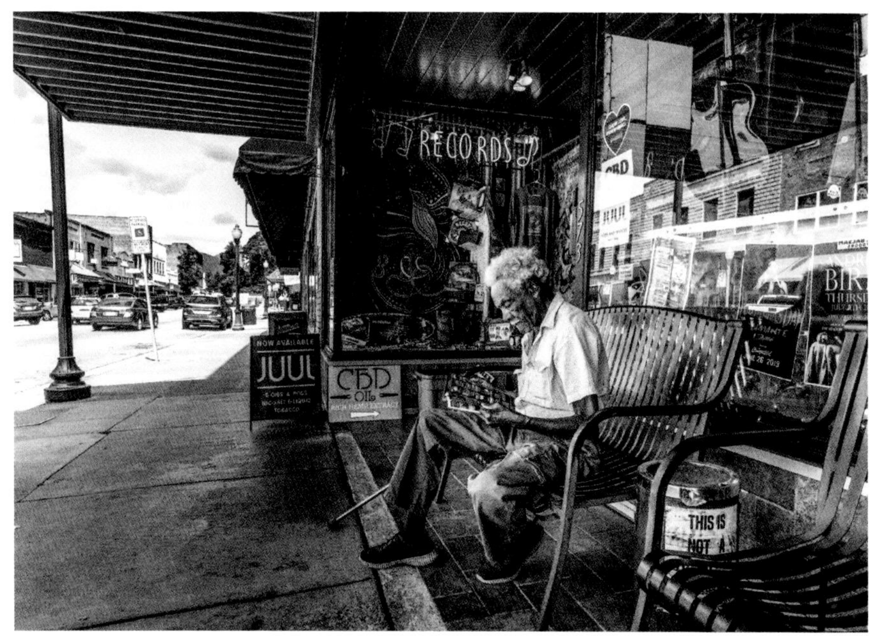

This gentleman is sitting in front of In Your Ear Emporium, a music store and smoke shop. June 17, 2019, Sylva, North Carolina.

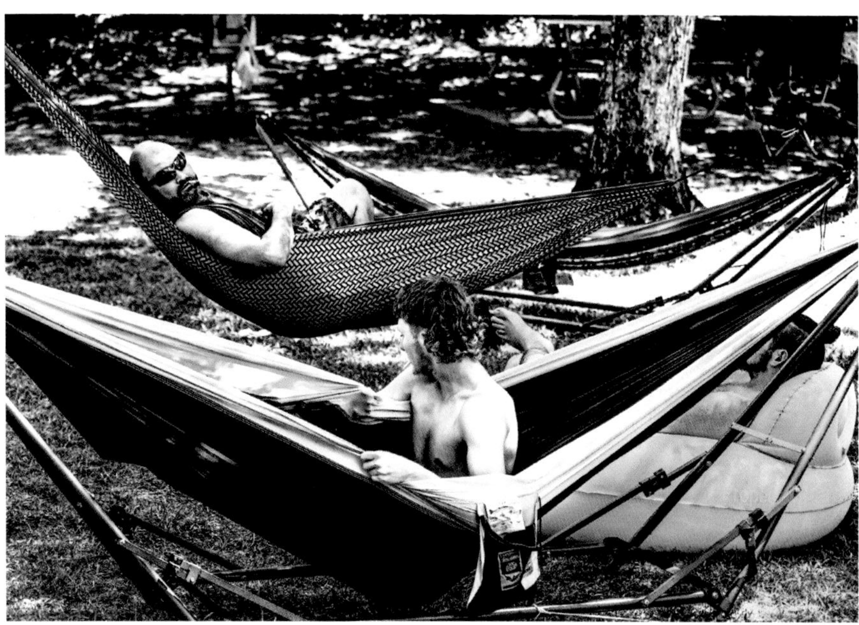

If you can connect eye to eye, so to speak, with the people you are photographing, the image gains power through that interaction. August 16, 2020, Deep Creek Campground in Great Smoky Mountains National Park.

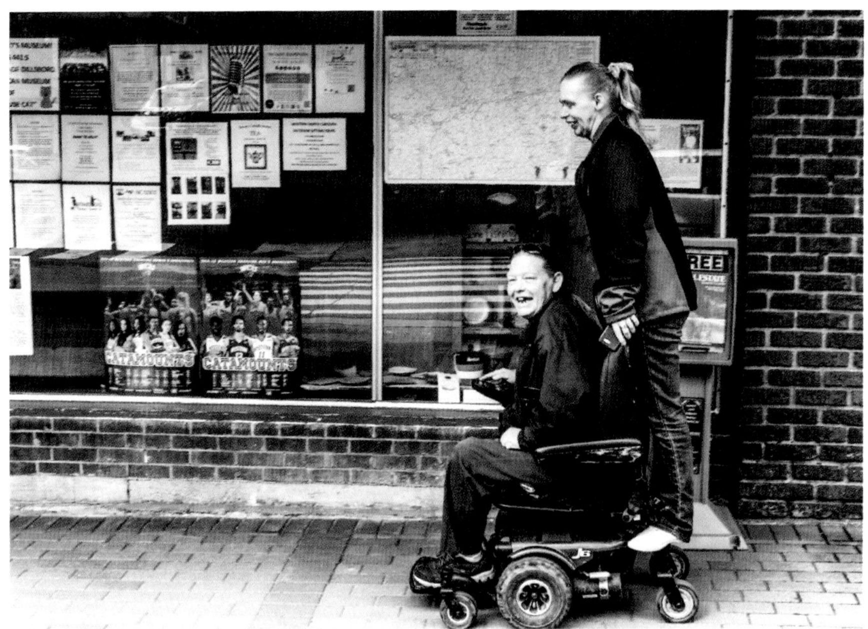

The mother is driving, and her daughter is hitching a ride on the back. They didn't have a car, so the scooter served as a substitute. I admire their sense of fun. February 19, 2018, Sylva, North Carolina.

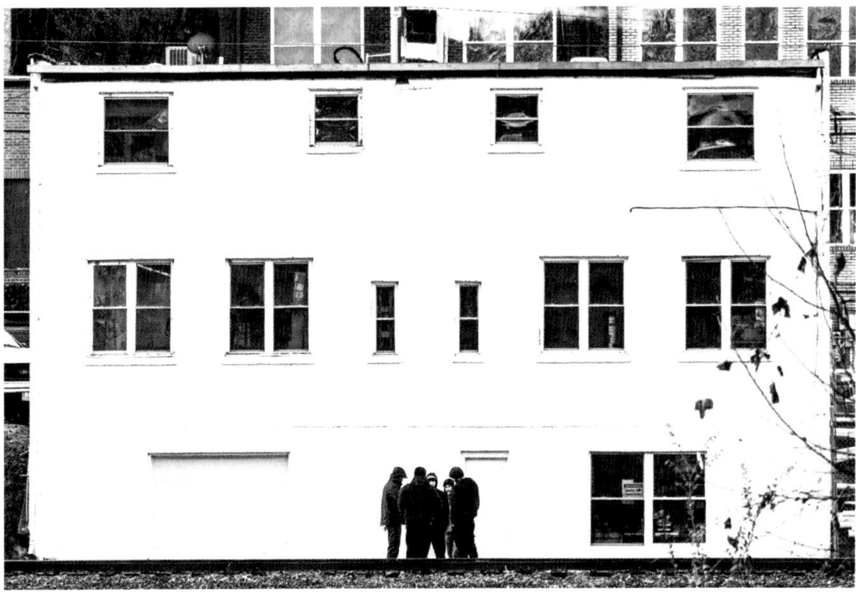

A group of workmen in front of Ward Plumbing, Heating and Air before their day gets fully underway. I was attracted to the figure-to-ground aspect in this image: light background with dark figures in front. If only more subjects cooperated and stood in front of light-to-dark or dark-to-light backgrounds. December 11, 2018, Sylva, North Carolina.

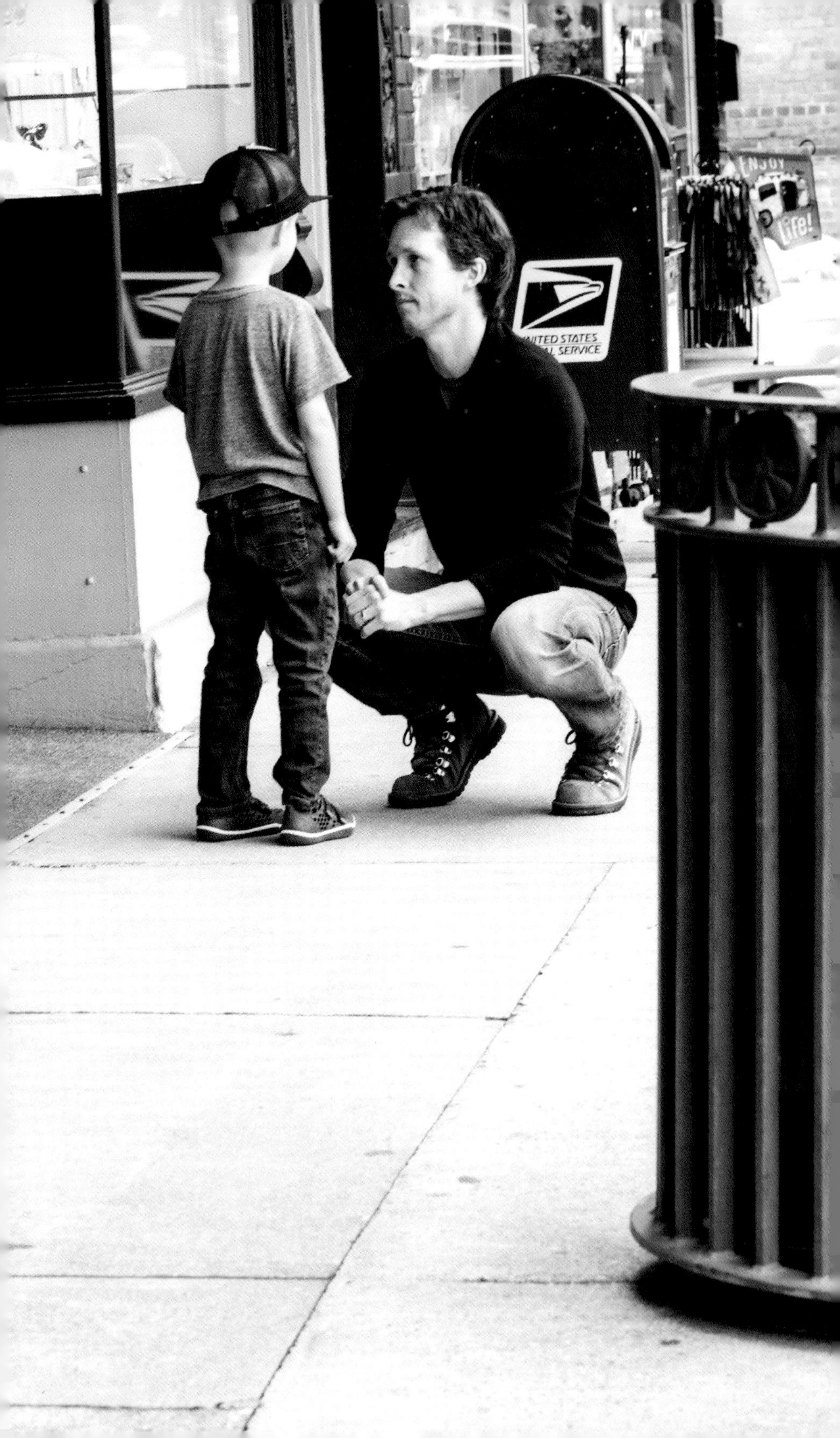
ENJOY
Life!
NITED STATES
AL SERVICE

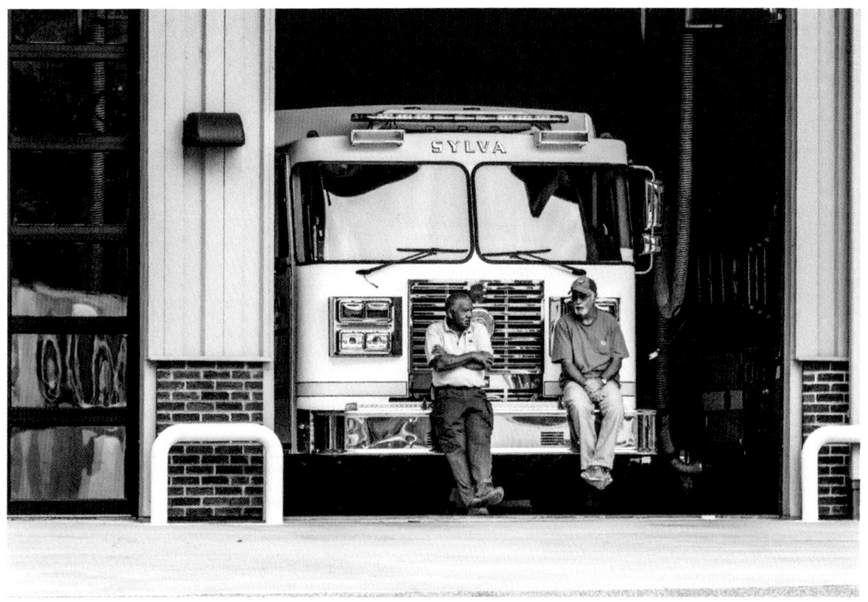

OPPOSITE My story is that this image captures a father listening to his son after cautioning him not to misbehave. You might look at this photo and have another story, one that is even better than mine. April 26, 2019, Sylva, North Carolina.

ABOVE Most of the firefighters in rural areas such as this are volunteers. With our busy modern lives, work commutes and such, it is getting increasingly difficult for small fire departments to recruit new members. October 8, 2019, Sylva, North Carolina.

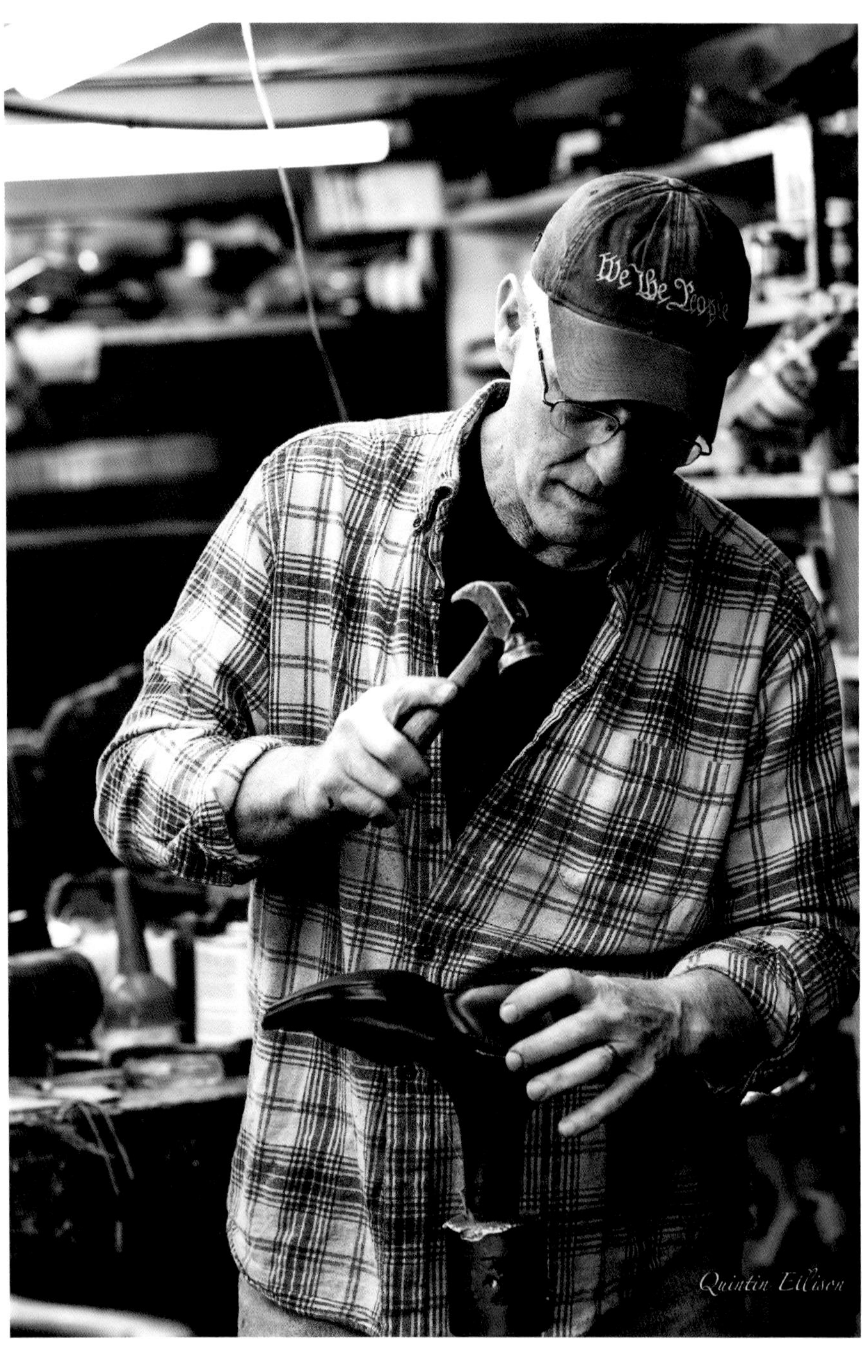
We The People
Quintin Ellison

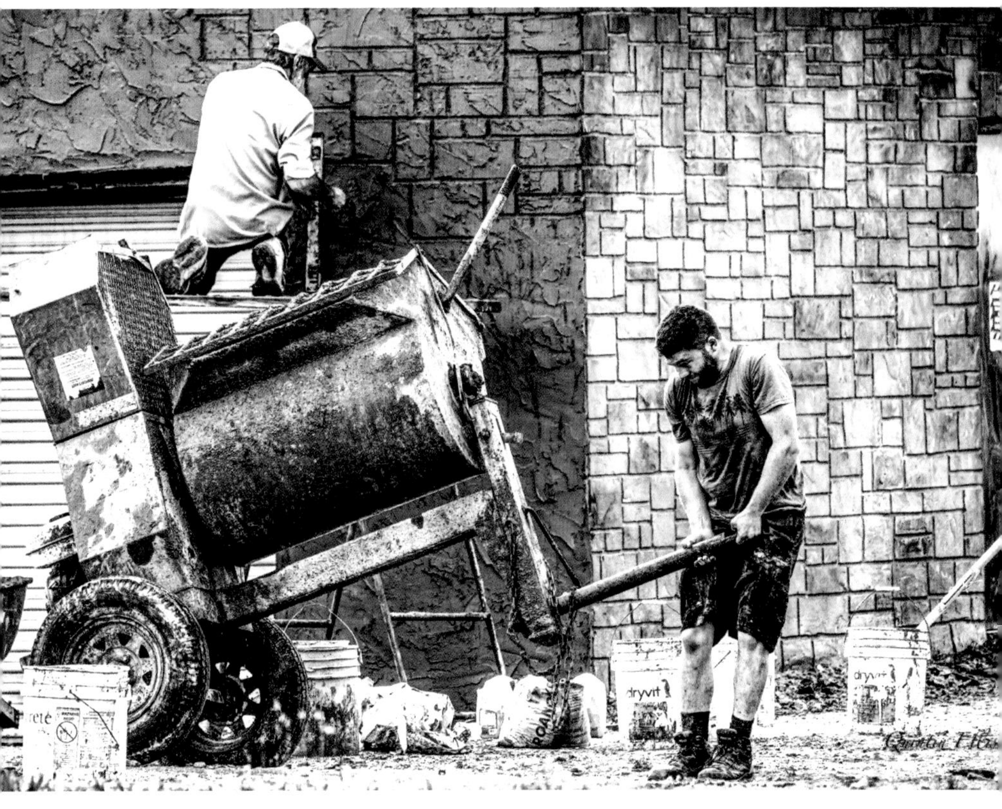

OPPOSITE Mike Fitzgerald is the only cobbler left in a seven-county area of Western North Carolina. He is a man who believes in public service. Mike served on the town of Dillsboro board for sixteen years, about twelve of them as mayor. April 16, 2021, Sylva, North Carolina.

ABOVE This image makes me thankful that I work mainly inside. My recollection is that it had been pouring rain. Still, these two were laboring to get the job done. June 29, 2020, Franklin, North Carolina.

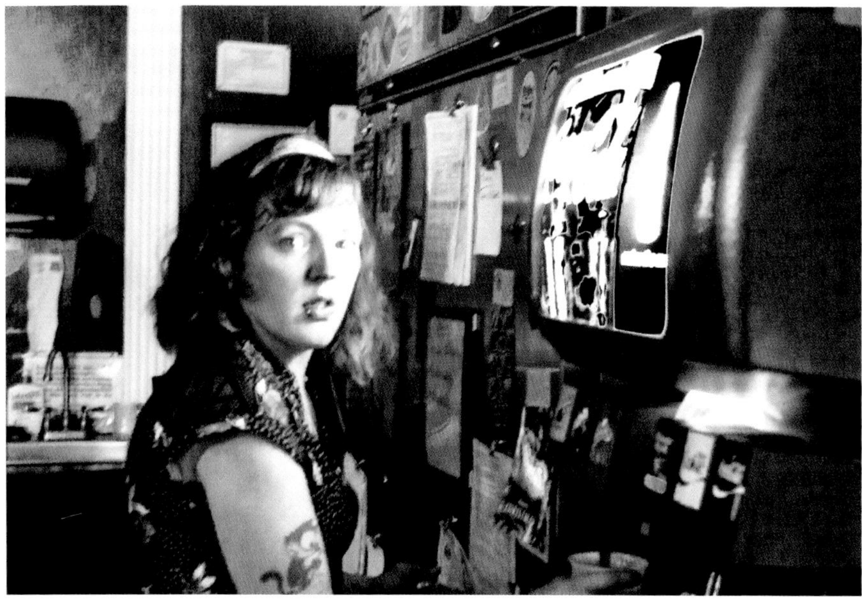

A waitress at the now-closed eatery Mad Batter Restaurant. Do you mind the out-of-focus look? I don't. For a long time, only sharply in-focus photographs passed my acceptability test. These days, I don't much care, as long as I think the image works.

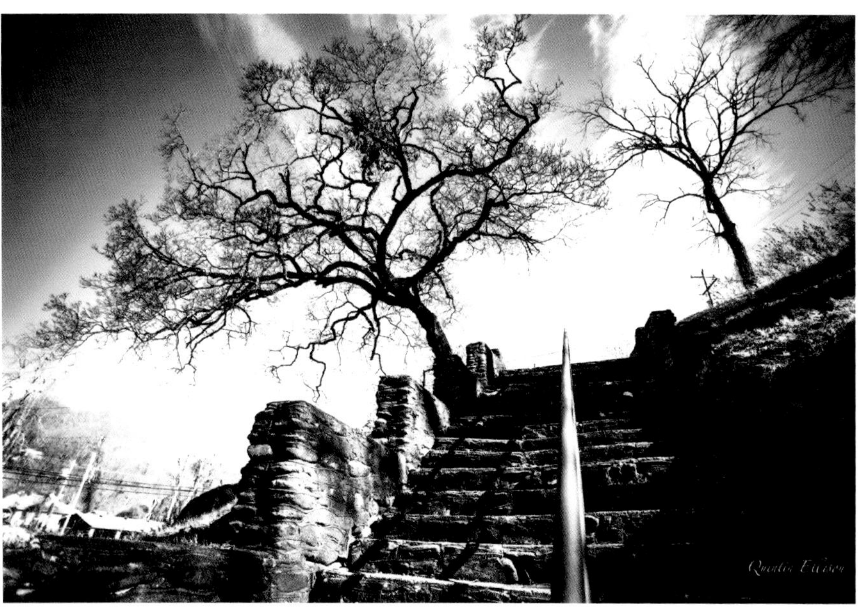

Dogwood tree and steps. I have repeatedly photographed this old dogwood (the tree to the left), in all seasons and from all angles. I believe this photo is the best of the lot. I used an old manual lens—you can see the distortion from the old glass, particularly on the left side of the image. January 31, 2019, Mark Watson Park, Jackson County, North Carolina.

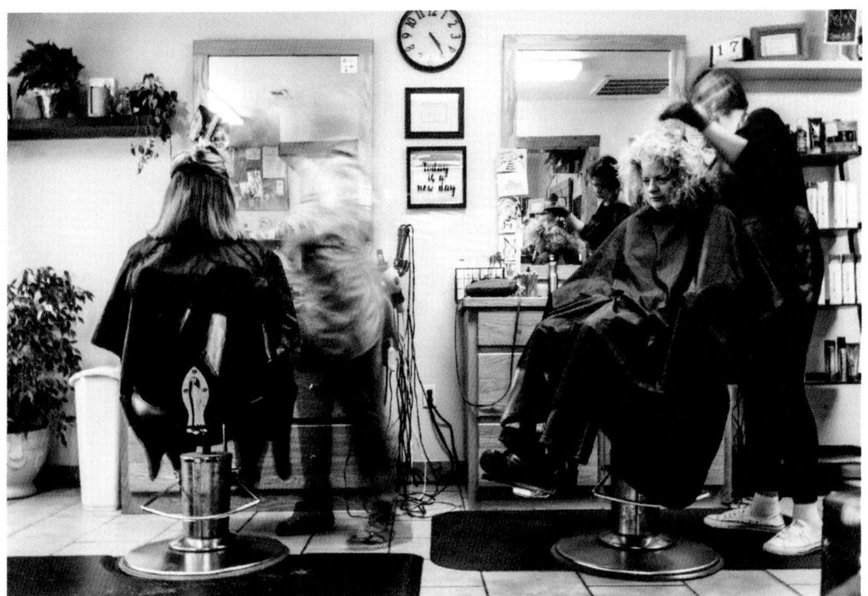

I remember sitting in this hair salon waiting to get my hair done and fiddling with my camera. I handheld a long exposure (to blur movement) and liked the result. December 17, 2018, Sylva, North Carolina.

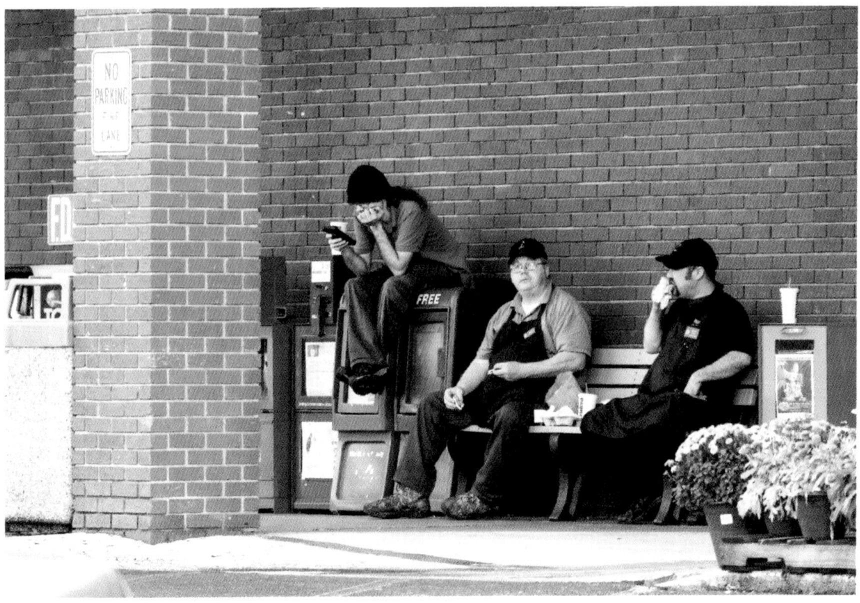

Lunch break. Workers outside a local grocery store. October 11, 2018, Sylva, North Carolina.

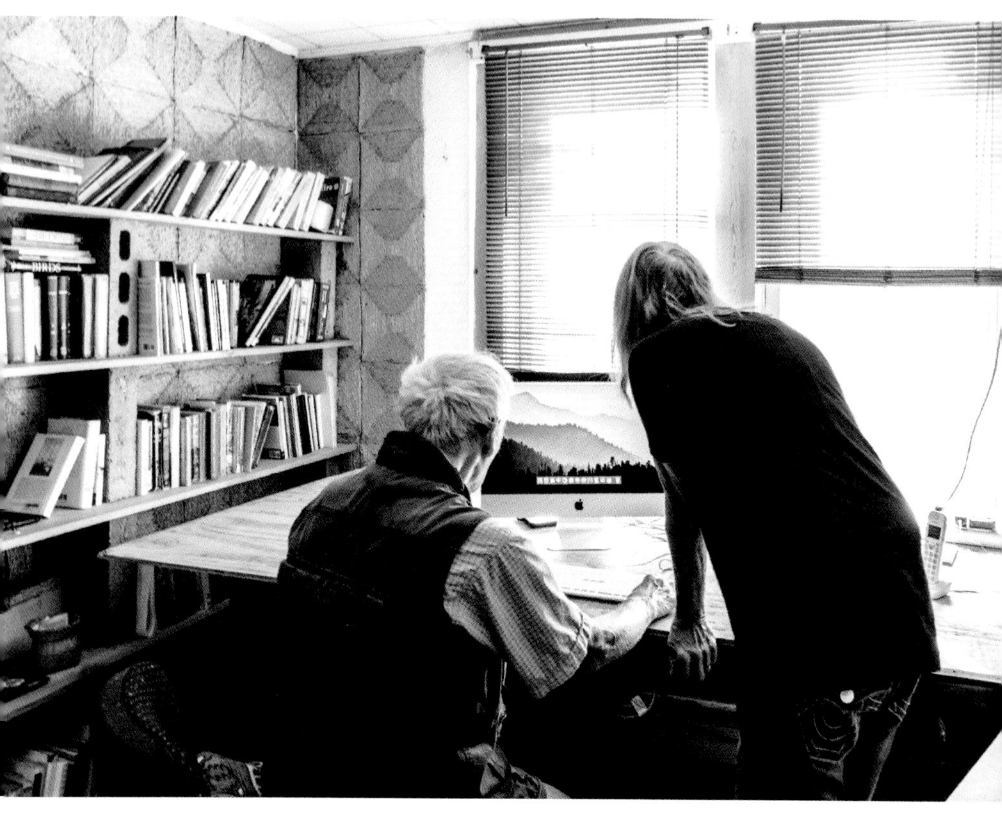

Mom and Dad at work in his office. Mom's studio and gallery is in the next room. September 6, 2018, Bryson City, North Carolina.

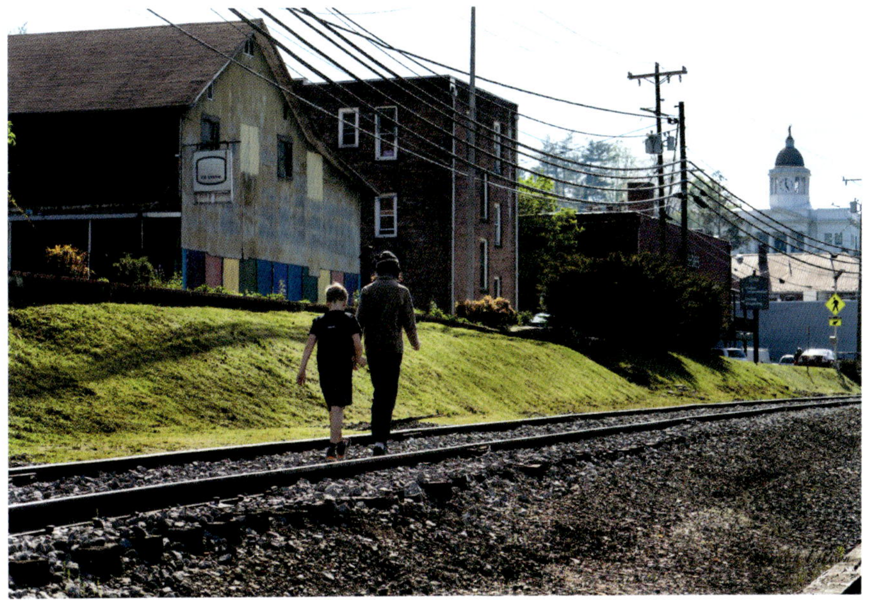

Two boys walk along the railroad tracks. April 21, 2019, Sylva, North Carolina.

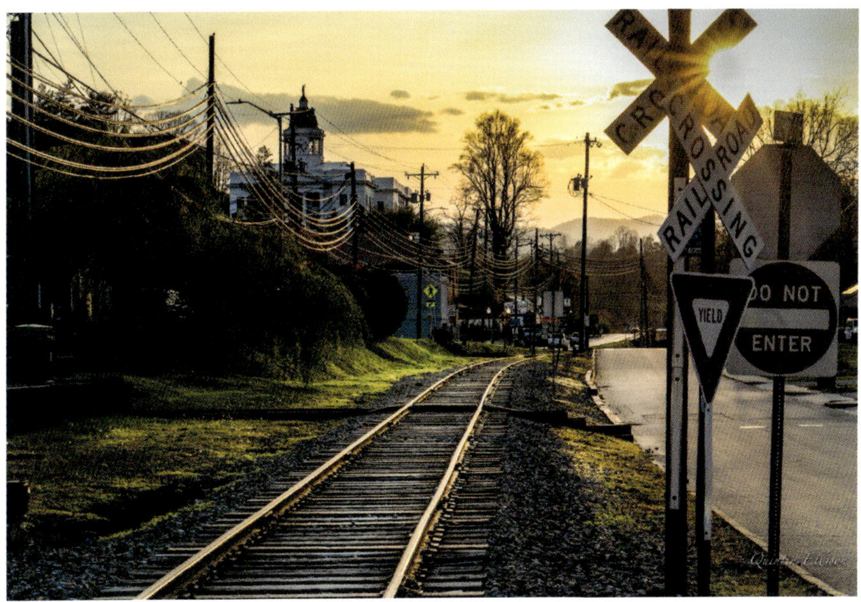

The historic Jackson County Courthouse to the left, railroad tracks in the center and Railroad Avenue on the right. The best bit is a setting sun that bathes the scene in warm yellow. April 7, 2021, Sylva, North Carolina.

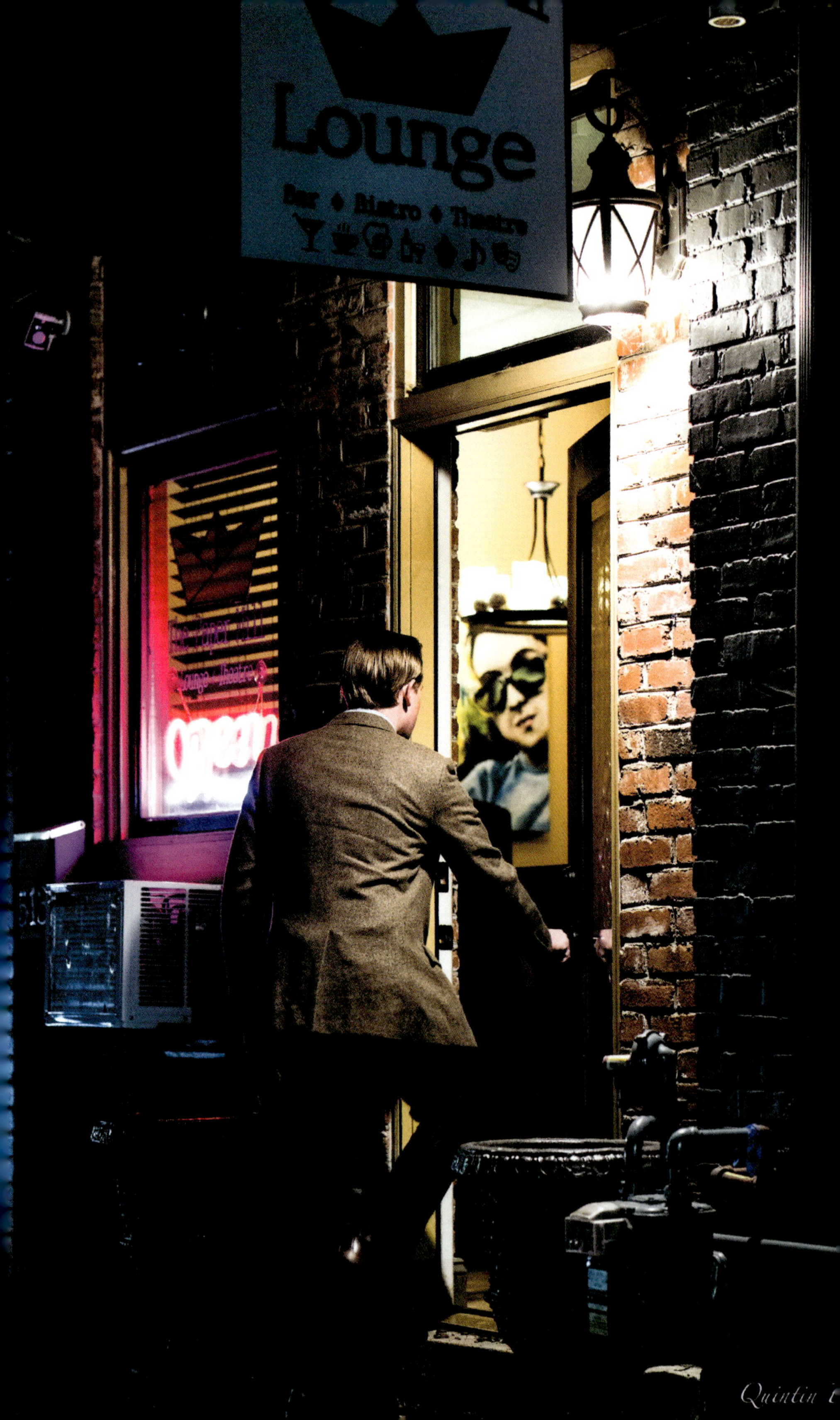
Lounge
Bar ♦ Bistro ♦ Theatre
OPEN
Quintin

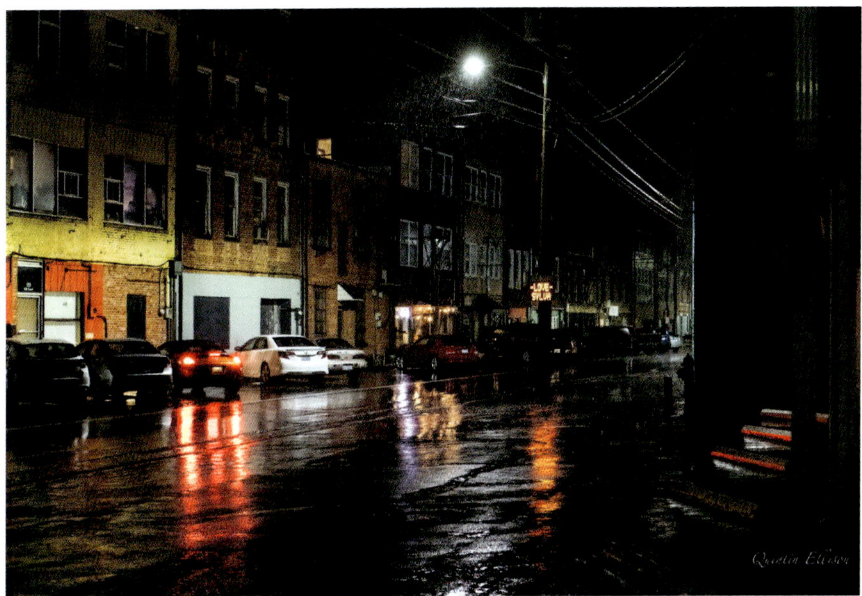

OPPOSITE At Papermill Lounge. I was returning from covering an event for the newspaper, decided to drive around for a bit and spotted this. The scene reminds me of an illicit speakeasy. February 4, 2019, Sylva, North Carolina.

ABOVE Sylva's police chief, Chris Hatton, called me one evening to suggest I take a photo of the department's newly installed radar-speed sign. It was pouring rain—adding to my lack of enthusiasm—but I went anyway. My reward was an image I treasure. March 17, 2021, Sylva, North Carolina.

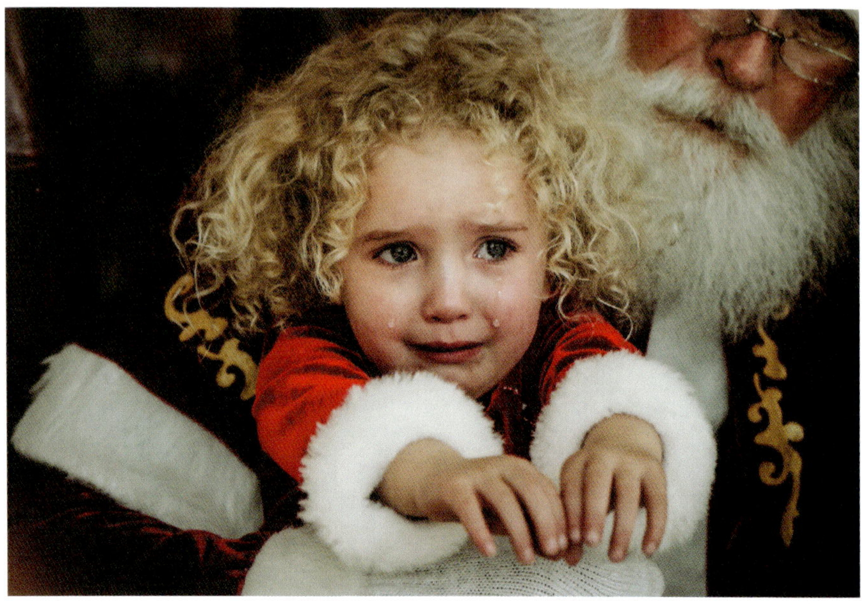

'Tis the Season: A small girl reacts poorly to a photo with Santa Claus. November 30, 2019, Sylva, North Carolina.

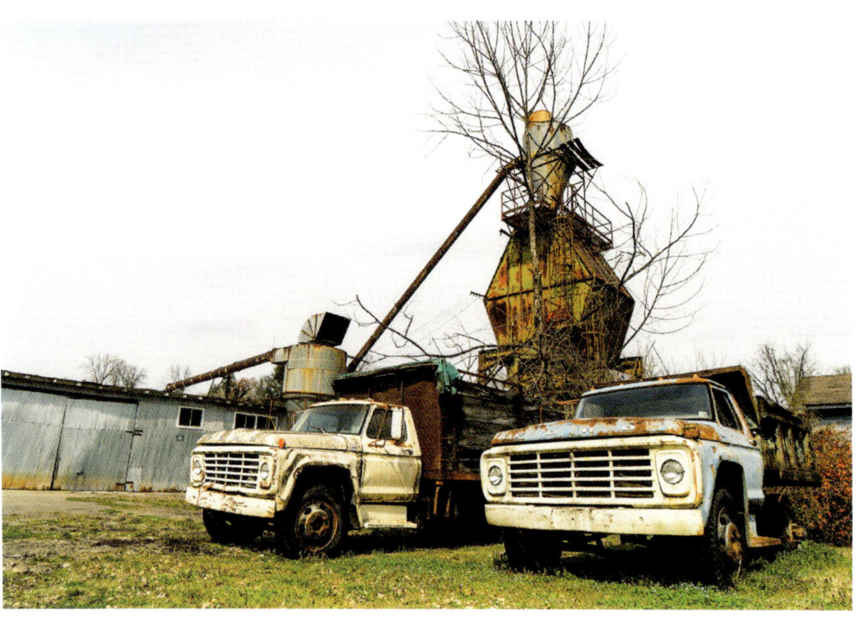

The colors of these two old trucks caught my eye. March 13, 2019, Bryson City, North Carolina.

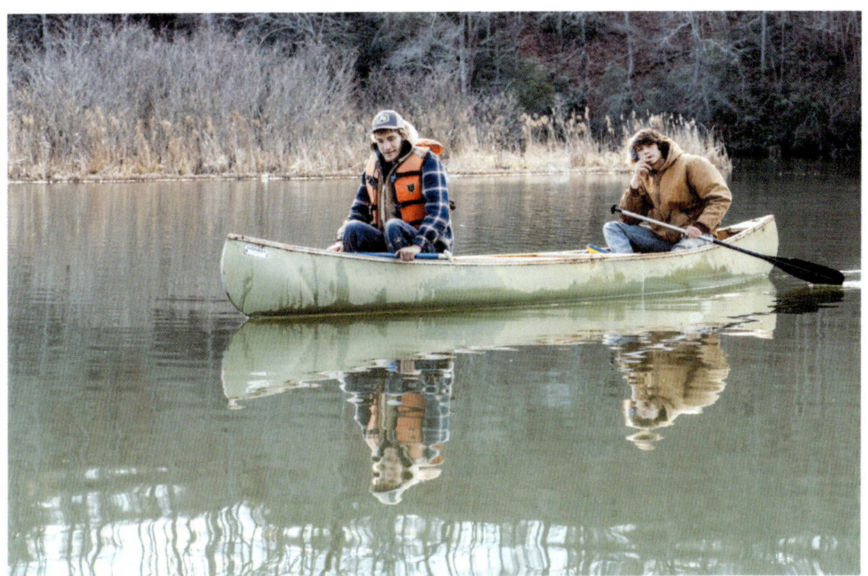

Two boys canoeing on Lake Emory in Macon County paddled in for a chat. This small, manmade lake is a great place to watch and photograph birds. A pair of eagles nests in a towering pine on the water's edge. January 11, 2019, Macon County, North Carolina.

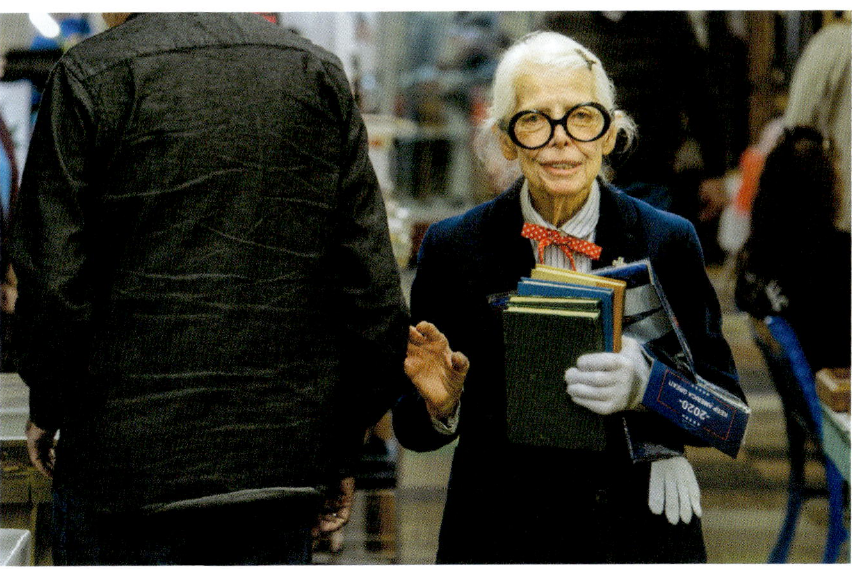

The late Dodie Allen at Uncle Bill's Flea Market near the Whittier community in Jackson County, where she kept a political booth to promote her conservative beliefs. Dodie was one of a kind. I liked her immensely. This photo was taken about seven months before her death. February 9, 2019, Jackson County, North Carolina.

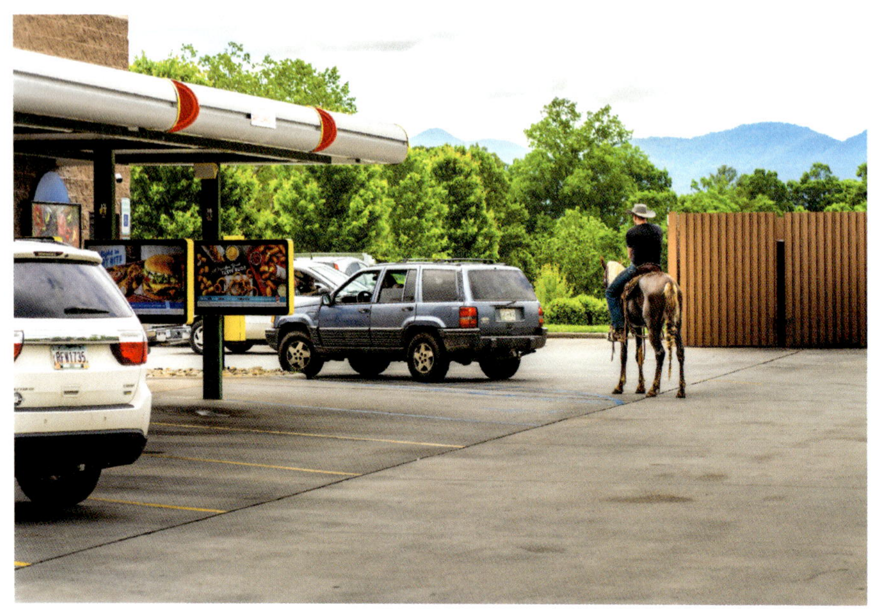

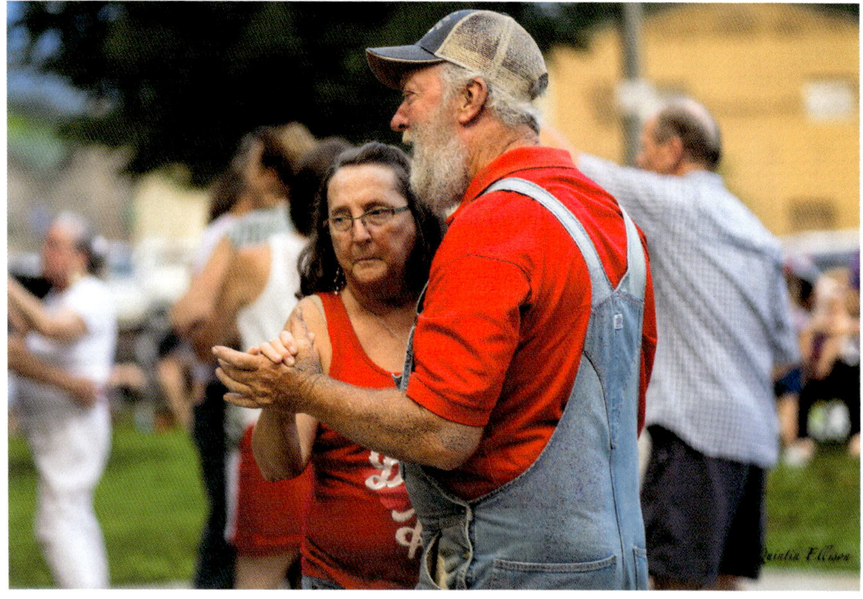

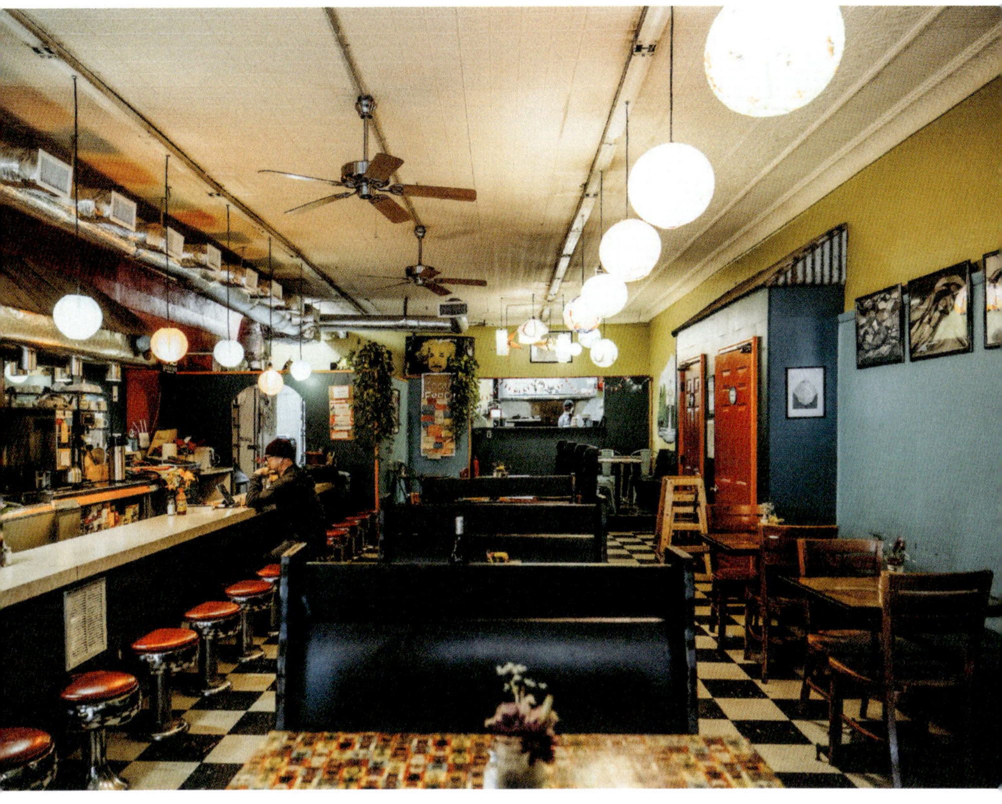

OPPOSITE, TOP A hungry cowboy waits his turn in the line at a fast-food restaurant drive-thru. June 5, 2020, Franklin, North Carolina.

OPPOSITE, BOTTOM A couple dancing at Concerts on the Creek in Sylva. Live bands perform on Friday evenings throughout the summer. I love the bright red shirts and, of course, the man's overalls. July 16, 2021, Sylva, North Carolina.

ABOVE Guadalupe Café was a favorite hangout for many in Sylva. Owner Jen Pearson opened the restaurant in the former Hooper's drugstore, closing it recently after twenty years in business. February 19, 2020, Sylva, North Carolina.

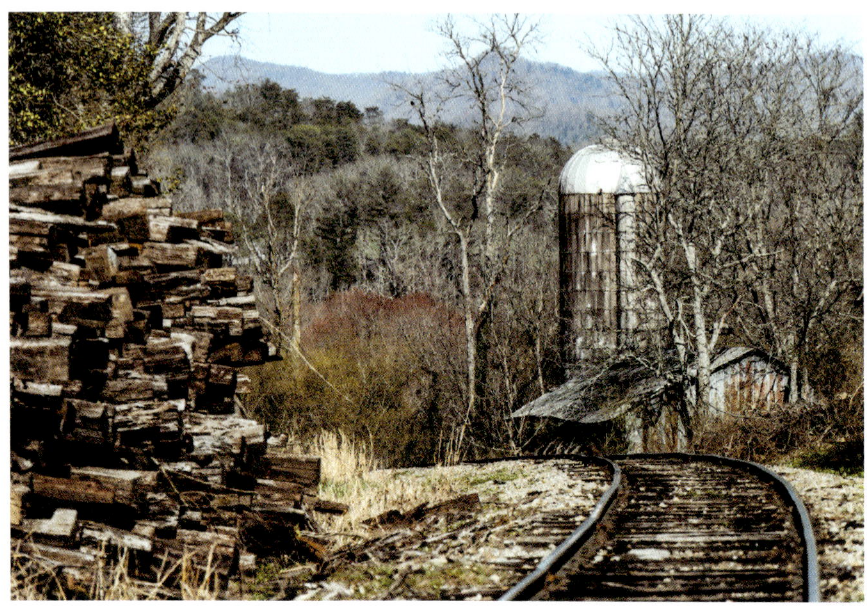

A silo and small barn speak to the long farming history at Kituwah, one of the Cherokee Indians' ancient mother towns. The Eastern Band of Cherokee Indians repurchased the 309-acre site in 1996. March 6, 2019, Swain County, North Carolina.

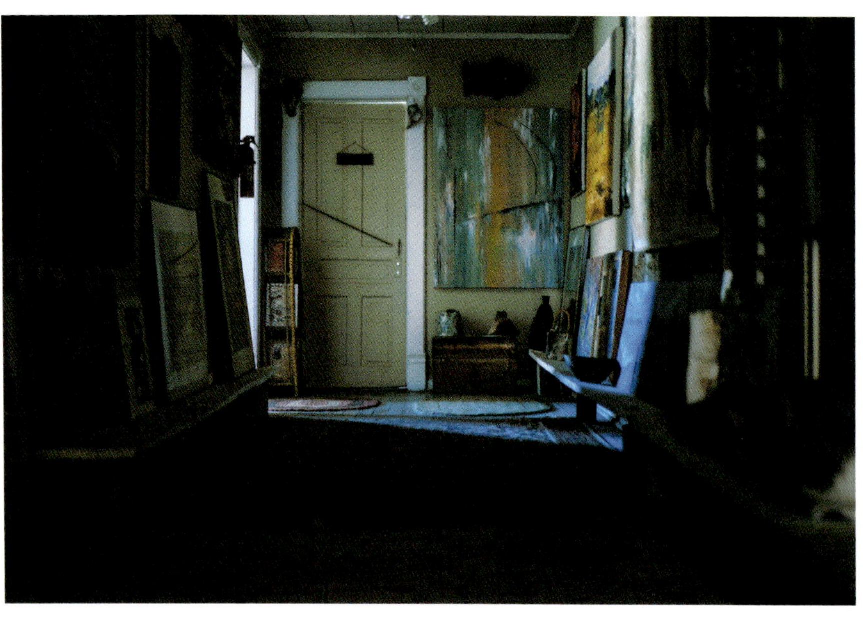

A photo of the interior of Elizabeth Ellison Studio and Gallery. April 22, 2019, Bryson City, North Carolina.

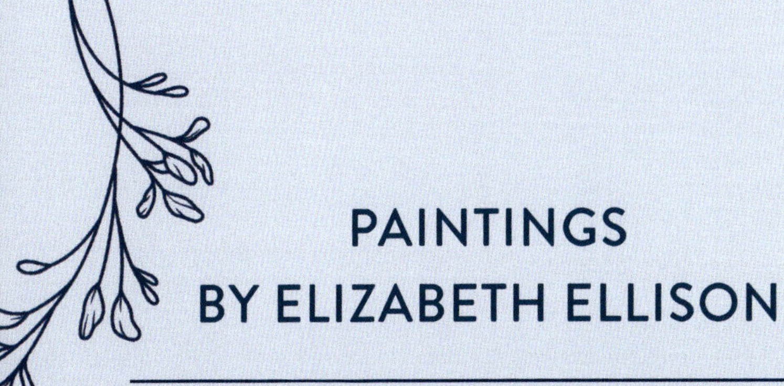

PAINTINGS BY ELIZABETH ELLISON

The Journey of a Painter

In 1973, George was teaching English at Mississippi State University in Starkville, Mississippi. In a graduate course, he asked his students to write a paper on a regional writer. They were to do the research and then present their paper.

Being George, who never did anything without significant preparation, he decided that he should also research a regional author, so that he would know what to expect from his class. I don't know why, but he chose Horace Kephart, who lived in and wrote about the Great Smokies and Southern Blue Ridge.

Kephart had left his wife and family behind, seeking a "back of beyond" to deal with his binge drinking and some mental health issues. In George and Janet McCue's *Back of Beyond: A Horace Kephart Biography* (Great Smoky Mountains Association, 2019), his life and move to the mountains were later thoroughly expounded.

And so, back in 1973, George traveled to Swain County and Bryson City to do the same assignment that he had delegated to his class. He fell in love with this area, and soon we decided to move with our family of three young children to Western North Carolina. George wanted to pursue his own writing career, and I wanted to paint. My only stipulation was that I never wanted to live anywhere but in the country—not in a town or city.

We found the cove we live in, and which we call Permanent Camp, on a hike along Old N.C. 288. We followed an overgrown wagon road along Lands Creek to a cabin, really a shack, built beside the creek. This became our home for nearly twenty-three years. We lived without electricity, and our water source was a spring up the branch from the cabin. We rented the cabin and about forty acres for thirty-five dollars a month. We bought the property in 1996.

This has been our base for more than forty years. It has been both our inspiration and an ongoing inspiration to various family members. Most of the property is now in a permanent conservation easement with the State of North Carolina.

The paintings and illustrations I have done through the years are a direct result of that move to these mountains. I painted in the cabin and in the fields until I opened my studio/gallery in Bryson City in 1984. George maintained his office in two rooms of this space until his health necessitated he move his office to our house, where he continued to write until his death.

I continue to paint in my studio and open the gallery to the public. My paintings are meant to reflect how I feel about my environment, which happens to be in these beautiful mountains. They are not photographic representations, as I often go where my brush and paints take me. In some way, I like to feel that I still capture the magic of each place I choose to depict.

Both George and I always believed/believe in what we share with people, be it through teaching or writing and, in my case, painting. We've hoped to instill awareness of nature's importance so that others, in turn, will want to protect and preserve it. Our daughter Quintin has joined us in this same mission with her photographic depictions of mountain living and the natural world in this region we call home.

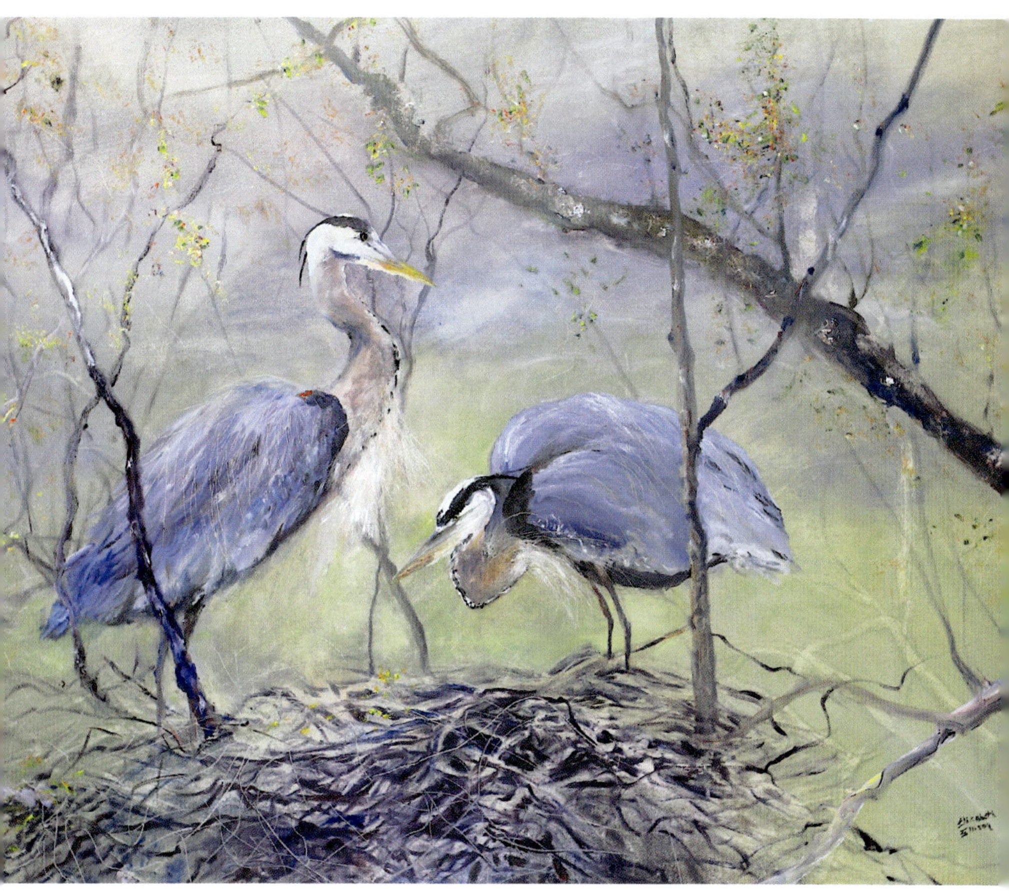

Herons Along the Tuckaseigee. Our daughter Quintin captured a beautiful image of nesting great blues beside a highway overpass. I often see them posing in the scrubby sycamores there. Lucky is the artist who has a gifted photographer in the family.

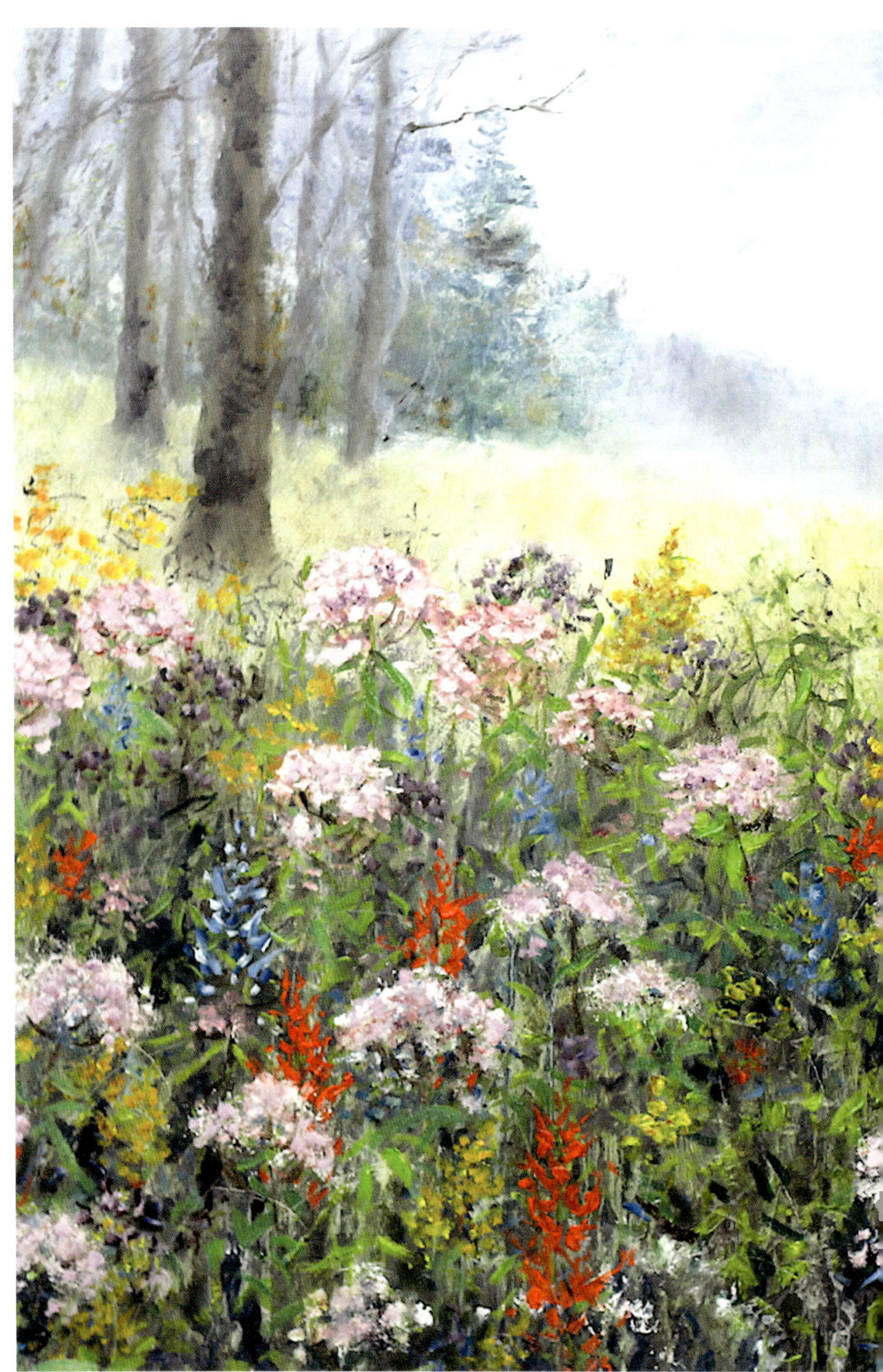

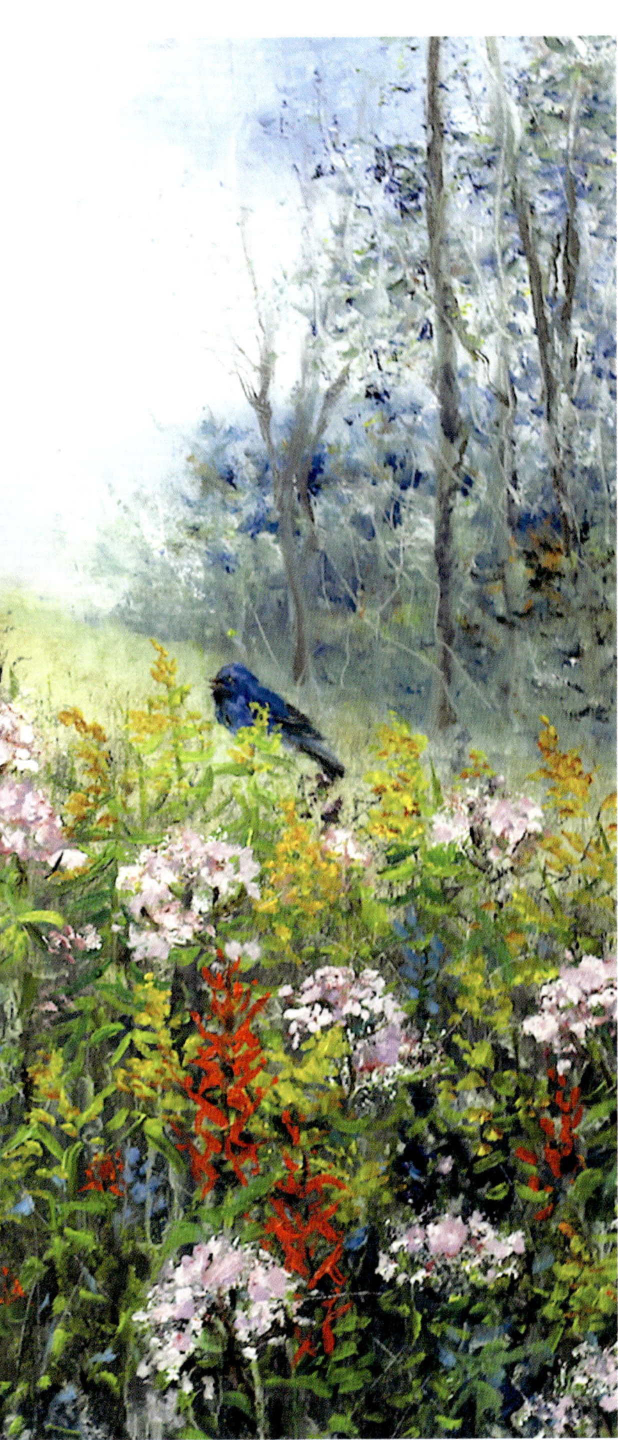

Indigo Bunting and Wildflowers. Driving along the Blue Ridge Parkway in the spring and summer, the road banks are often abloom with wildflowers. If you are fortunate, there might be an Indigo bunting perched among them.

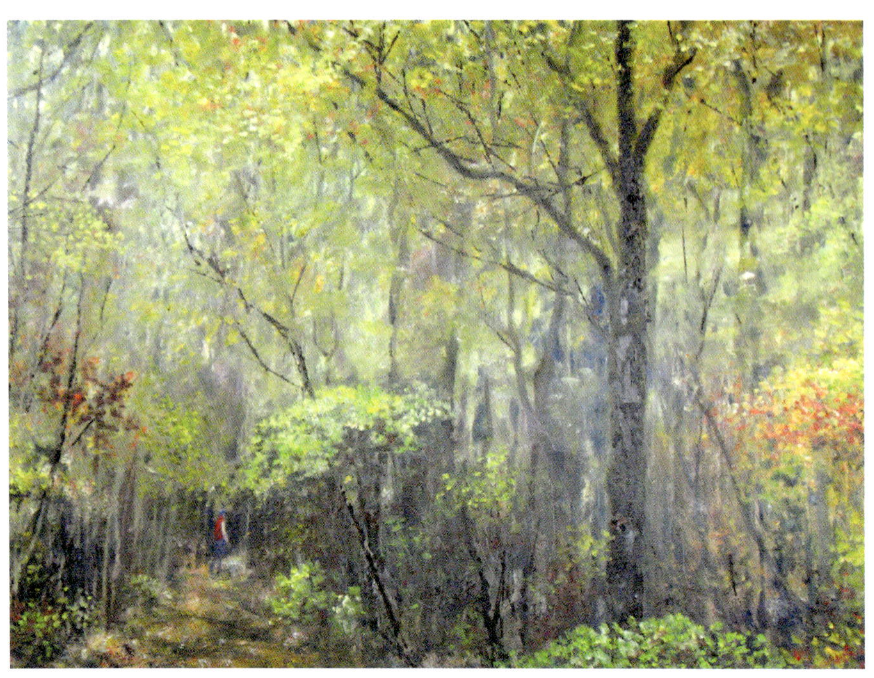

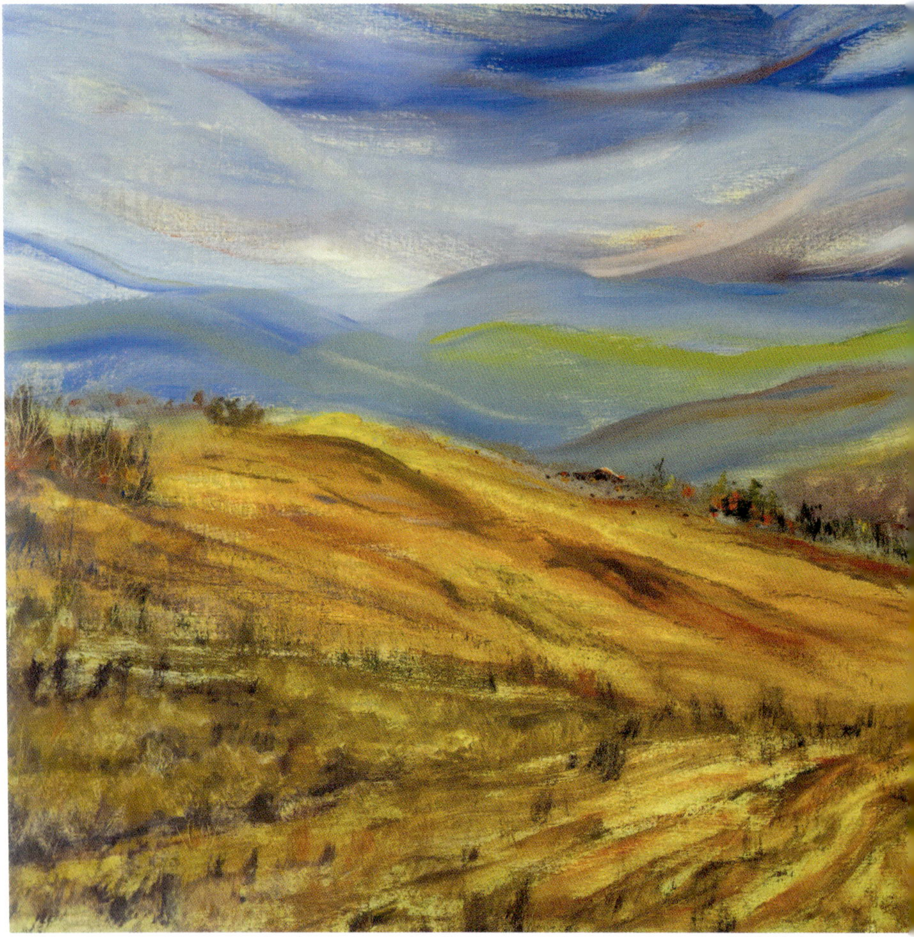

OPPOSITE *The Magic of Walking.* A walk in the mountains is a sure cure for almost any down feeling. I find it clears my head and allows me to, perhaps, contemplate the meaning of life. Often I visualize subjects that I might wish to explore in my paintings and think about possible ways to go about it.

BELOW *Happy Valley.* The warm colors of fall inspired me in this rural landscape. In my mind, anything is possible, and it makes me happy to think about bright colors, happy horses, happy cows and a bit of a fire in the big house. And just look at that happy sky!

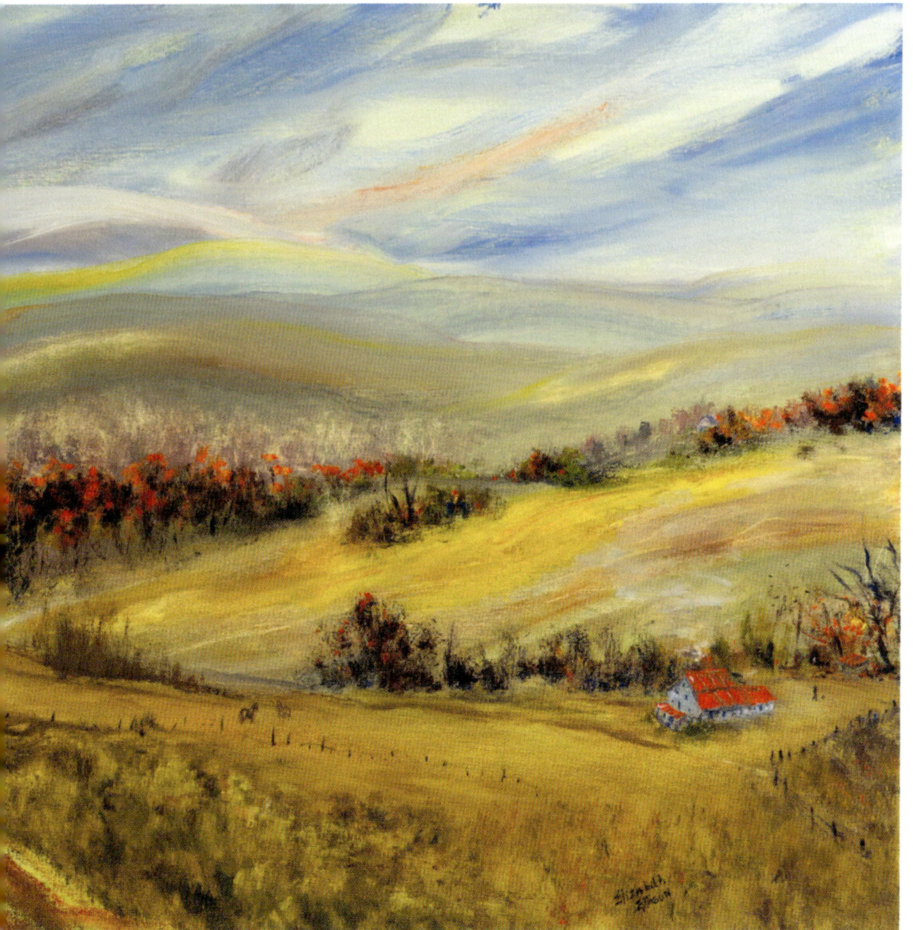

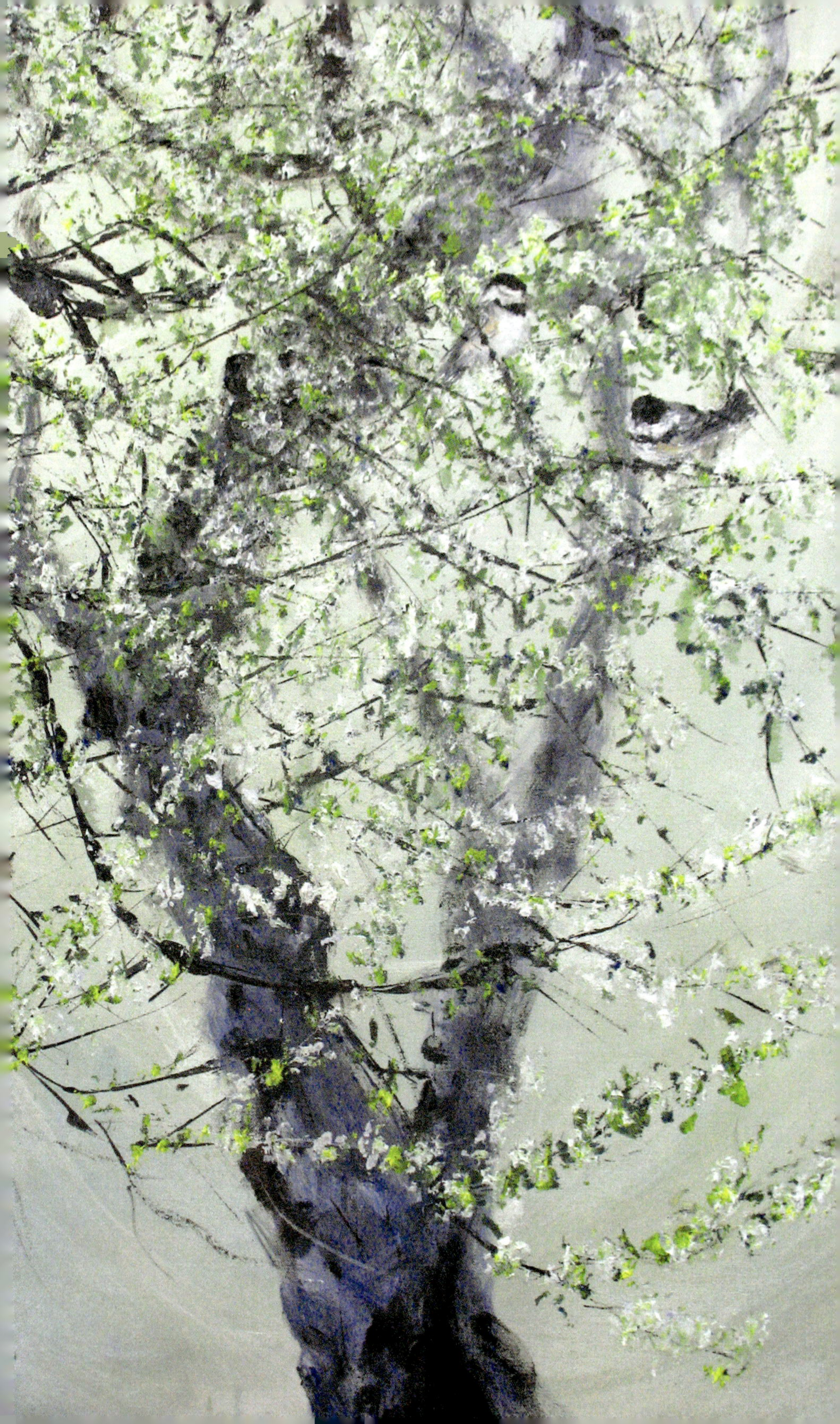

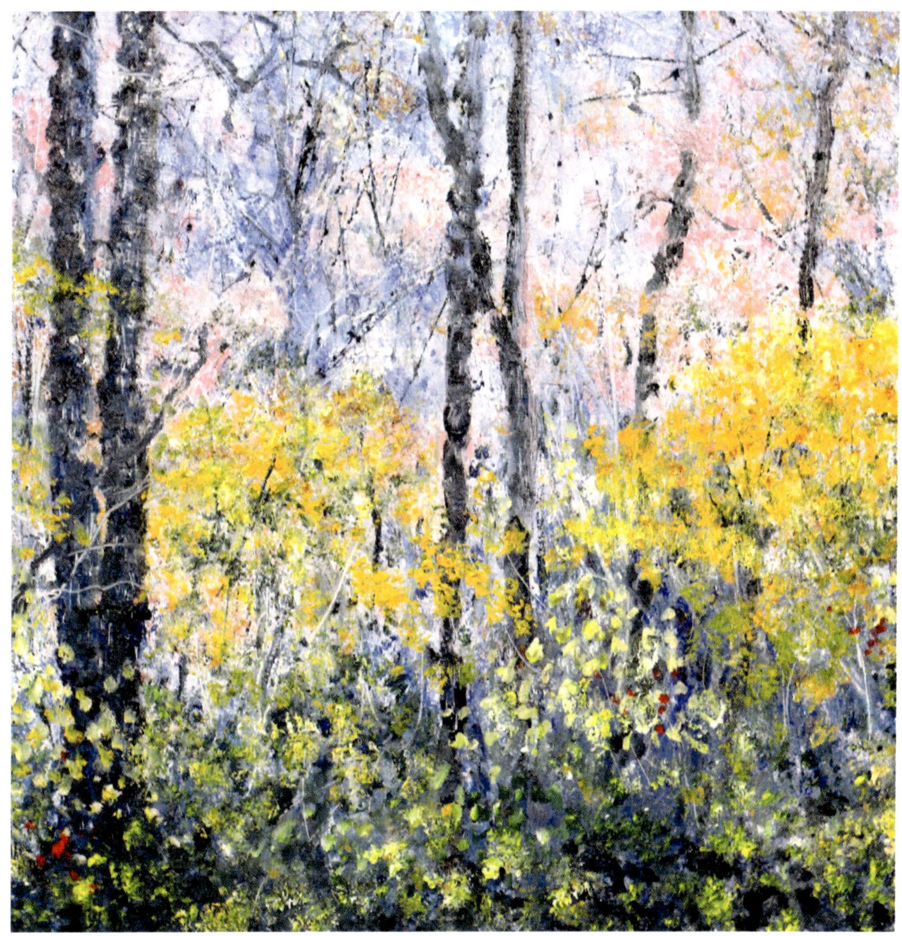

OPPOSITE *Plum Blossoms and Chickadees.* The white blossoms with perching chickadees give early spring new promise.

ABOVE *Beside the Trail and Above the Creek.* I often plan my work on morning walks along our horse trail, and October colors lend an extra glory to these physical and mental excursions.

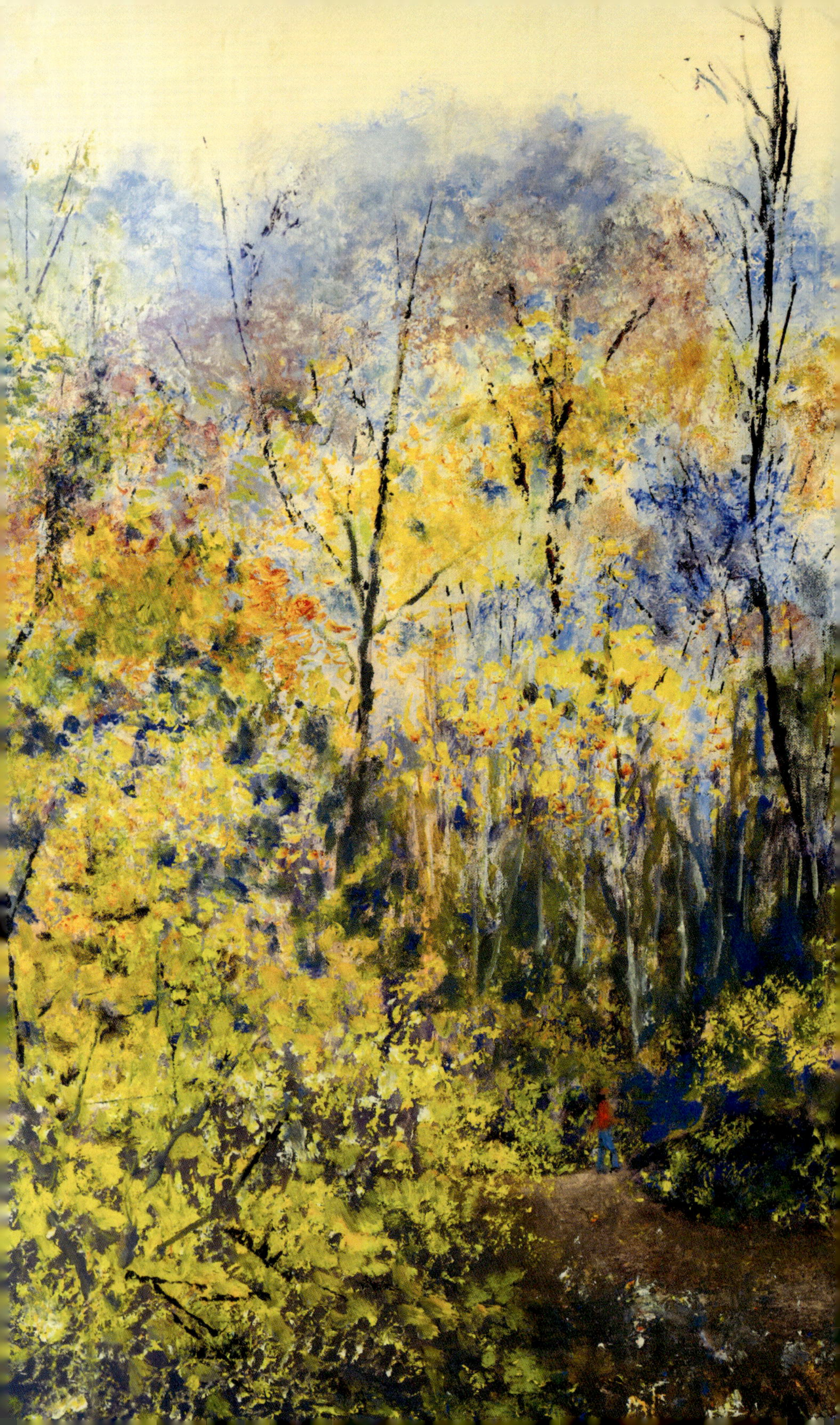

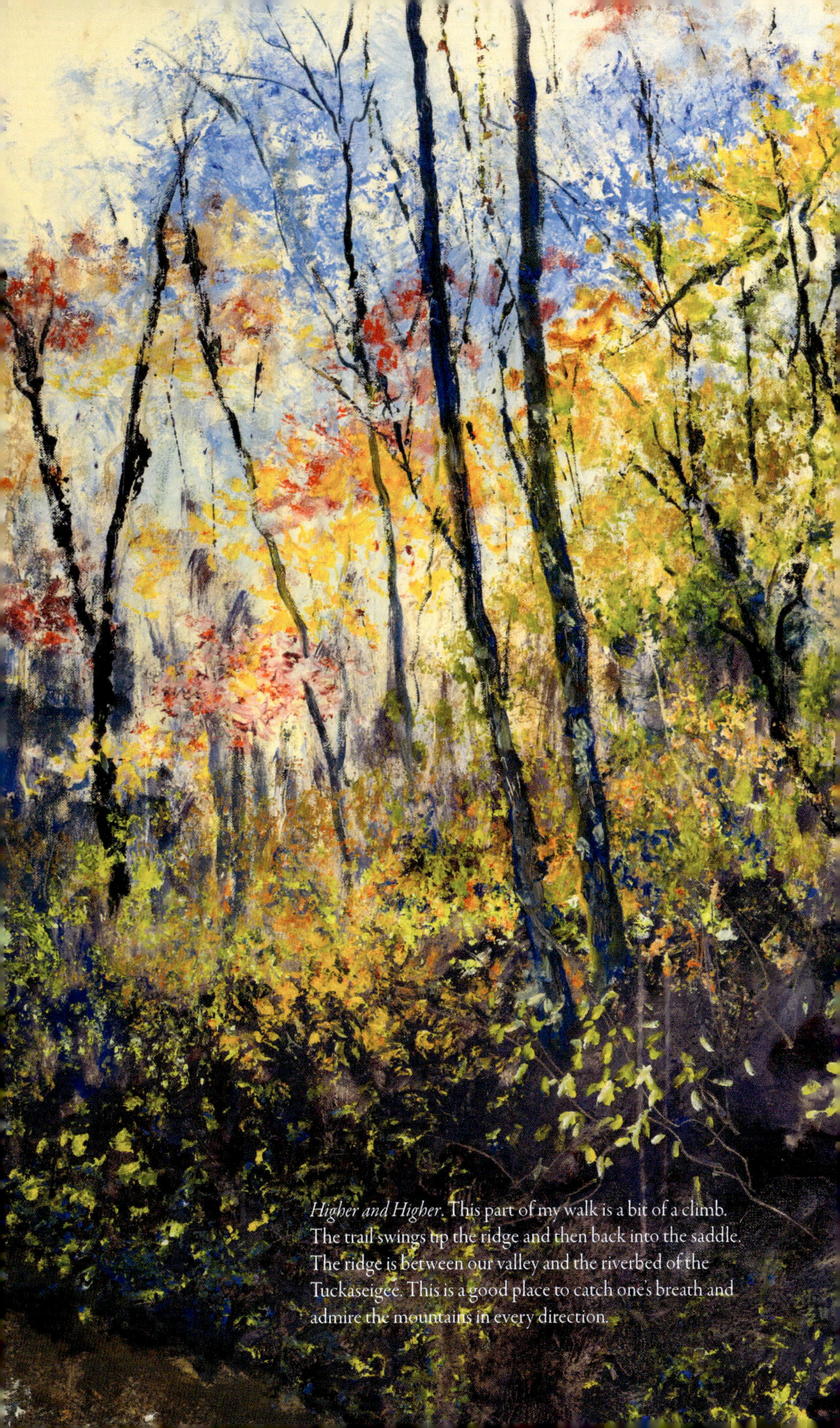

Higher and Higher. This part of my walk is a bit of a climb. The trail swings up the ridge and then back into the saddle. The ridge is between our valley and the riverbed of the Tuckaseigee. This is a good place to catch one's breath and admire the mountains in every direction.

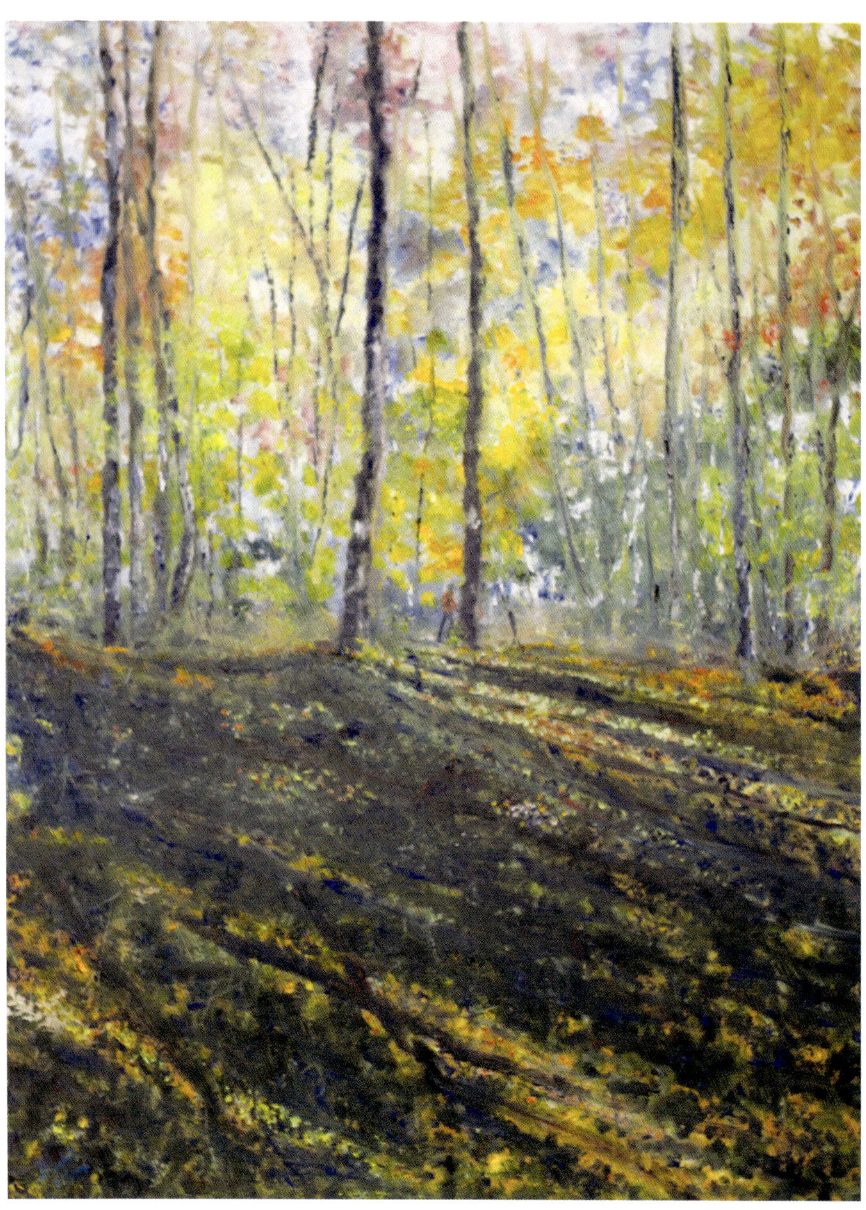

Land of Blue Shadows. The shadows help to depict the light in a nearly flat portion of the trail before it climbs again. In a bit, I will be looking into Great Smoky Mountains National Park. This is about as close as one can get to heaven, I would say.

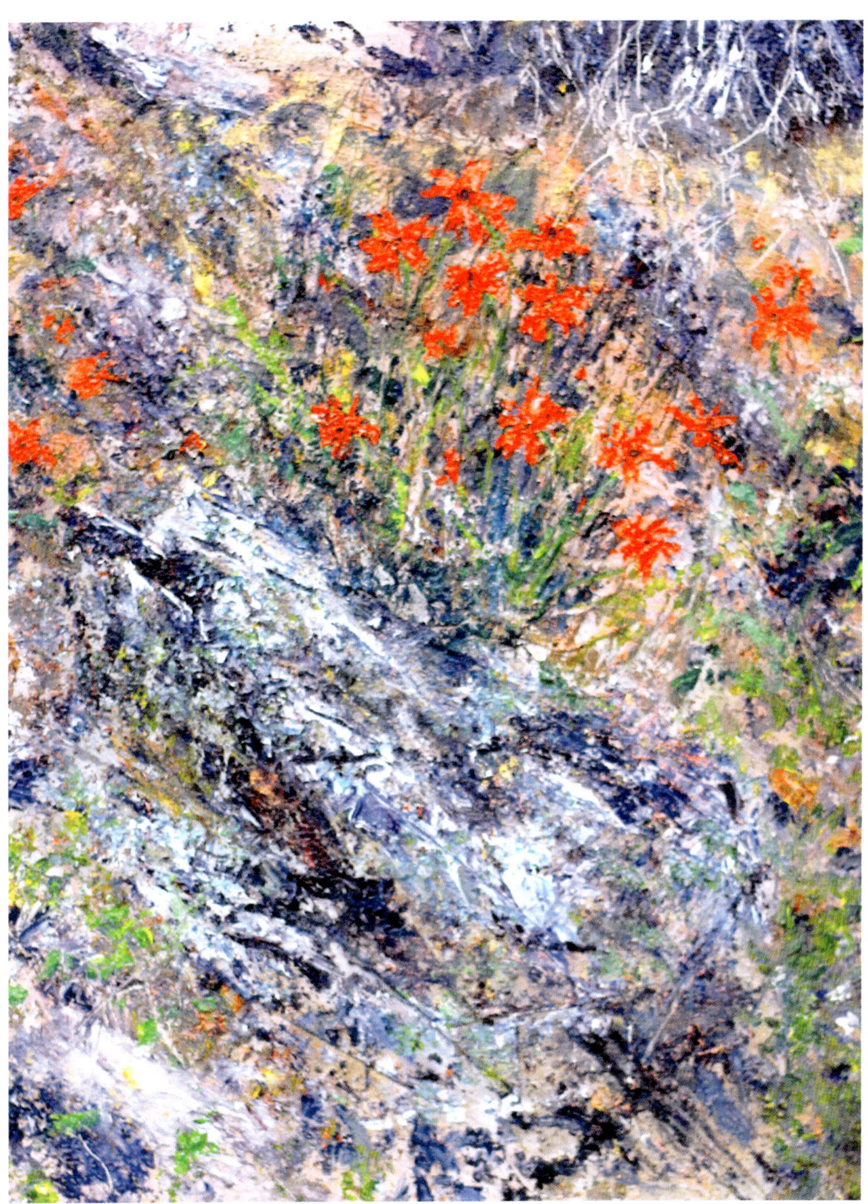

In a World of Texture, Fire Pink Floats.

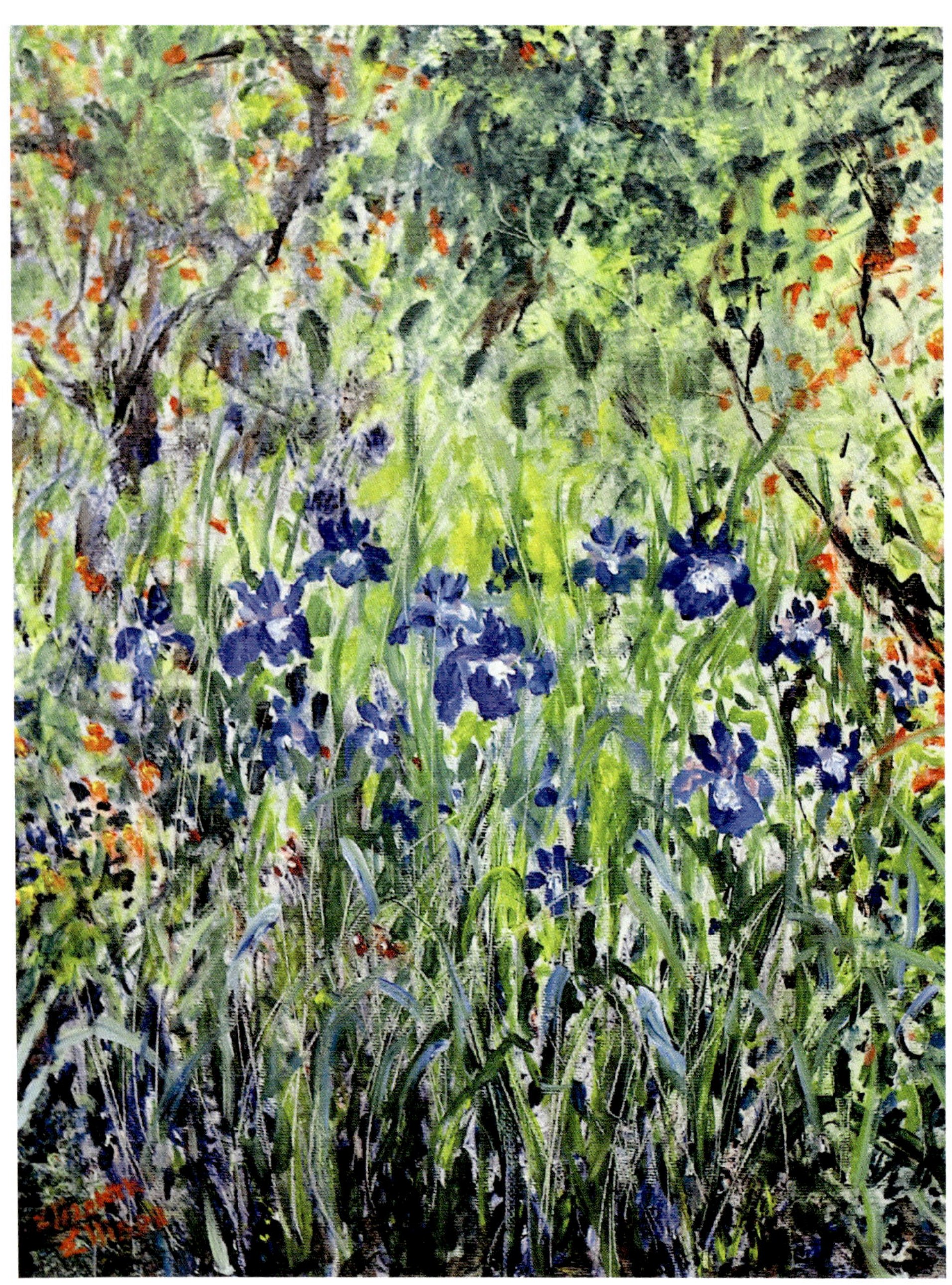

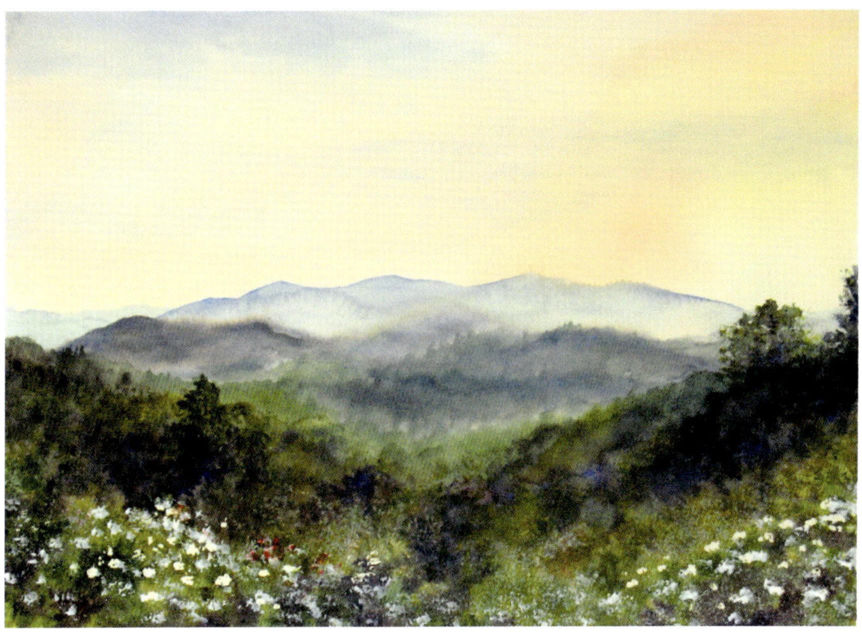

OPPOSITE *The Garden at Permanent Camp.* My garden might appear chaotic, but it harbors life for a lot of critters and gives me pleasure when I walk past. I find it perfect!

ABOVE *Mile High in the Smokies.* The view is from a pullover on Balsam Mountain that goes by that designation. From there, it seems as if you can see forever.

FOLLOWING *Breathe.* How does it make you feel when you are near bamboo, cattails and the creatures that live or visit there? It just makes me want to breathe deeply and smell the air.

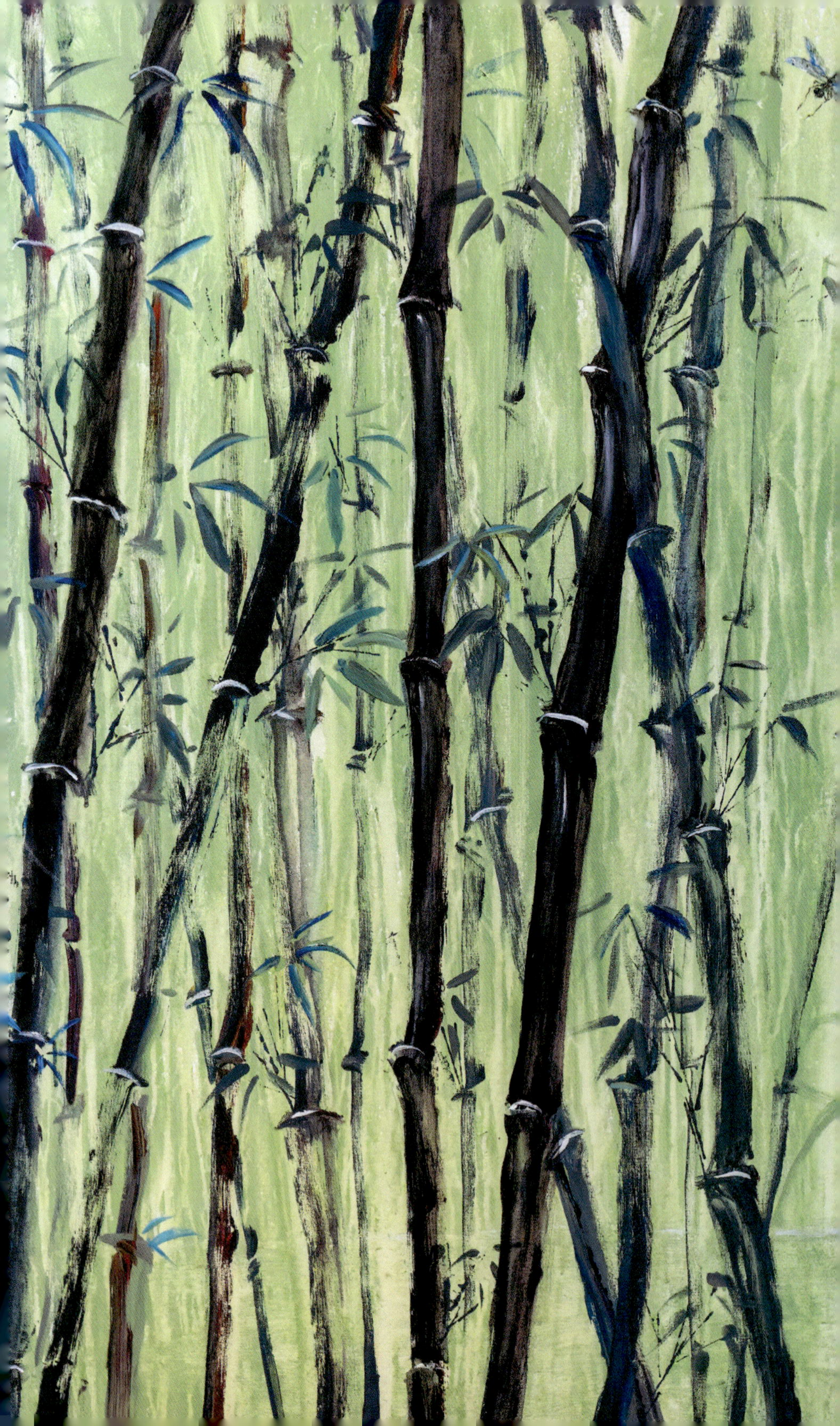

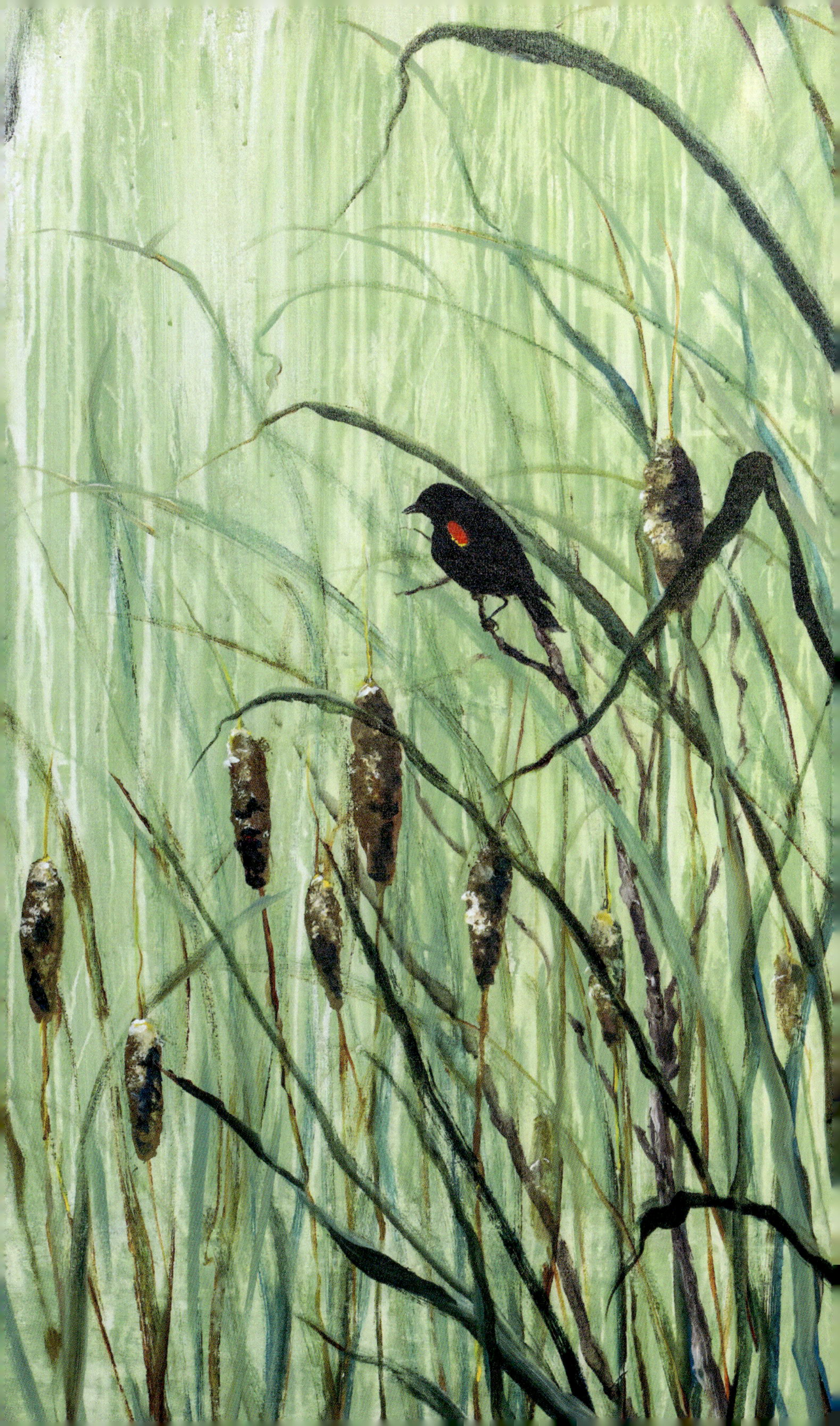

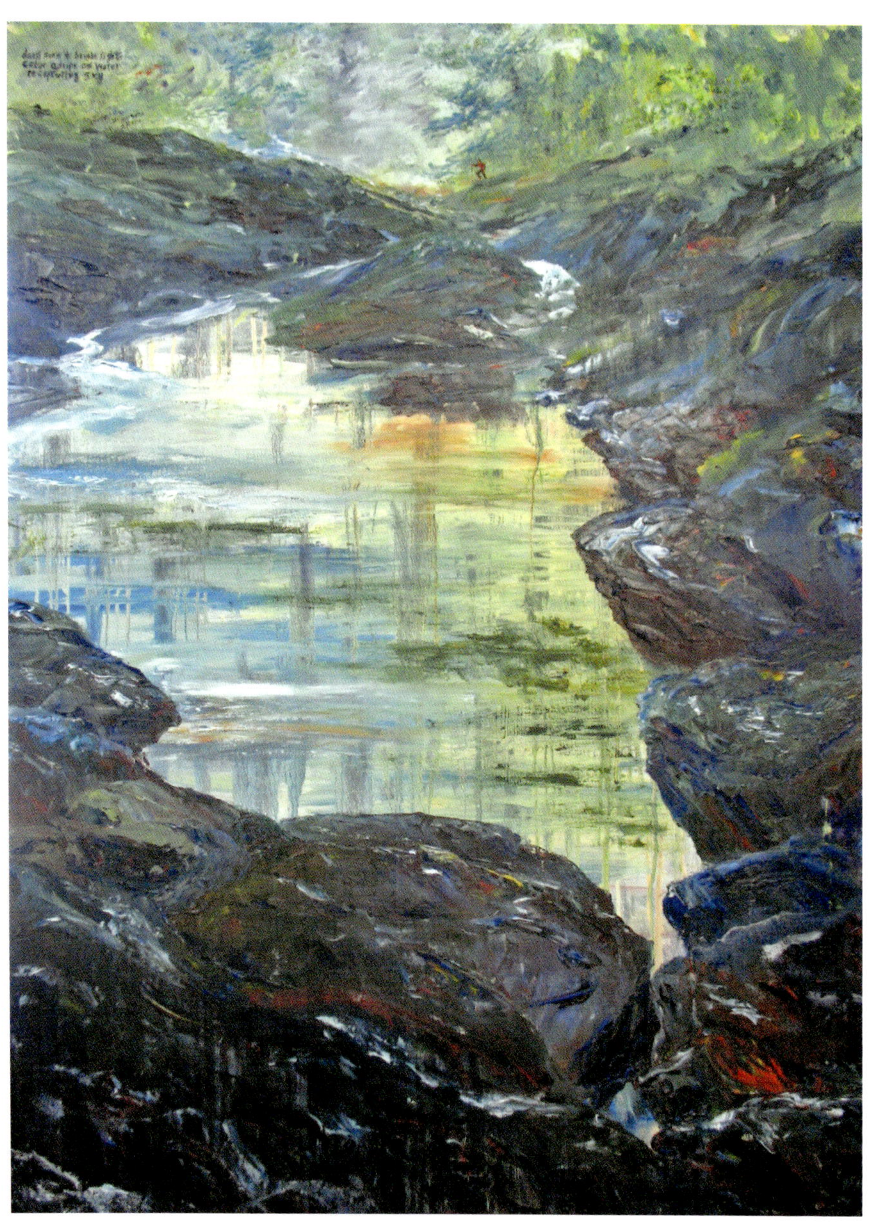

ABOVE *"Dark rock & bright light/Color adrift on water/Recapturing sky"*: The haiku is by my soulmate, George Ellison. This painting is inspired by a rock climbing/hopping trek up the Tuckaseigee Gorge. It is where Bonus Defeat is located and is an awe-inspiring gorge formed by nature using force of water.

OPPOSITE *Boulder Field Along the Appalachian Trail.* The painting is inspired by a grouping of boulders that you pass while hiking the trail in the Nantahala Mountains.

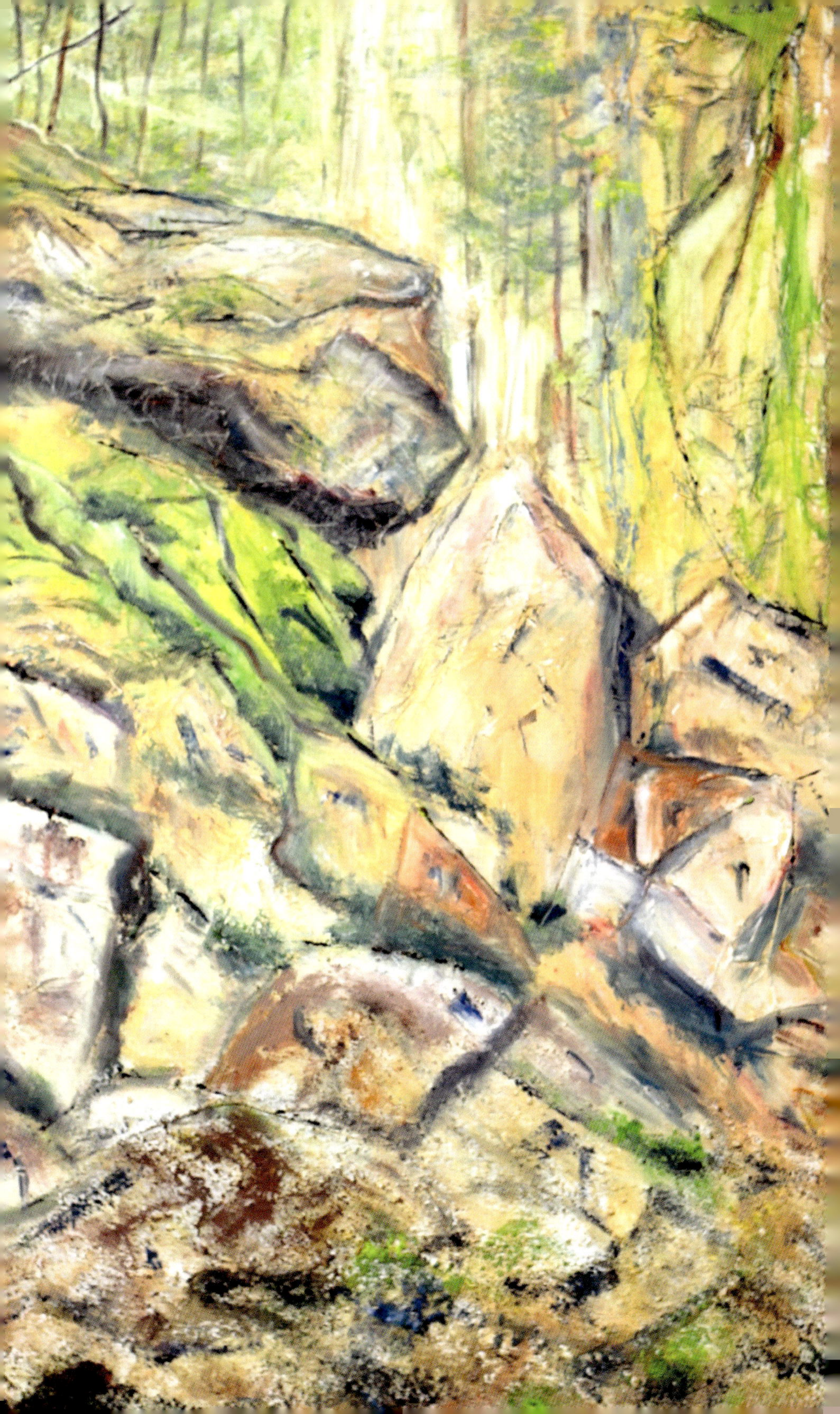

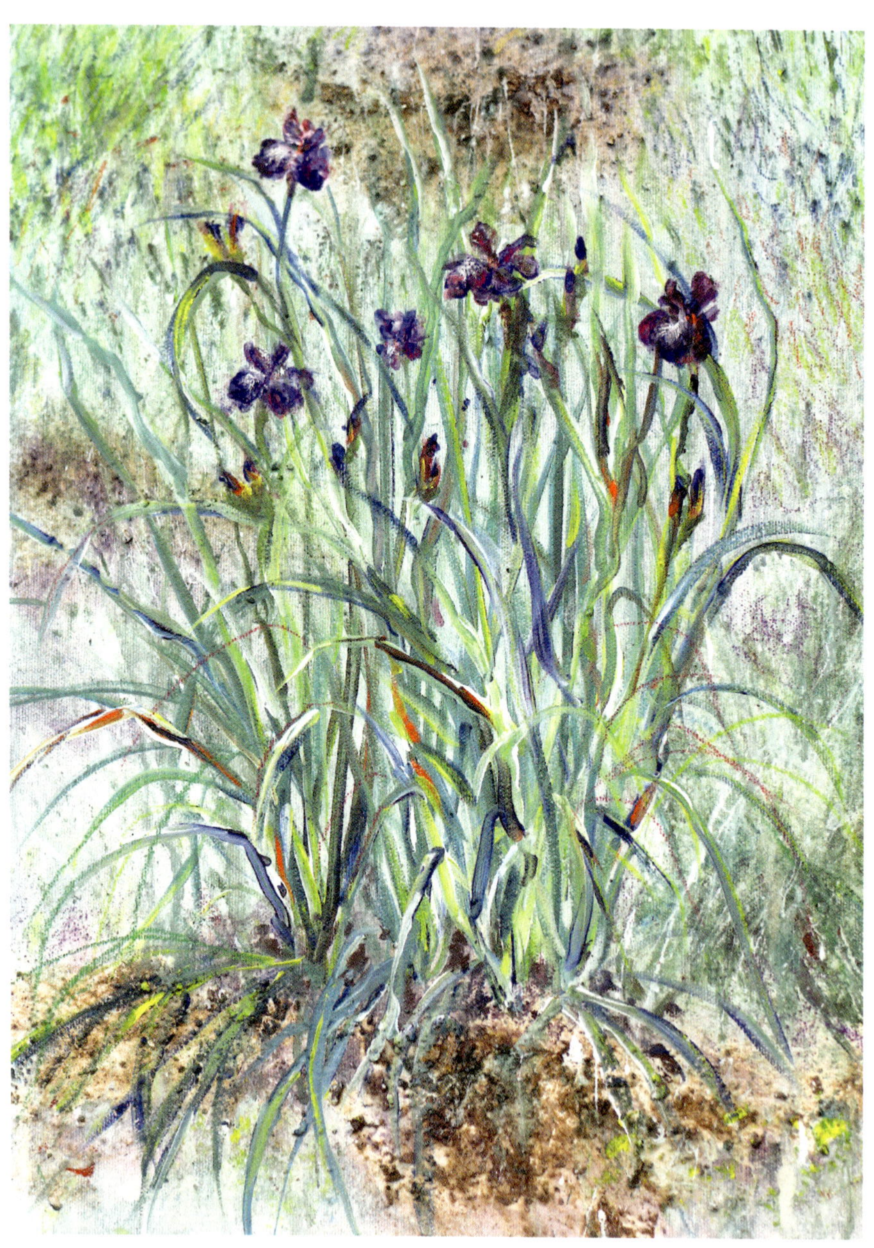

Iris, Goddess of Sea and Sky. I painted this in homage to the goddess.

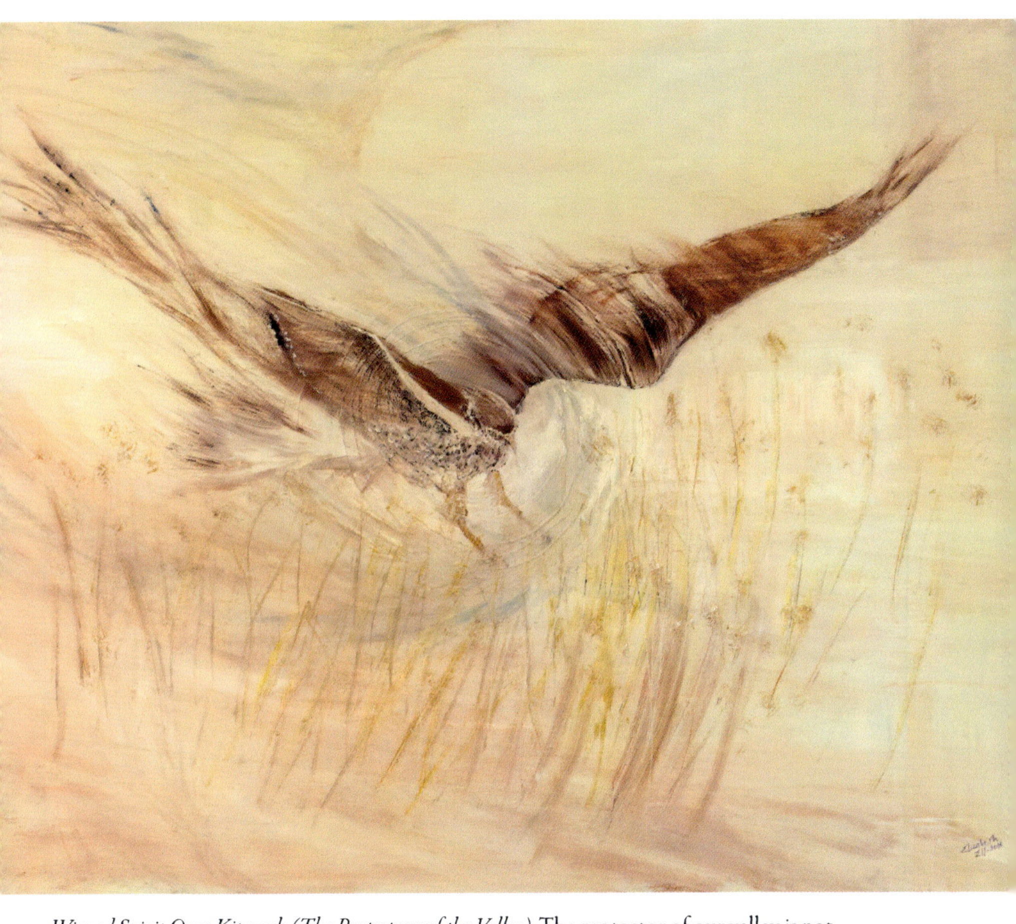

Winged Spirit Over Kituwah (The Protectress of the Valley). The protector of our valley is not Thunderbird, but rather a female Marsh Hawk. The spirit hawk glides over the valley and rises above the ridges where the forest grows. We feel the rush of her wings when the wind blows from the west, and we rejoice to have her with us always.

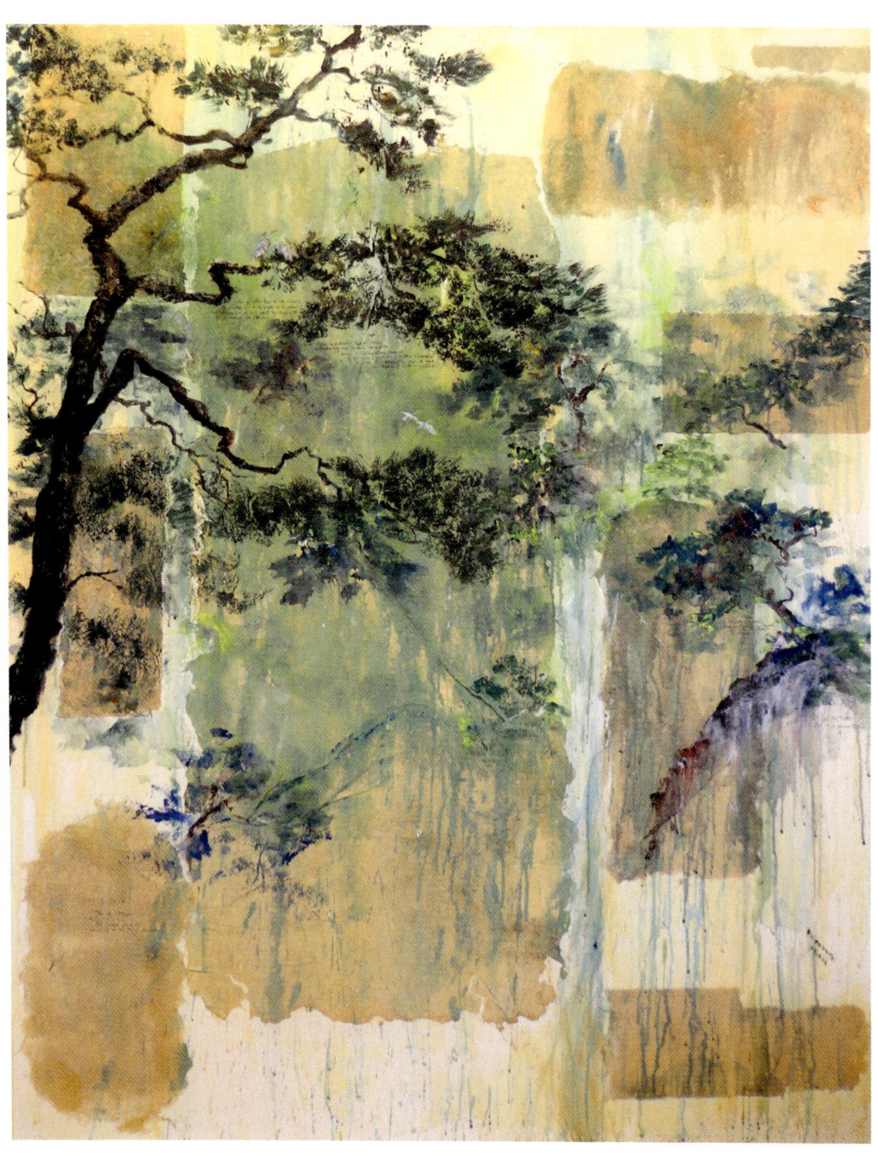

Contemplation on the Meaning of Tao. As soon as I picked up paint-laden brushes, my path totally changed, and the result is what you see. In the painting, I incorporated a quote from *The Mustard Seed Garden Manual of Painting* (Gai Wang, 1679, translated and annotated by Mai-mai Sze, Princeton Bollingen Paperbacks, 1956). This quote is the mantra for my paintings and in my life.

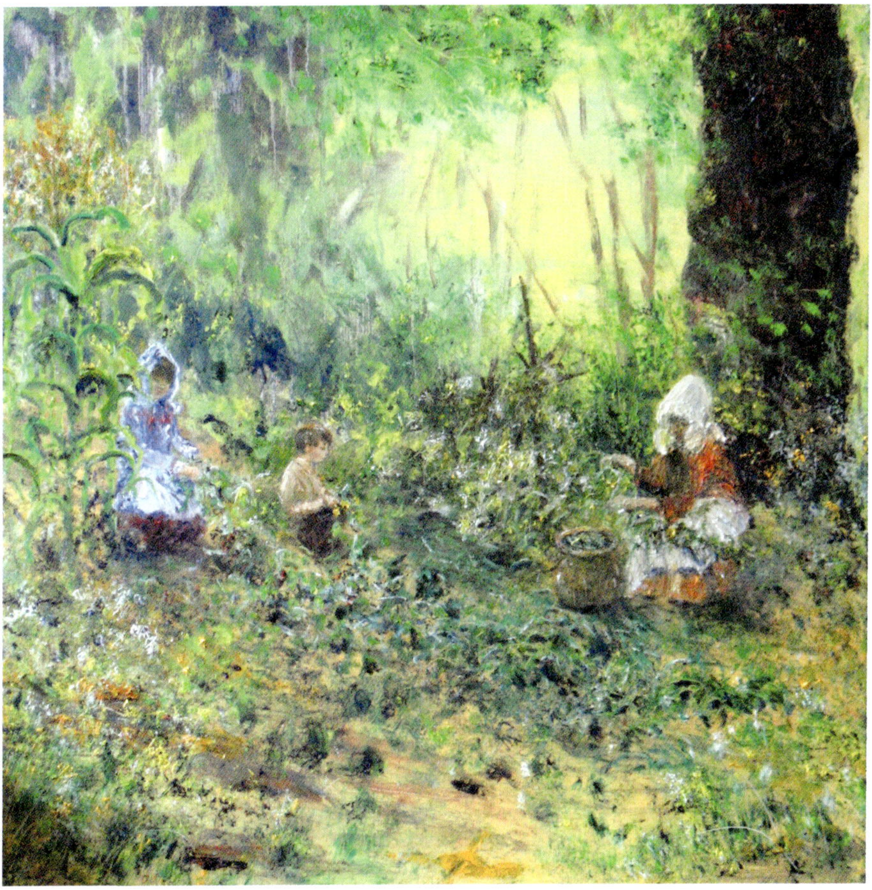

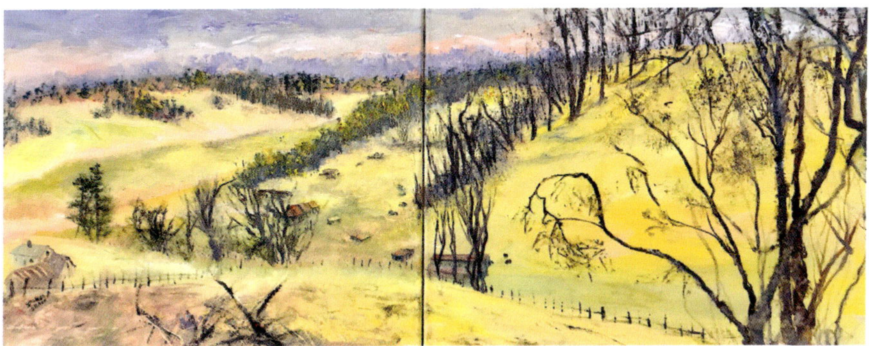

TOP *Helping Out.* This is from a scene painted on location (initially in watercolor and, later, in this small oil painting) at the filming of the 2000 movie *Songcatcher,* directed by Maggie Greenwald Mansfield (Lionsgate Films).

BOTTOM *Among the Rolling Hills/Kennith's Farm.* The words to Van Morrison's song so perfectly describe the way Kennith Wike lived. A good person who did right by everyone who had dealings with him. We enjoyed some good horseback riding adventures, and his spirit lives on in the small cove he called home.

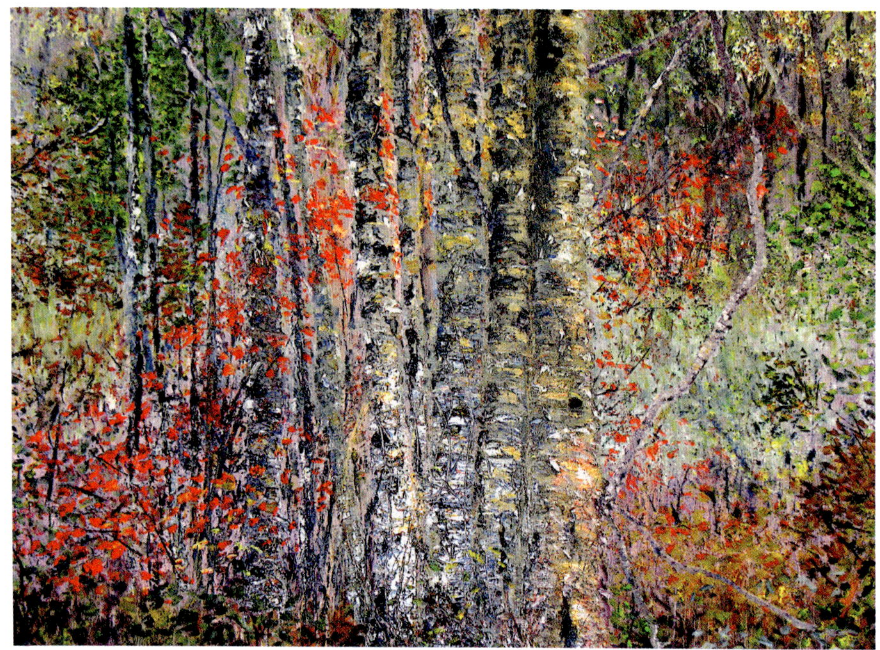

ABOVE *Higher Ground. Alarka Laurel* (Big Laurel) is located at more than four thousand feet and is a high-elevation bowl or "hanging valley." The maintained meadow is about three miles across. These birch trees grow alongside the dirt road beside the meadow, which, in fall, is filled with mauve, tan and brown grasses. I think they are mostly big bluestem and little bluestem, and Canada goldenrod is interspersed with the grasses. When there is a breeze, which there often is, the waving vegetation juxtaposed with calm birch trees is lovely.

OPPOSITE *Beauty Surrounds Us.* Having painted a watercolor of our valley for the cover of one of George's books, *Mountain Passages* (The History Press, 2005), I wanted to revisit the idea in oil. The cove has been our haven for many years, and we like to feel that we have been a fitting partner to the land and all it represents. It is now in a permanent conservation easement with the State of North Carolina. That means this small valley through which Lands Creek meanders will be here for future generations. They, too, will feel the joy of being surrounded by glorious beauty.

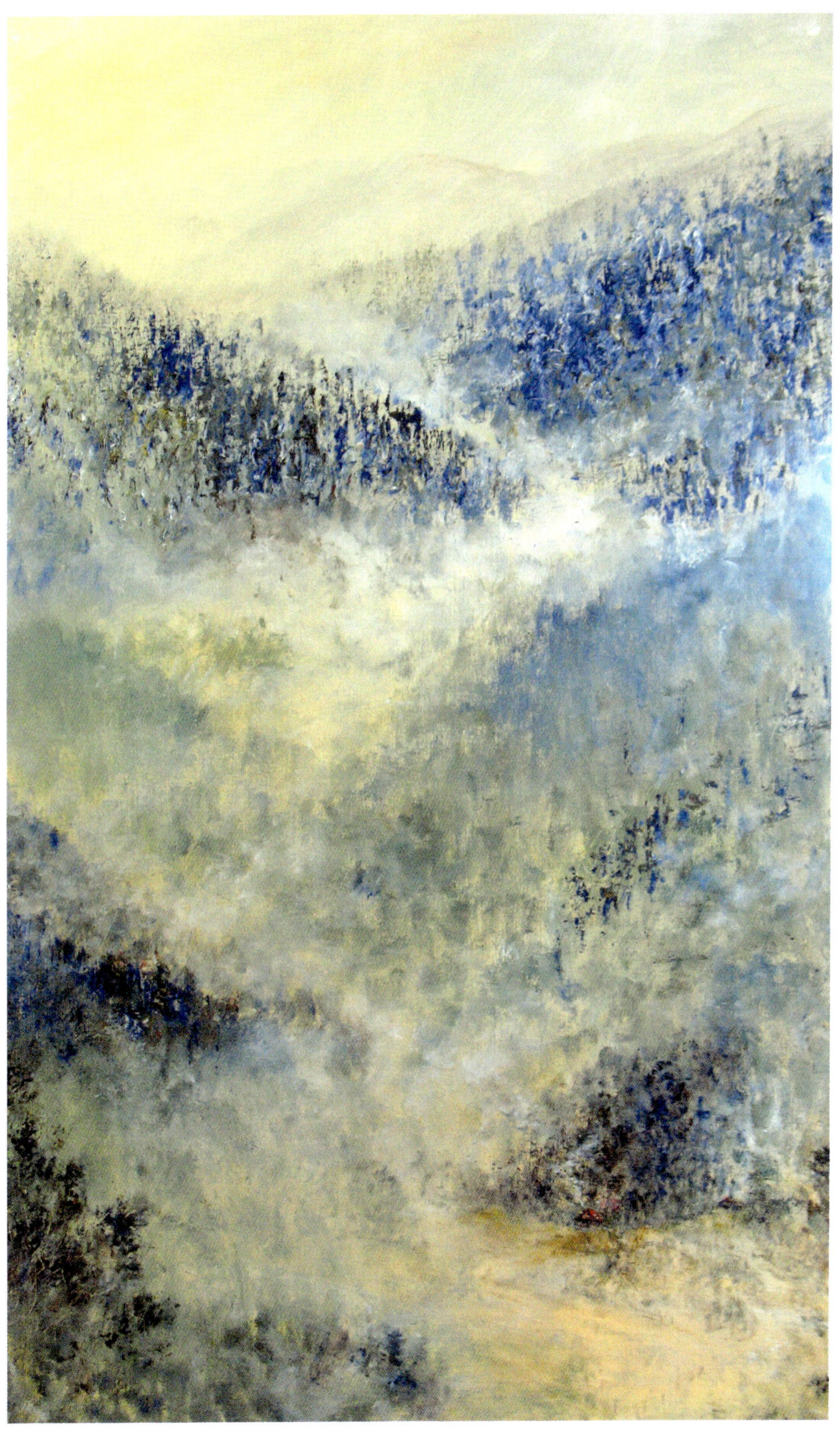

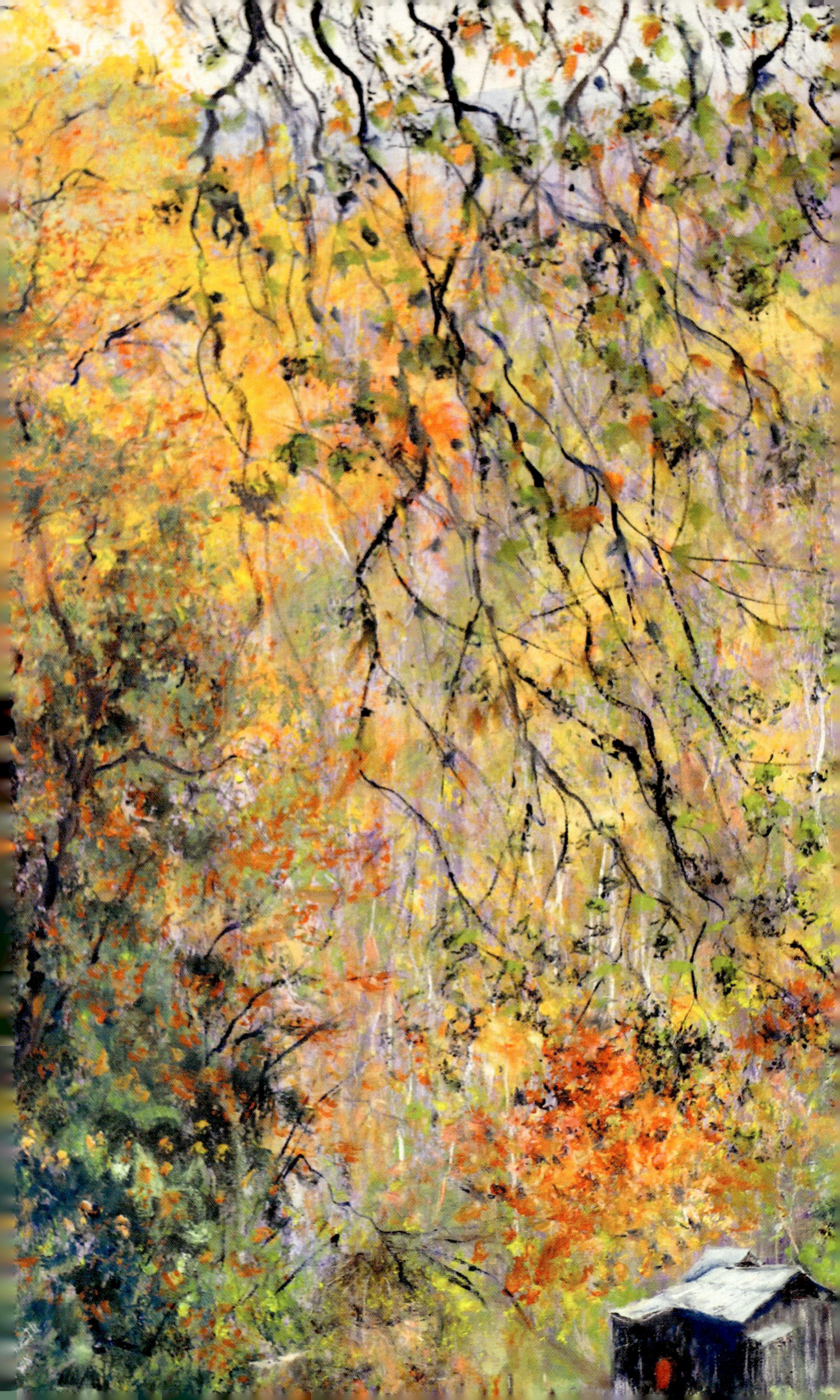

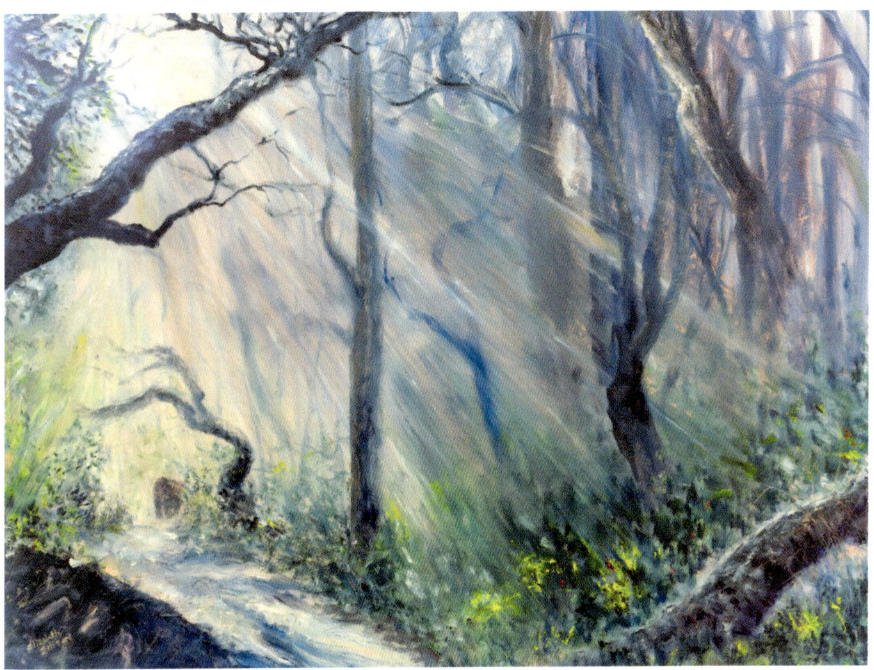

OPPOSITE *From the Gate.* Upon entering Permanent Camp, the name of our cove, you first encounter the tack room and barn where I care for my horse. The road continues to our home, which overlooks the creek. In conservation studies, the land was described as steep to rolling; I guess that is because the high ridges reach down into the valley. It is completely forested, except for a few acres alongside Lands Creek. There is much inspiration for creative endeavors without ever leaving the valley.

ABOVE *At Higher Elevation.* I was near Wayah Bald in Macon County when I walked into these woods. It felt mysterious and exciting, as if I were entering a special place where spirits roam—not spooky, just intriguing.

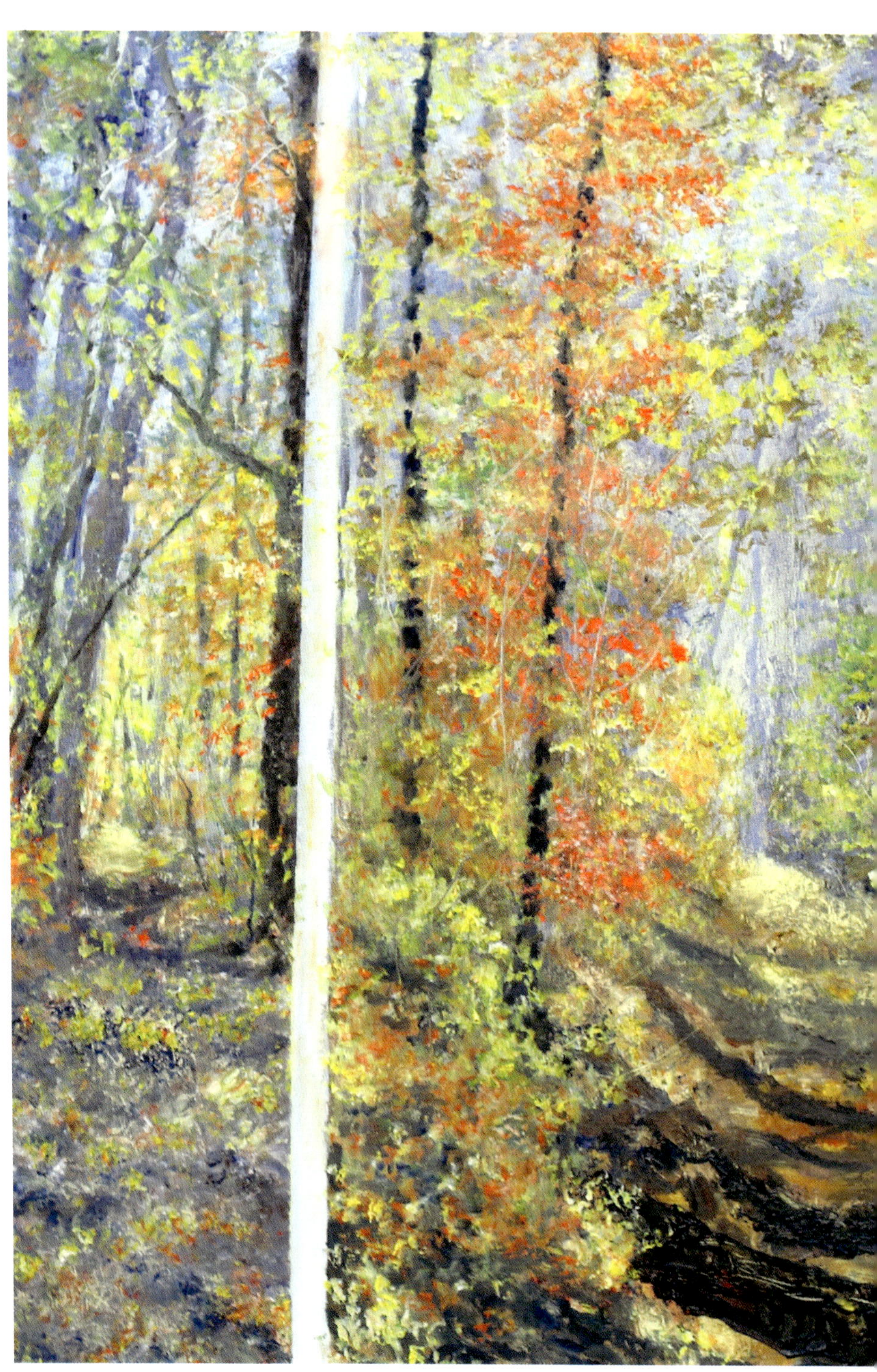

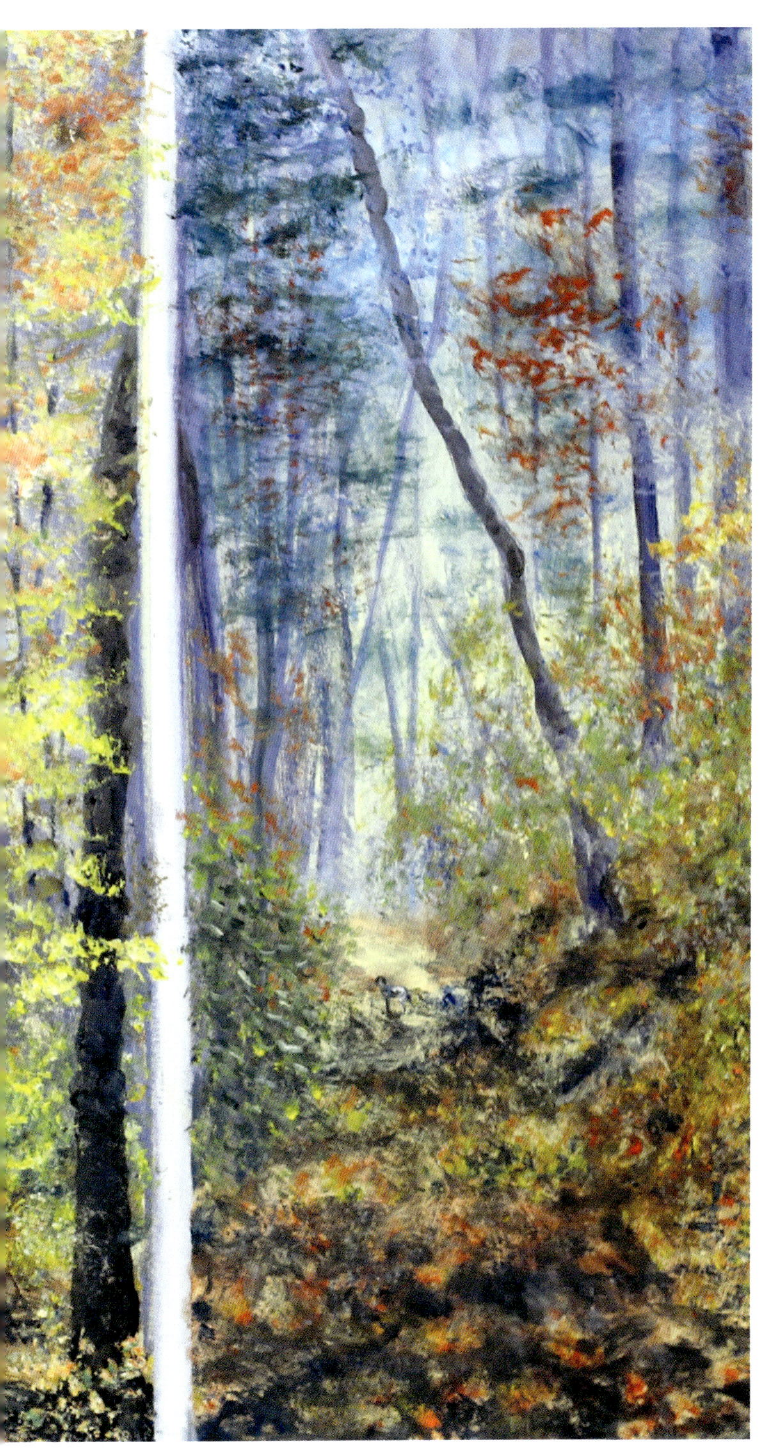

On the Trail with LinaBlue. I divided the canvas as if this were a triptych to convey the feeling of trail walking on our property. Traveling from left to right, from the high ridge, one turns onto the spur trail, then into a small cove. Finally, you make the return to the creek valley with LinaBlue leading the way.

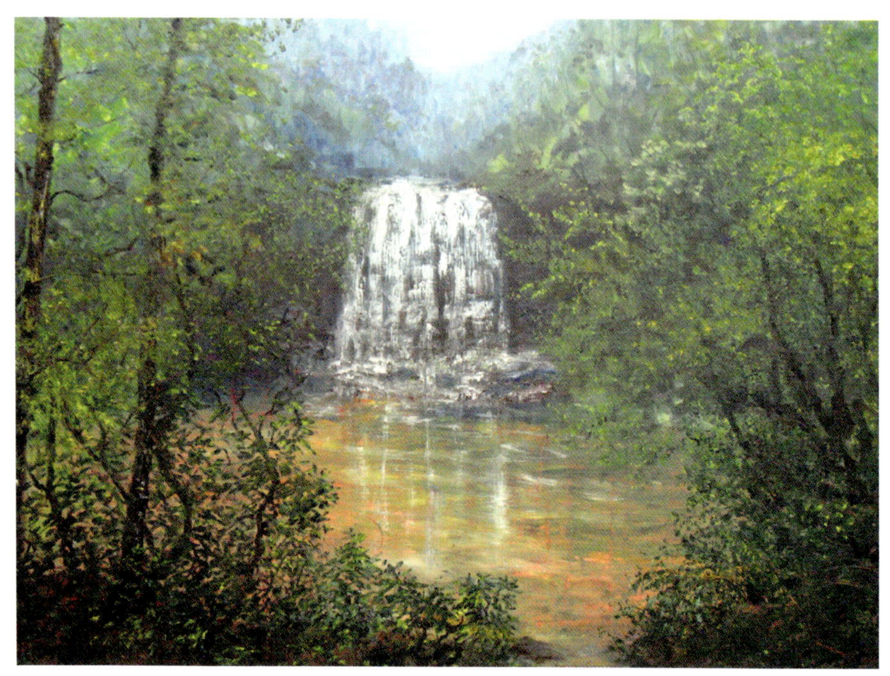

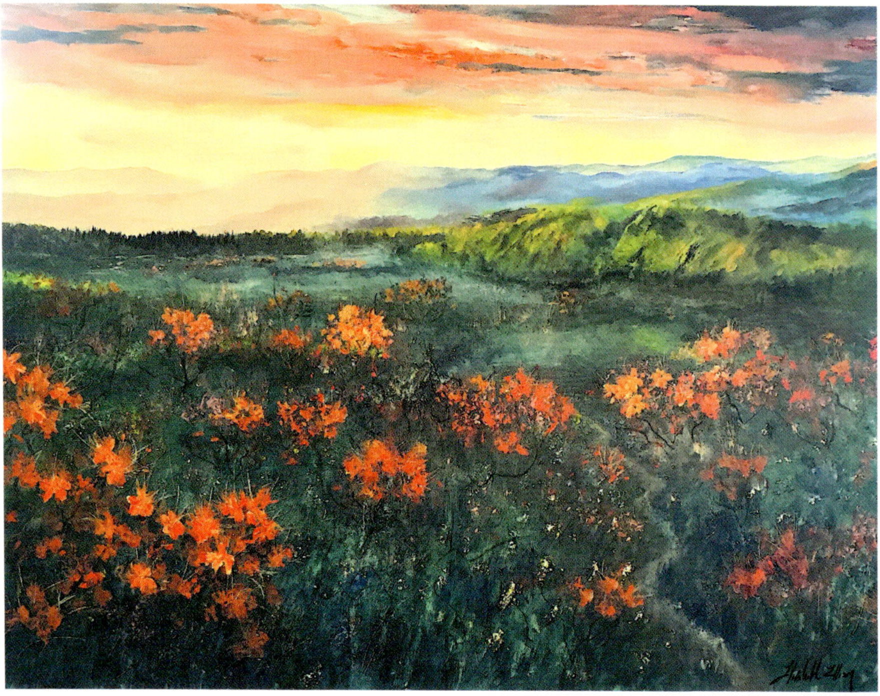

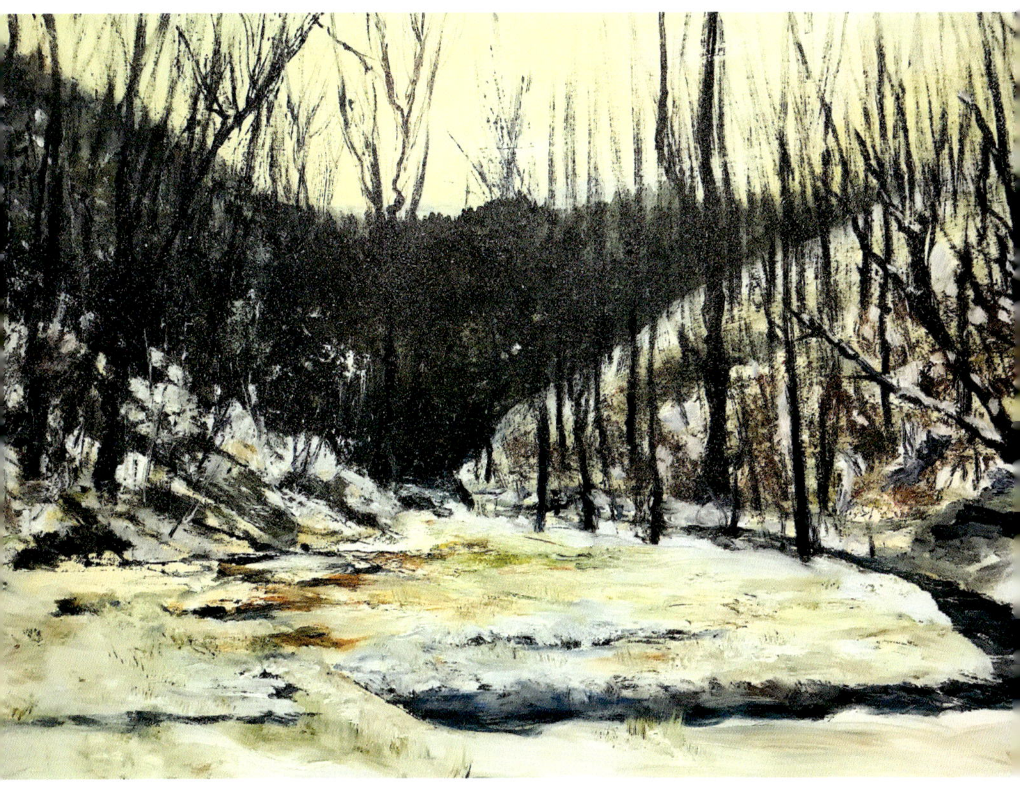

OPPOSITE, TOP *Where Water Falls*. Schoolhouse Falls is a small waterfall in Panthertown Valley—I think about twenty feet or so—but it is so lovely. The water is stained brown with tannin, but it is very clean. Because of the colors and the mysterious glow to the painting, it looks like a setting from a much earlier century, and that fascinates me.

OPPOSITE, BOTTOM *Enter Dawn*. Gregory Bald is renowned as a destination in the Great Smokies, and you can steep your soul in the beauty of the wild azaleas that flourish there. I chose to pay homage to Eos, Greek goddess of dawn. I know Eos is associated with roses, but this dawn beamed on the Smokies and onto our flame azalea.

ABOVE *Across the Creek*. The view from our deck is of a small field across the creek. We have a sturdy footbridge to cross the creek into the field. It is a pathway for us and our German shorthaired pointers, as well as fox, deer and the occasional black bear. We often see wild turkeys feeding in the field and the occasional great blue heron. The lovely winter view of melting snow reveals the warm colors of the grasses and paths, and it is enough to almost warm the chill of winter air.

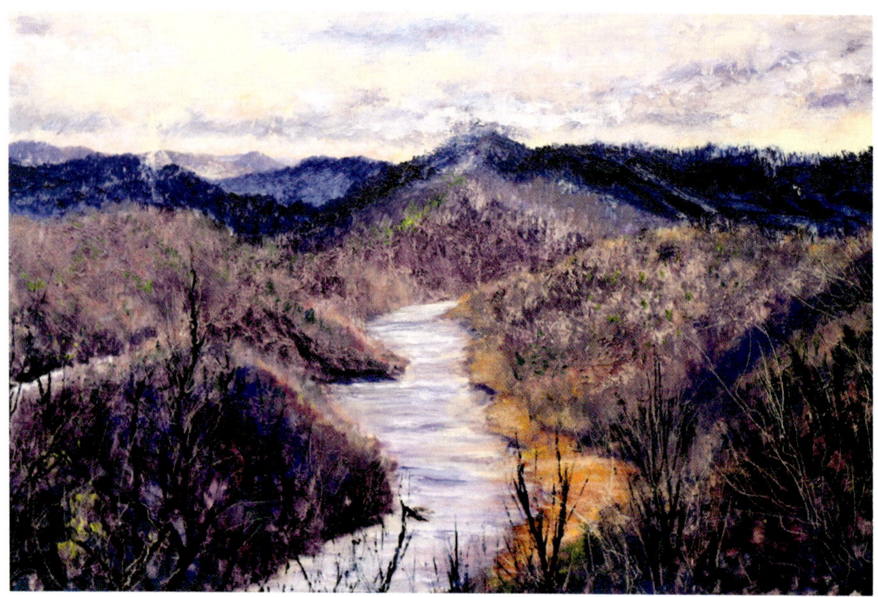

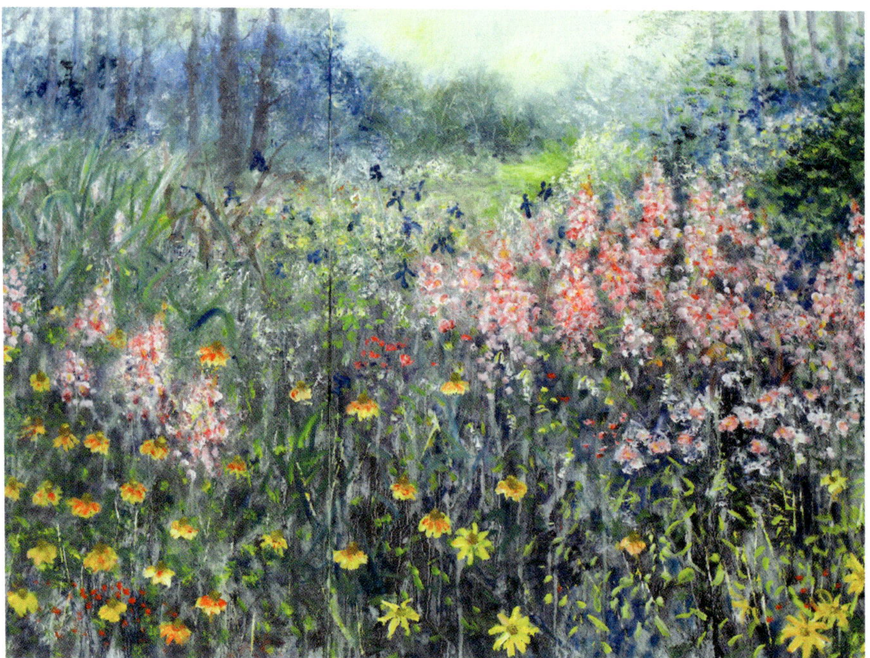

TOP *Horseshoe Bend.* The horseshoe bend in the Little Tennessee River can be seen from N.C. 28 in Swain County. The colors of winter enhance the reflective glow of the flowing river. This bird's-eye view is worth pulling over beside the road to enjoy.

BOTTOM *February Dreaming.* I have to admit that dreary days are part of winter in the Southern Appalachians. It helps to visualize the coming days of spring and the future abundance of showy wildflowers.

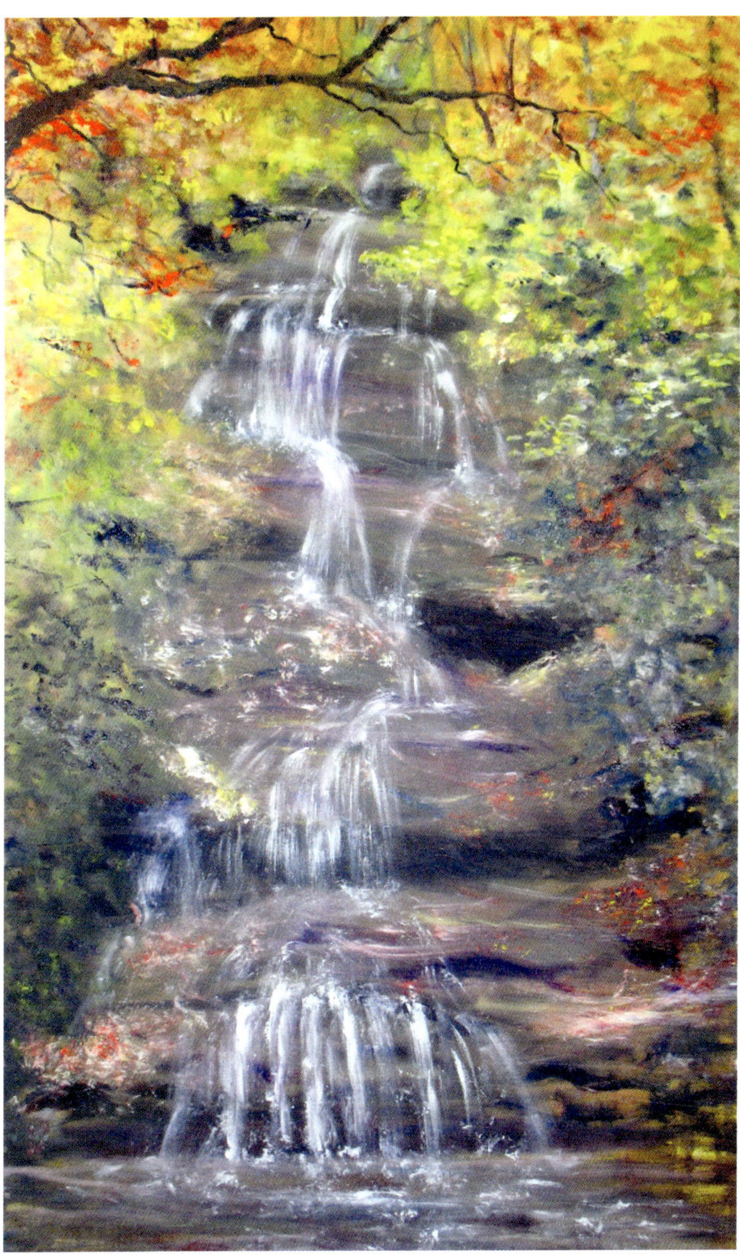

Fall Reflections. Tom Branch (or Tom's Branch) Falls is a short hike up the trail, beginning at Deep Creek Trailhead just north of Bryson City. It is an easy walk, and benches are provided at the falls. It is a good place to enjoy the sounds of the fairly large creek, rushing by to converge with the Tuckaseigee River. This is also a good place to set up an easel or make an entry in your nature journal, if you keep one. I have done both. I also just love sitting there beside the creek.

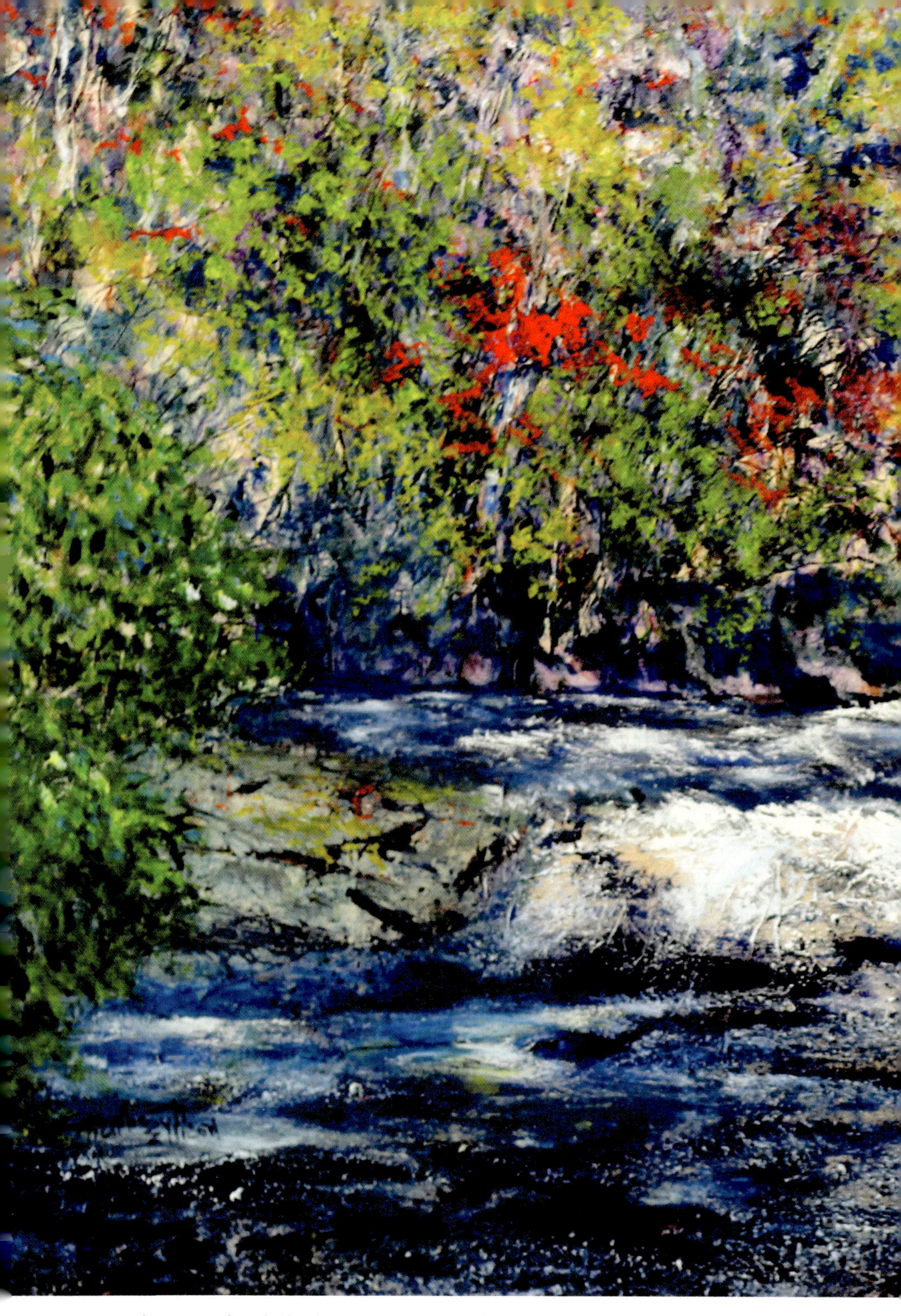

From the First Bridge. The bridge across Deep Creek provides an excellent view of Big Rock and the rushing water. Upstream just a bit is a great swimming hole that locals and tourists have used for decades. I love to paint where the roaring stream makes a turn to continue on its journey to the Tuckaseigee River and, from there, into Fontana Lake.

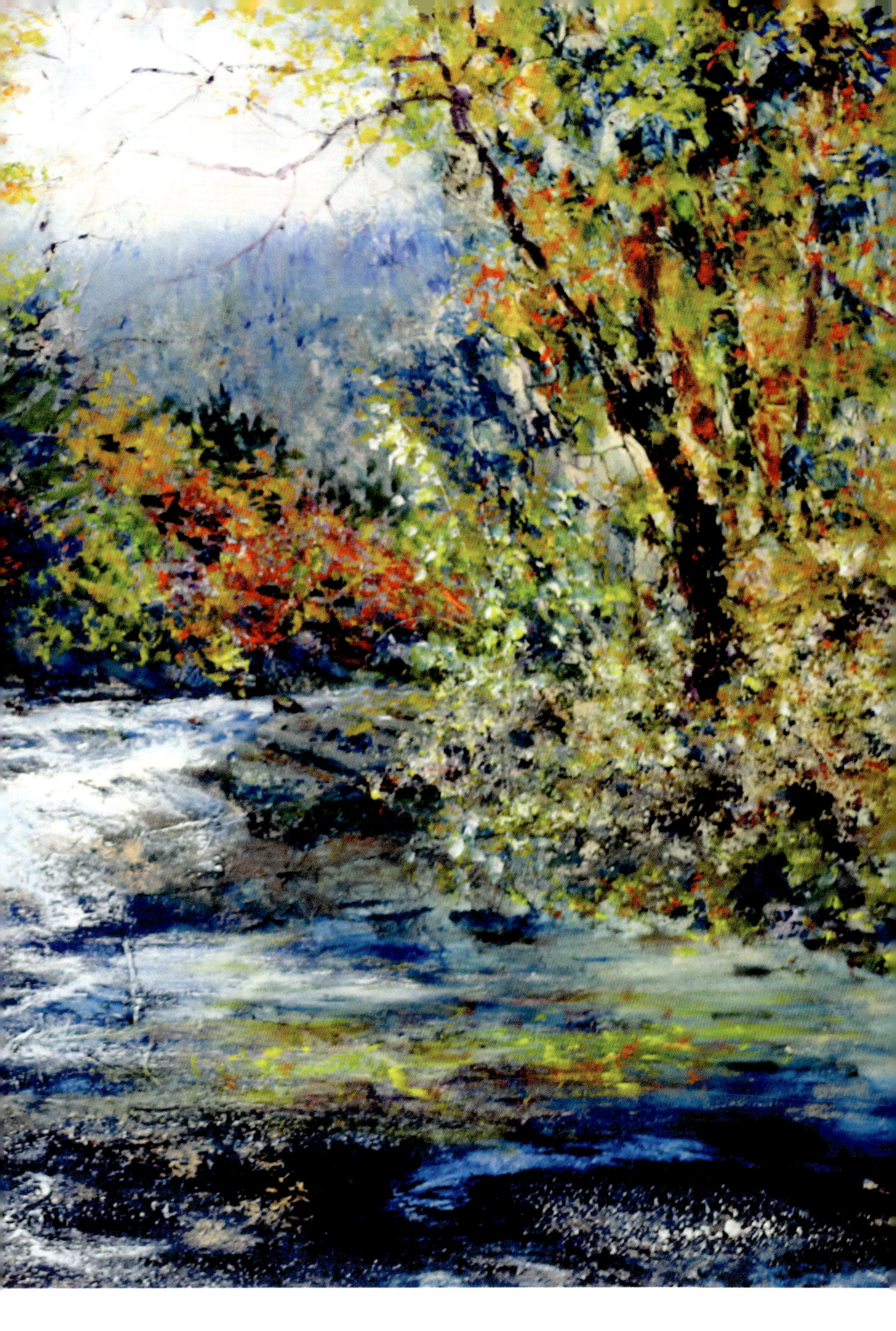

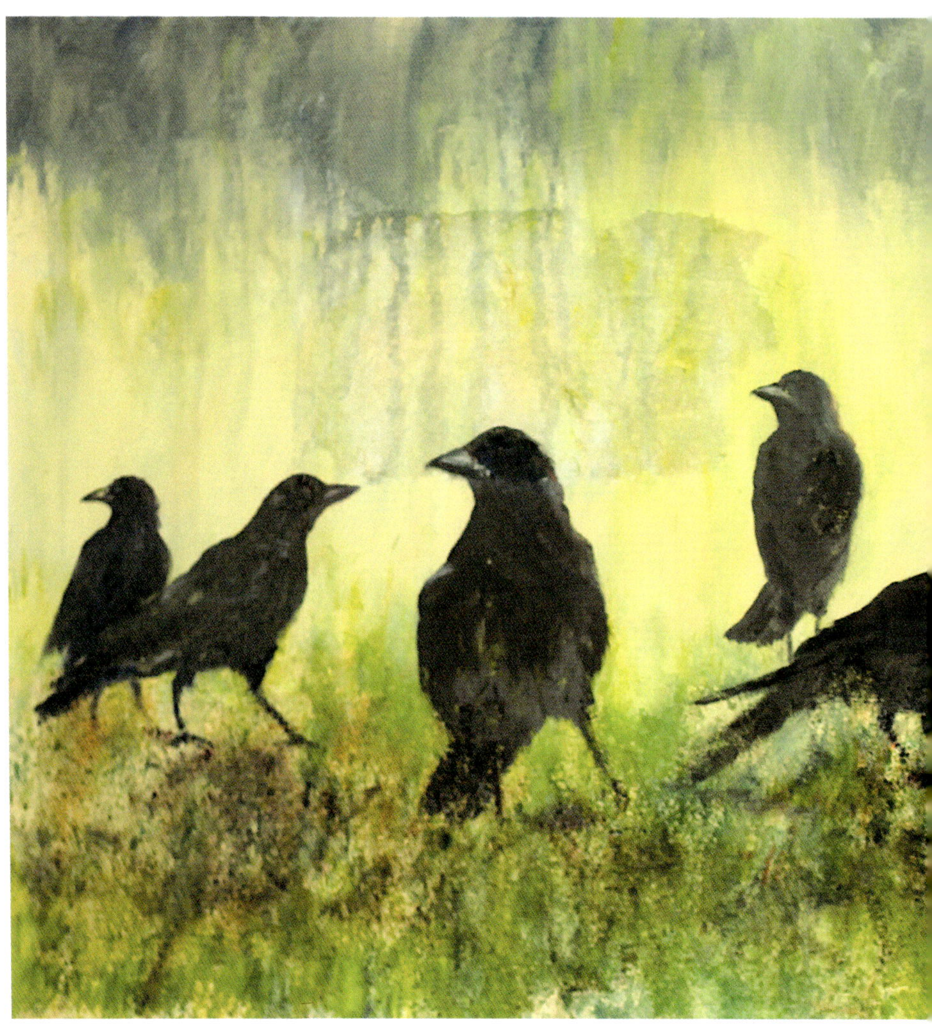

A Congress of Crows. I actually think they do accomplish things, in contrast to our human congresses—perhaps with a lot of undue noise, but crows have much to decide. Is there a red-tailed hawk that needs to be driven from the valley, for instance, or where are the best pickings for food today? We have about fourteen resident crows. It seems as if they are always up to something. We find them immensely entertaining. They enjoy the field across the creek from our house, and they love to fly onto the deck railing to see what is going on with the resident humans. And I love to paint them.

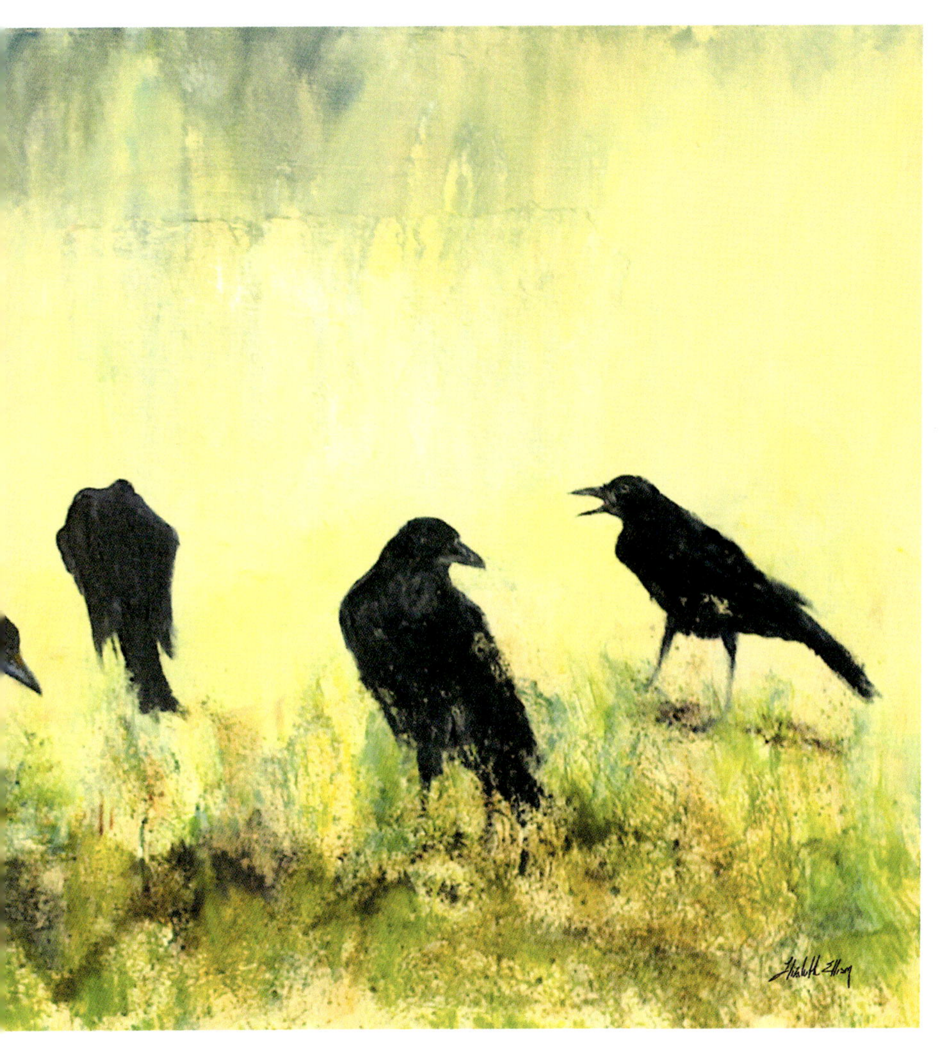

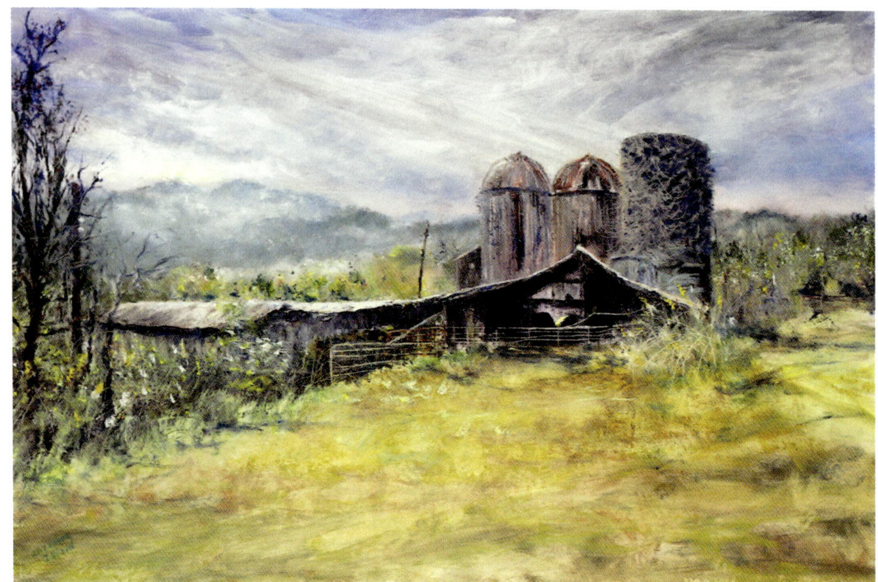

ABOVE *Kituwah Barns at the Fields.* We often bird the fields at Kituwah, and we can feel the sacred nature of these acres, the traditional motherland of the Cherokee Indians. The barns were there before the Cherokees bought back this land. They have preserved it for the people so that they will not forget who they are and what they stand for, and in hopes they will not lose their reverence for the natural world. This painting is based on a photograph our daughter Quintin took and allowed me to use as reference. I love the small touch of sunlight on hay inside the barn. I also wanted to work out how to portray the vines wrapping around the silo.

OPPOSITE, TOP *September in the High Country.* The views are incredible from Blue Ridge Parkway as nature changes her seasonal cloak. This particular view is toward Pisgah mountain range from near Balsam Gap.

OPPOSITE, BOTTOM *The Old River Road.* Permanent Camp, our home, is about a mile up Lands Creek from old N.C. 288, once the main road to several towns and quite a few settlements. Alcoa Aluminum Company purchased the land for the dam at Fontana, capturing the waterways to form Fontana Lake. Old Lands Creek bridge is visible in winter and early spring. Beyond the dark cliffs in this painting, you see the entrance of Lands Creek. The bare tree on the left is a black willow. It is almost submerged when the lake is full, yet still the tree survives. This painting is partially a song to the tree, which bears witness to the changing river levels, as well as to other seasonal changes.

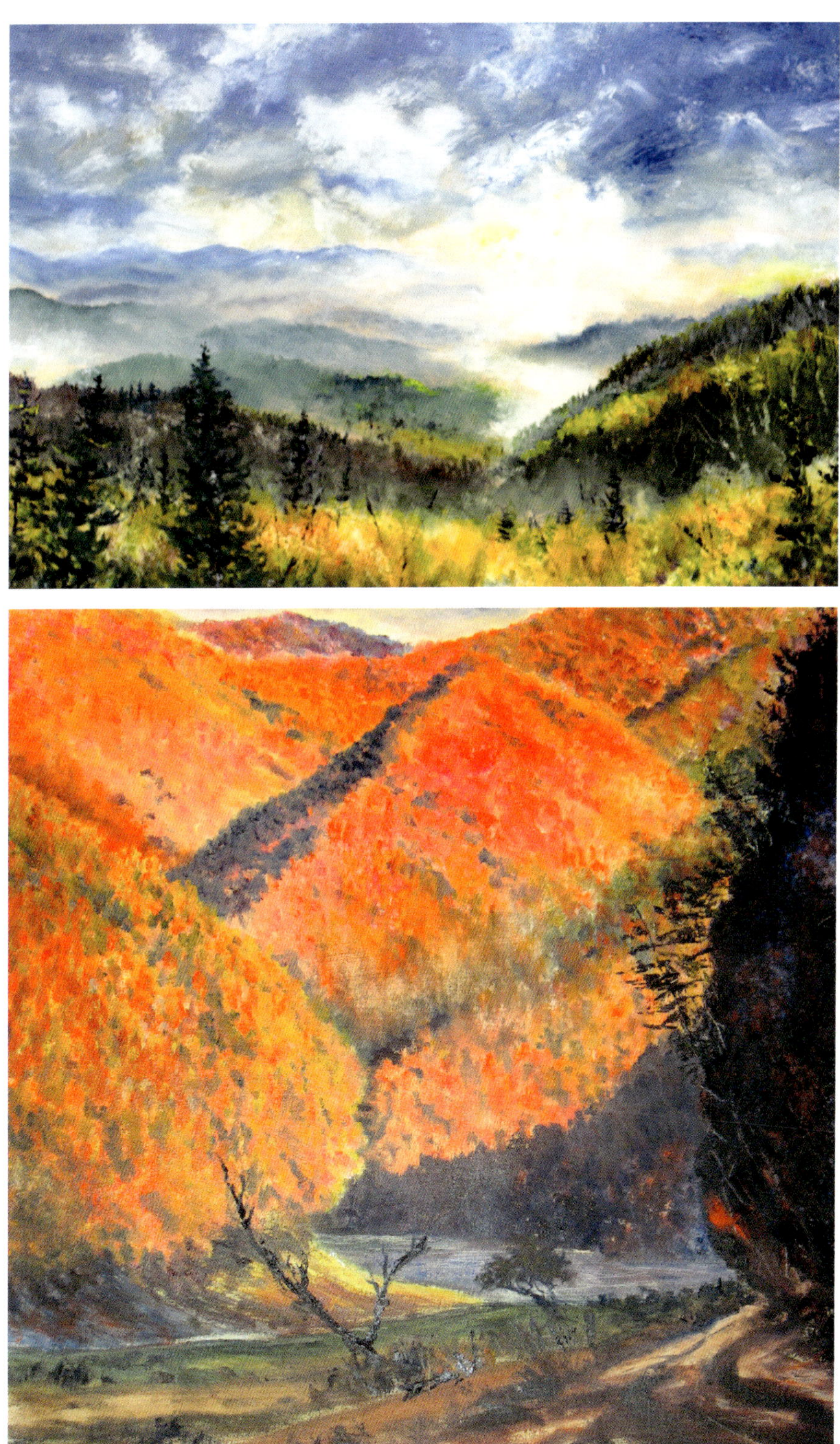

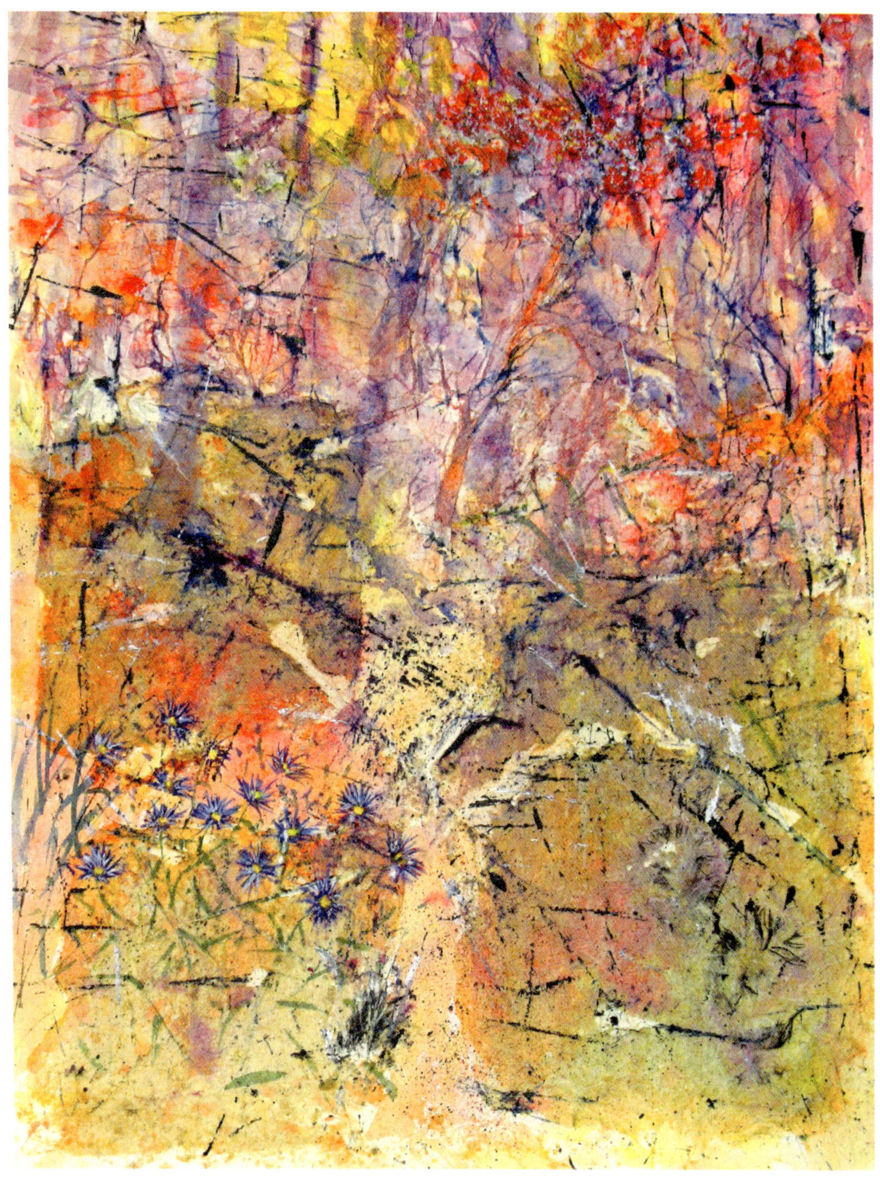

ABOVE *Farewell to Summer*. Asters are colloquially called "Farewell to Summer." This is a seep on one of our back trails that is often filled with sunlight when I take my trail walks in September. There are often downed trees and scattered debris in this area, as well as the fall asters lit by the sunlight. I used mixed media to portray how I feel at this particular pause on my walk.

OPPOSITE, TOP *The Tuckaseigee in Fall Glory*. I decided to paint the river at a point where it flows wildly past old N.C. 288. Instead of painting in a traditional manner, I used a painting knife, tissues, sponge and my fingers. Unorthodox, maybe, but I think it helped to convey the energy of the water. And it was fun.

OPPOSITE, BOTTOM *Birds in Winter Wind*. Who dares to attempt to paint the wind? I dared.

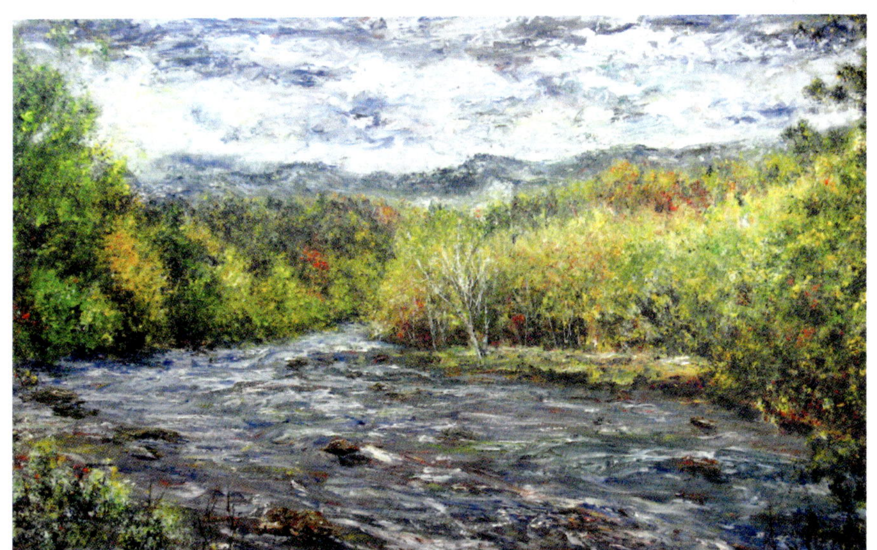

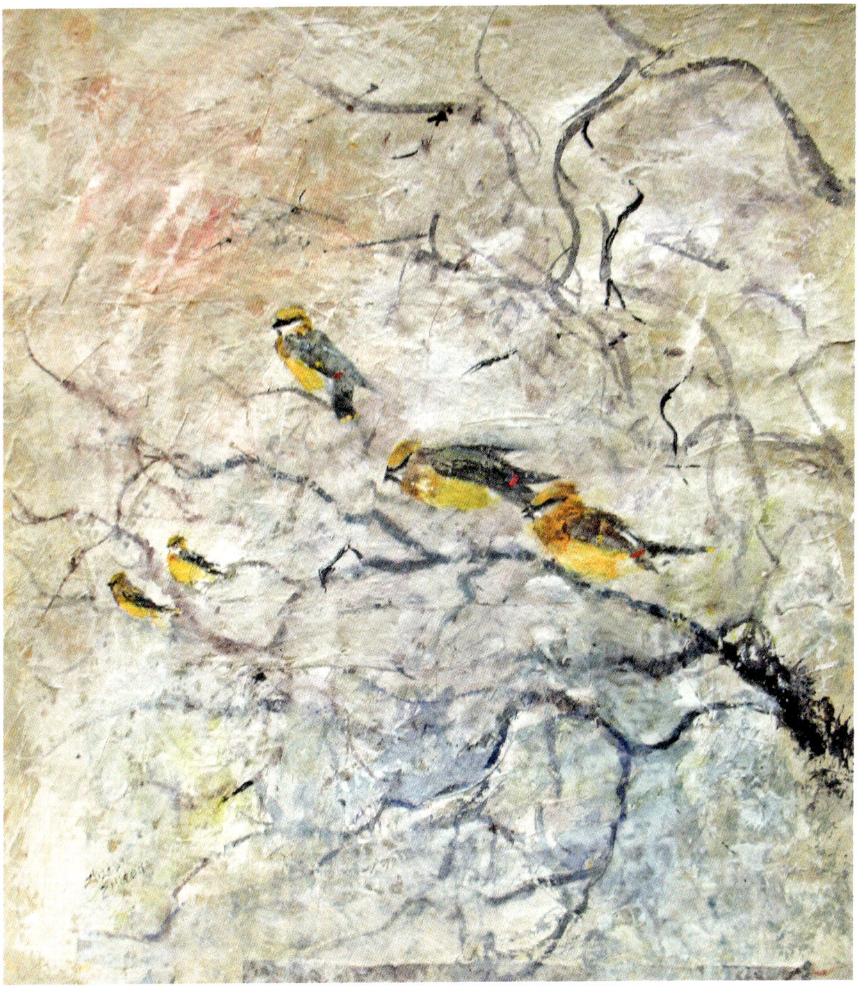

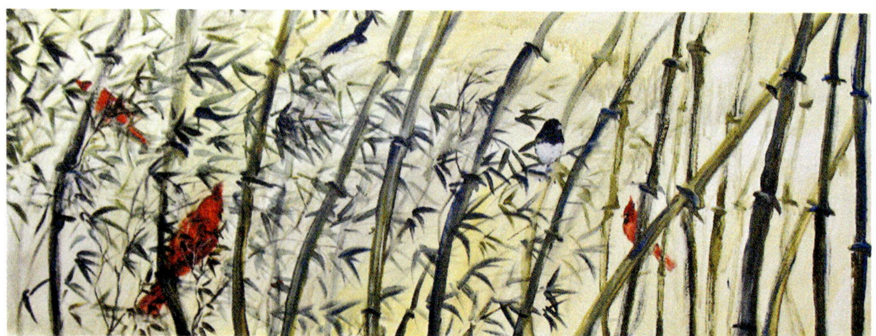

Ann's Bamboo with Birds. My friend Ann Smith loves bamboo and has planted many areas with the clumping variety. There was a stiff wind on this day, and birds were seeking shelter among the swaying bamboo canes. Ann incorporates canes and leaves of bamboo in her fine art assemblages. Occasionally, we make paper from the canes, which we both use in our art endeavors.

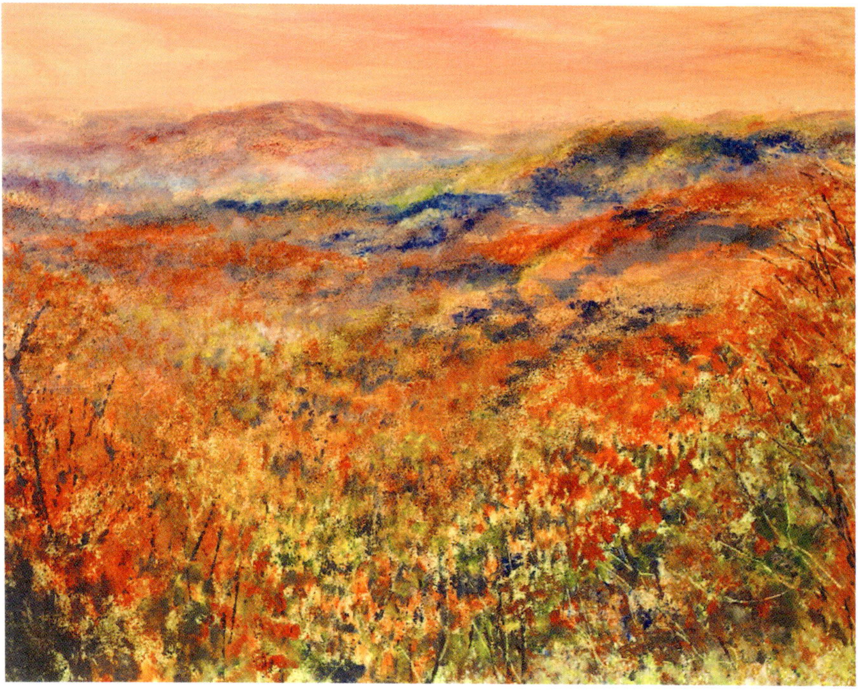

Light Floods the Mountains. Someone once said that painting is all about the light, and I mostly agree. Along with depicting light, I also love to paint with warm colors. It makes me happy.

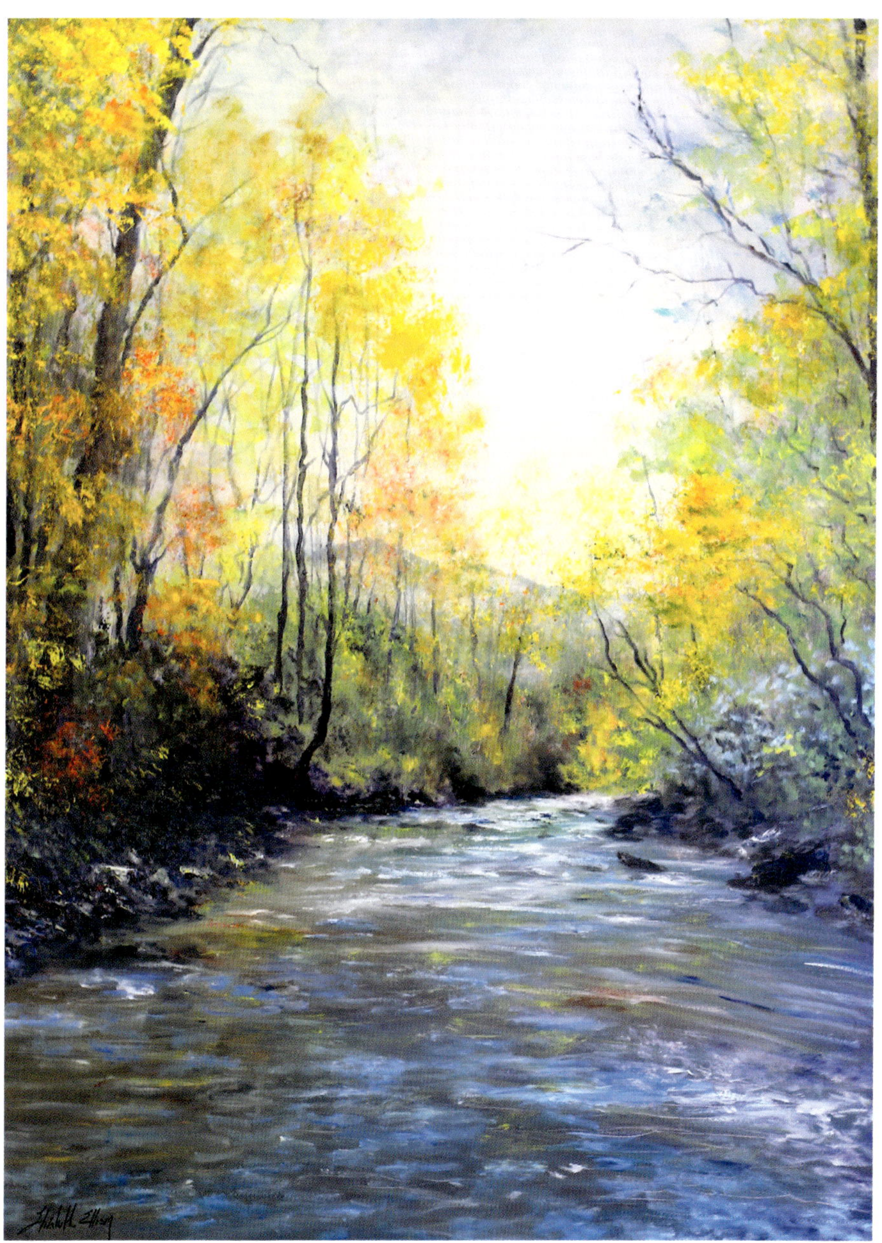

Downstream. The Tuckaseigee River flows through the small town of Bryson City. I have a lovely view of the river through my upstairs studio window. The colors reflected on the surface of the clear water constantly change with the light. On this day, the water seemed relatively still and peaceful.

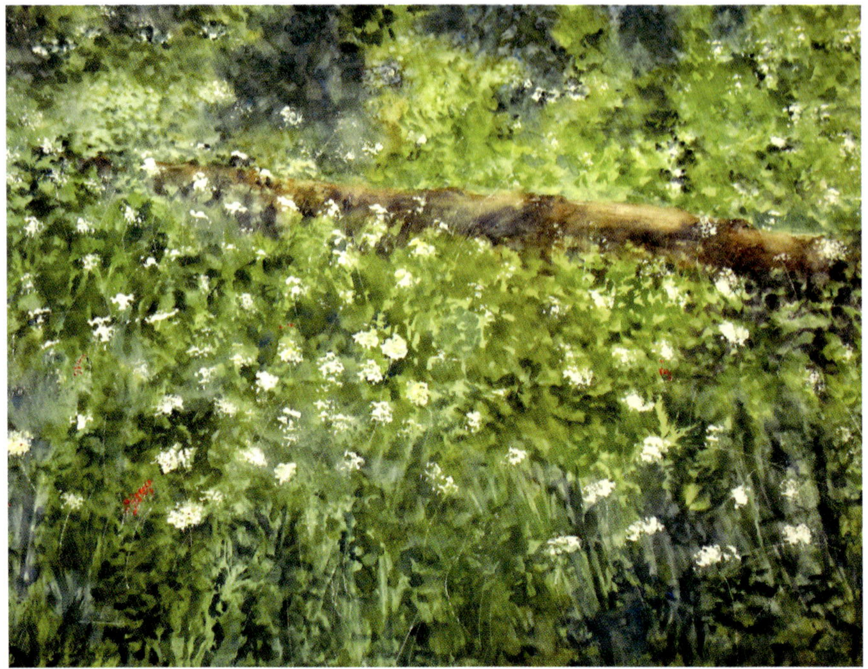

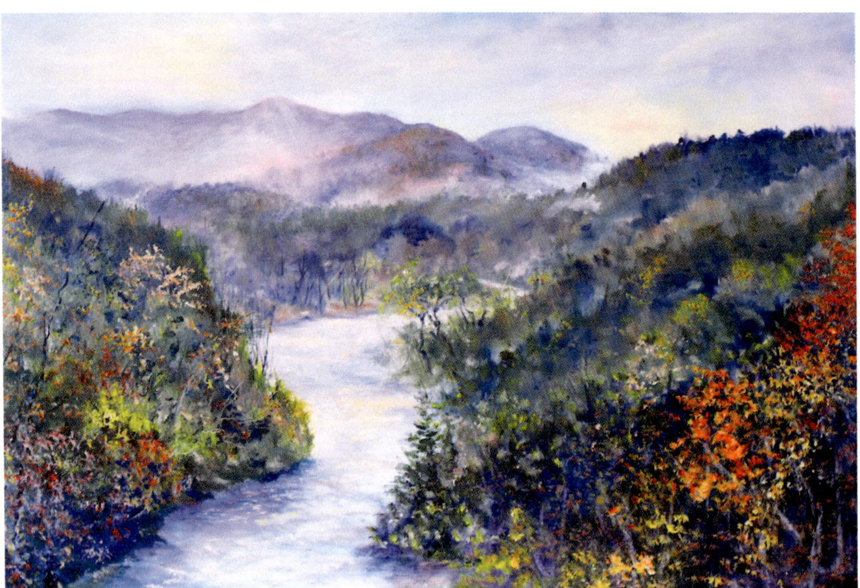

TOP *Flowers for the Fallen*. On the way home from the studio, I spotted this fallen tree in a small clearing. Queen Anne's lace added natural decoration. The combination of the tree and flowers made me feel both sad and happy. Regeneration, and the cycle of life and decay, keeps this earth in existence as we now know it.

BOTTOM *The Tuckaseigee from the Ridge/Old 288*. A view from the saddle of the ridge above our house. This is the place where I love to pause and catch my breath on my morning walk. The trail continues to climb, but I feel refreshed from the pause and lovely view.

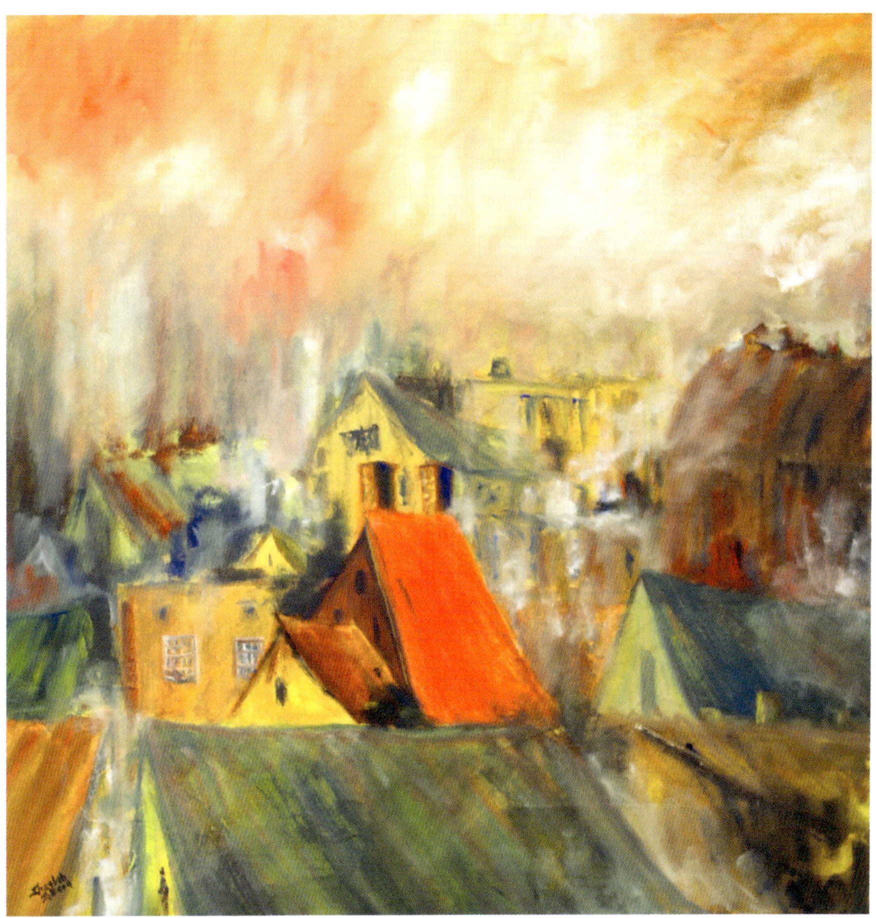

ABOVE *House with a Red Roof/Breaking Light.* Years ago, while waiting for George to return from a business call in the *Asheville Citizen-Times* newspaper building, I noticed a house with a red roof in Asheville's Montfort District. I made a drawing on a discarded envelope. I later painted a since-sold watercolor based on this drawing. I found the sketch a few years ago and did another painting, this time in oils. I incorporated some old buildings from the River Arts District in Asheville and added a few other buildings that are actually located in Bryson City. I do not paint many urban scenes, but I am glad I did this one—a nice, warm feeling there.

FOLLOWING *Just to Know It's There.* Charlies Bunion is one of the jagged cliffs that are underlain with Precambrian metamorphic rock known as Anakeesta. Anakeesta rock produces sulfuric acid when exposed to the elements. If it reaches streams and rivers, it can create acidic conditions and harm aquatic life. I find the rocks themselves beautiful with tones of blues, violets and ochre (a range of brownish yellow or red colors). We have Anakeesta rock on our property. I ground some and crumbled it onto my canvas, using an acrylic gel that seals the rock and adheres to the canvas. So, the rock itself helps to color this depiction of Charlies Bunion.

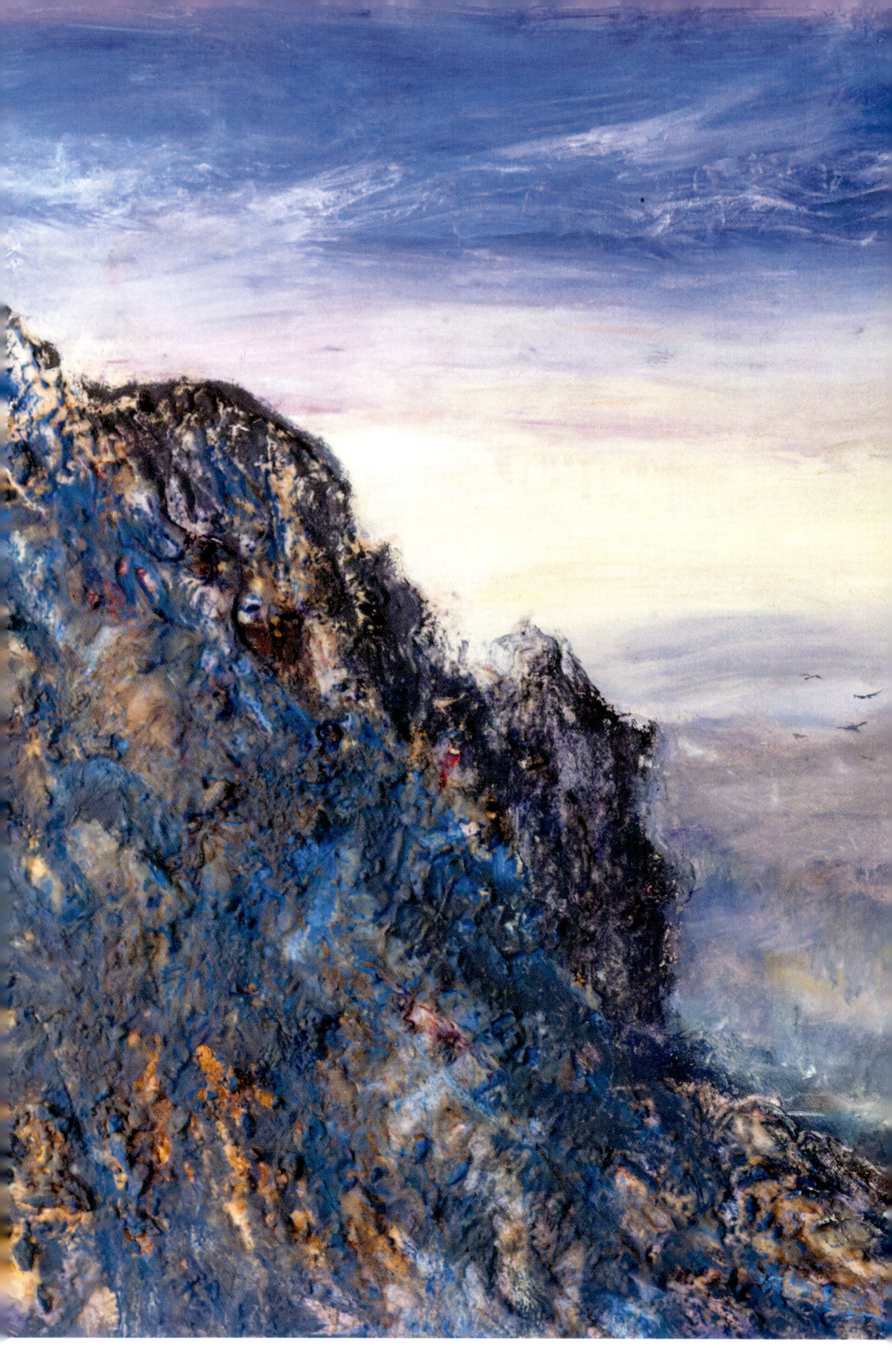

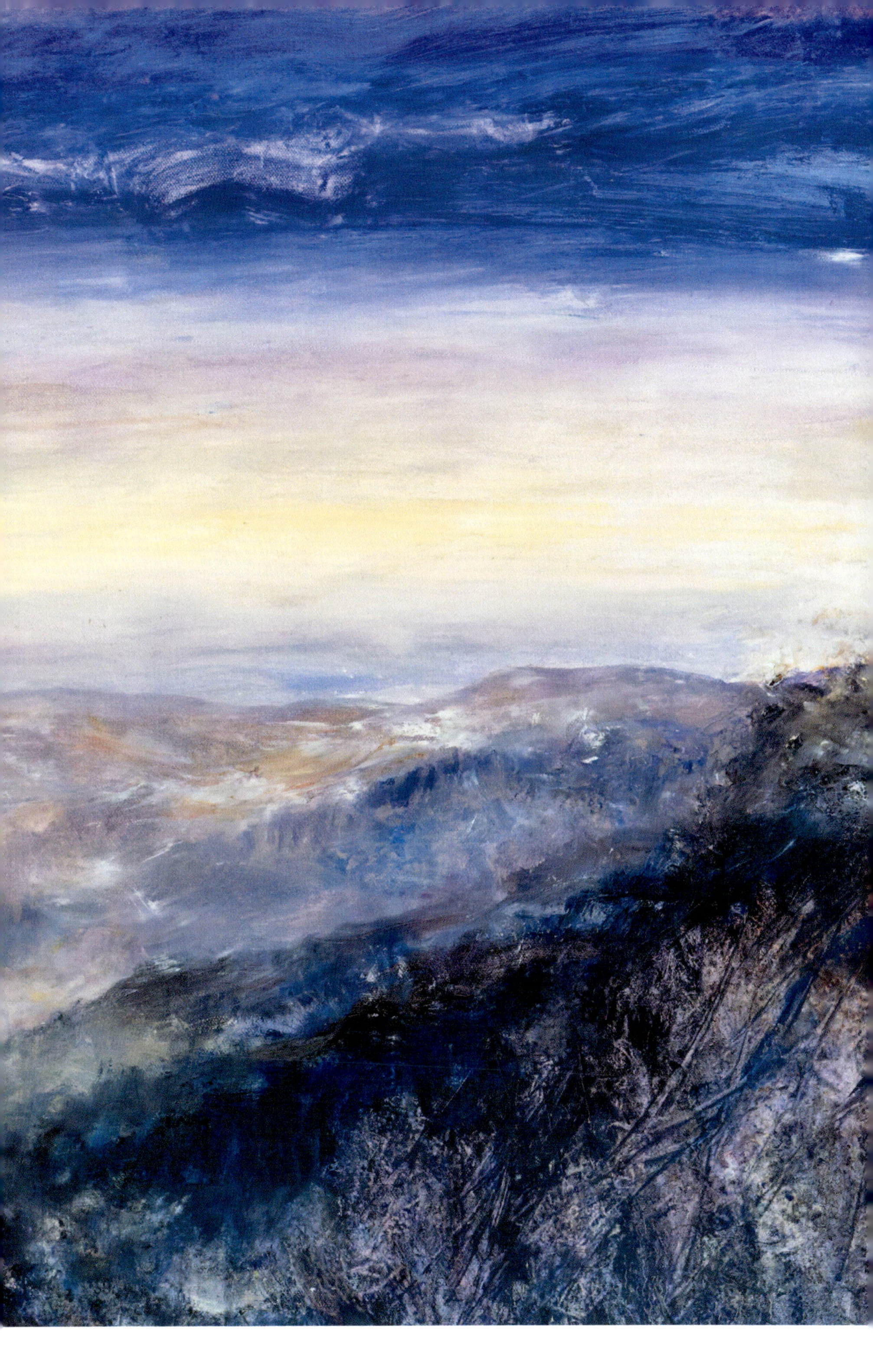

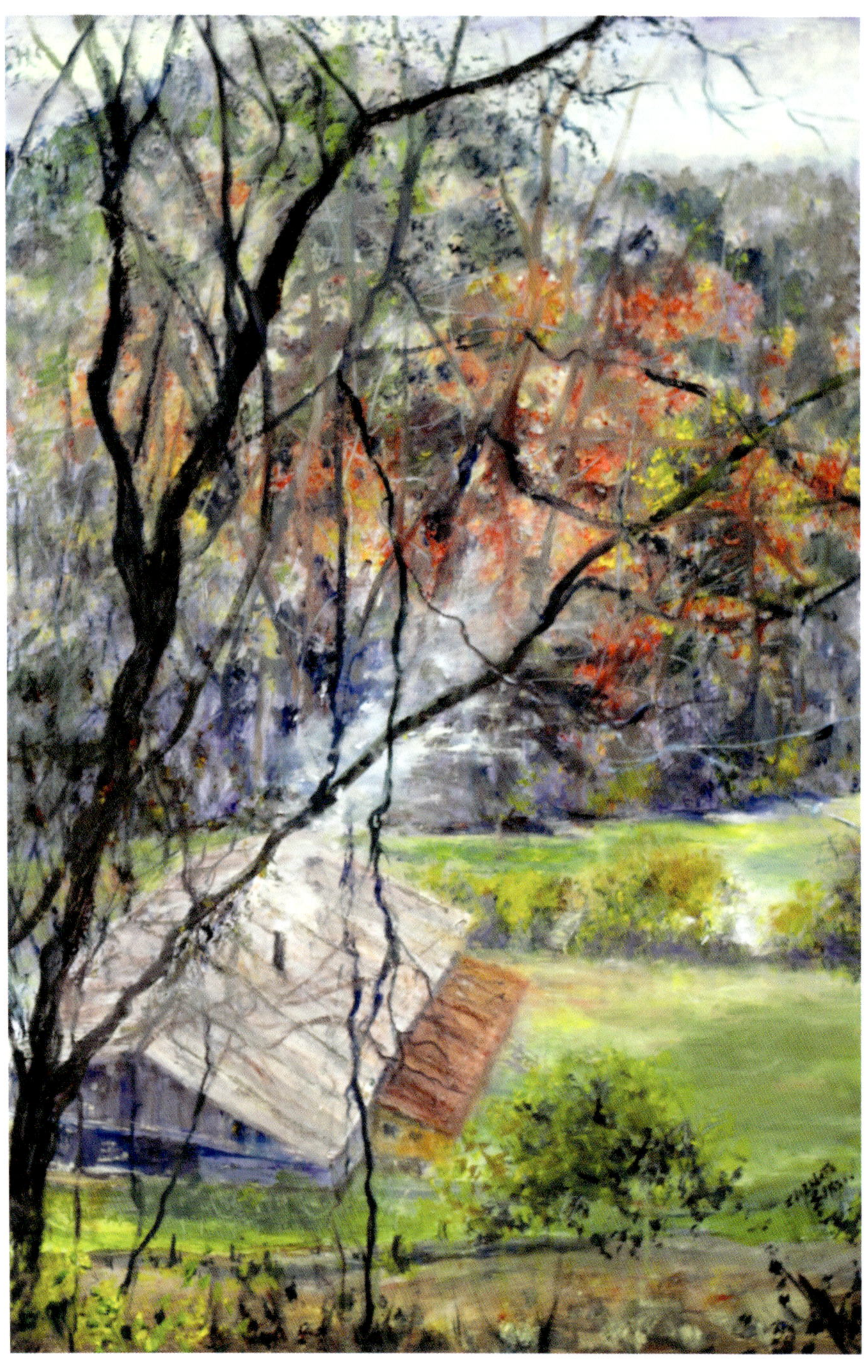

Take the Road Through Windy Gap. You leave Windy Gap and descend steeply into the Lands Creek watershed. Our small abode is located in what George called a catchment basin because of the high ridges that drain water and sediment into the creek. From there, the water carries it into the Tuckaseigee River and, ultimately, to the Gulf of Mexico. The creek makes a sharp turn near our house and enters the Great Smoky Mountains National Park and Fontana Lake.

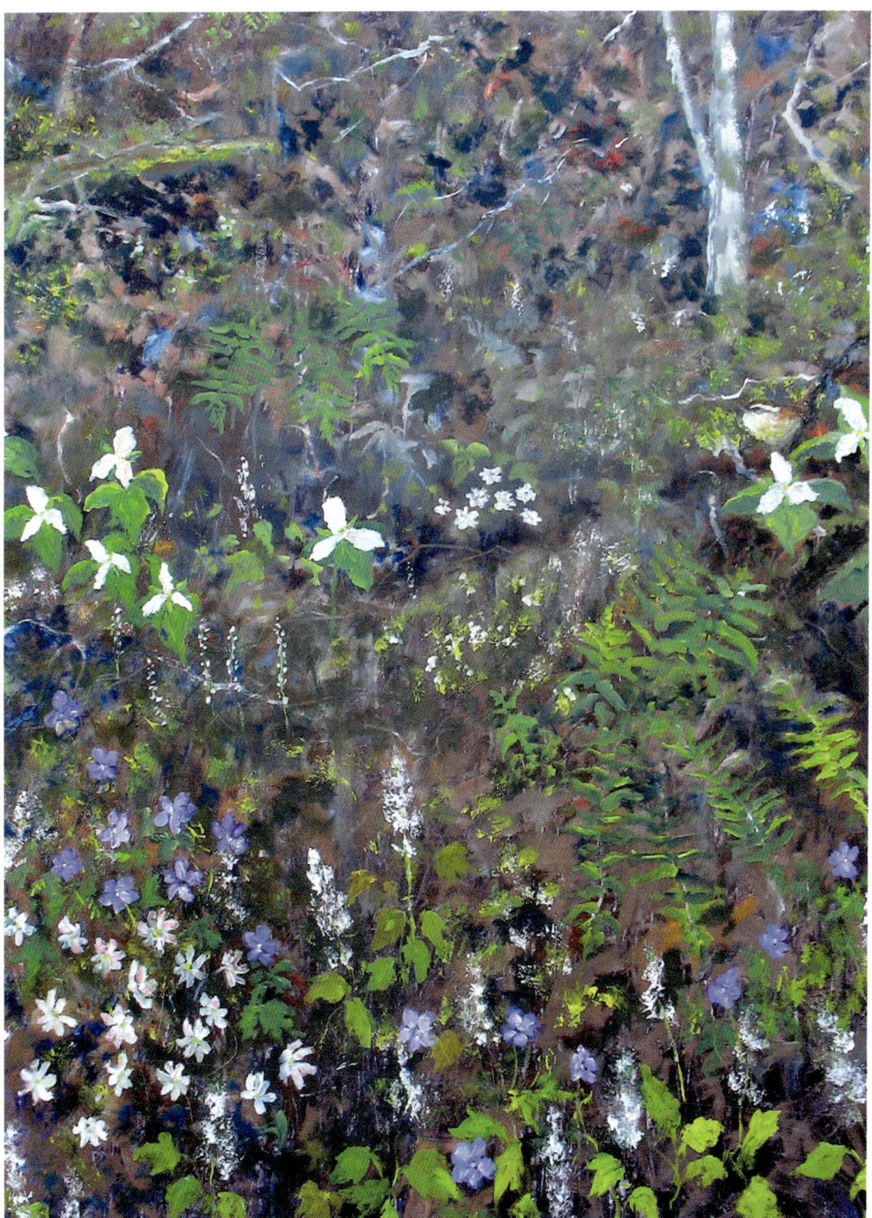

The Bank with Wildflowers and Wren. The bank depicted here runs a short distance beside Lands Creek before turning into the park. The rock formation consists primarily of gneiss (made up of feldspar, quartz and mica). The soil is very rich, and in the spring, there are so many different wildflowers it is lovely. Our resident Carolina wrens love this area. We are particularly pleased to have the area permanently protected.

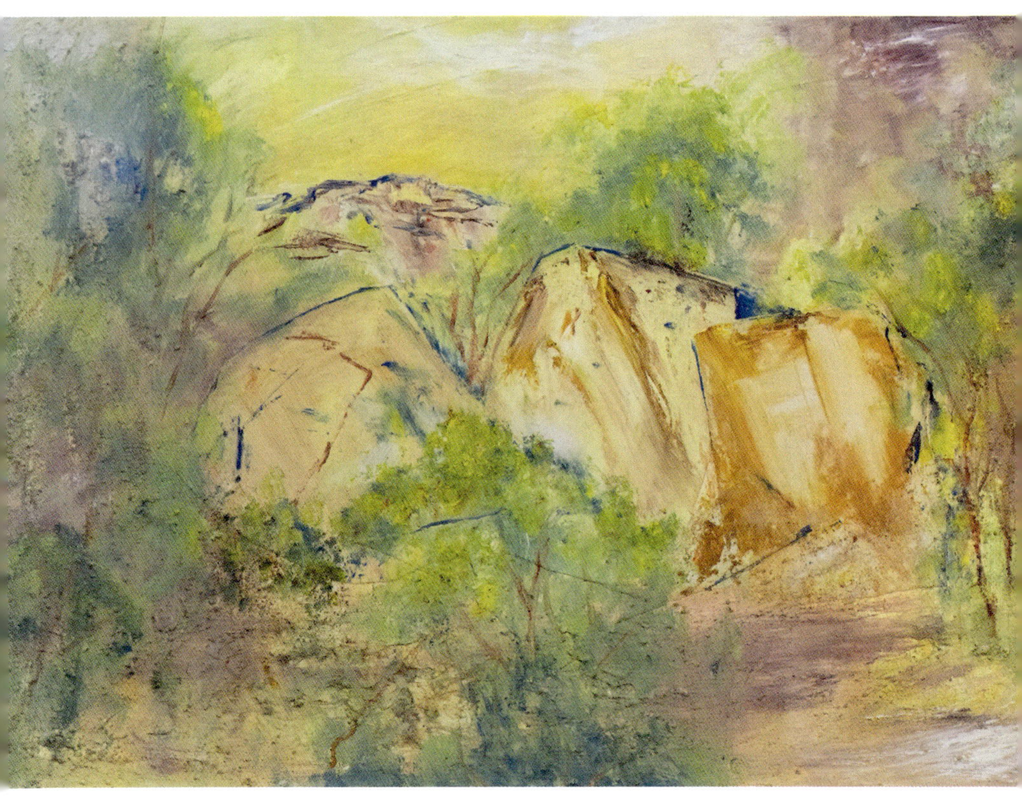

ABOVE *Boulders/Jackson County (The Garden of the Goddesses)*. Some of the rock formations near Whiteside Mountain in Jackson County seem worthy of harboring ancient spirits. I like to think they are there, drifting among the boulders.

OPPOSITE *Almost Floating*. On the last trip I made to Mount LeConte Lodge with my friends Pat and Philip Chamburs, the trail that descends to Alum Caves was seriously washed out. I had to cling to the cable that is attached to rocks beside the trail (the trail has since been repaired). I do not like heights or feeling almost suspended in space, so I looked straight ahead in order to not freak out. Then the hikers ahead of me stopped and started taking pictures. Maybe I started composing this painting then—I had to get my mind on something other than the open space beside me.

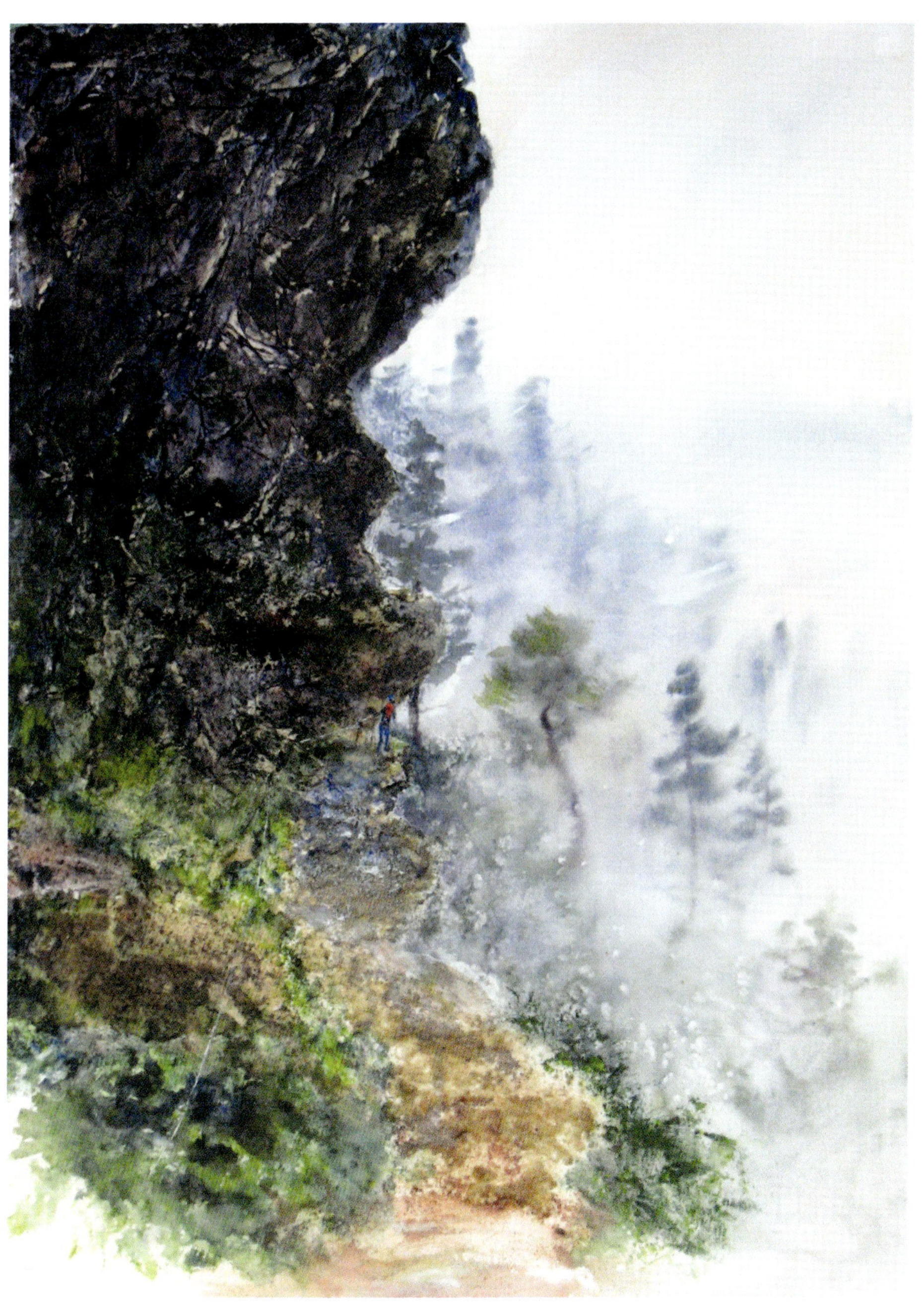

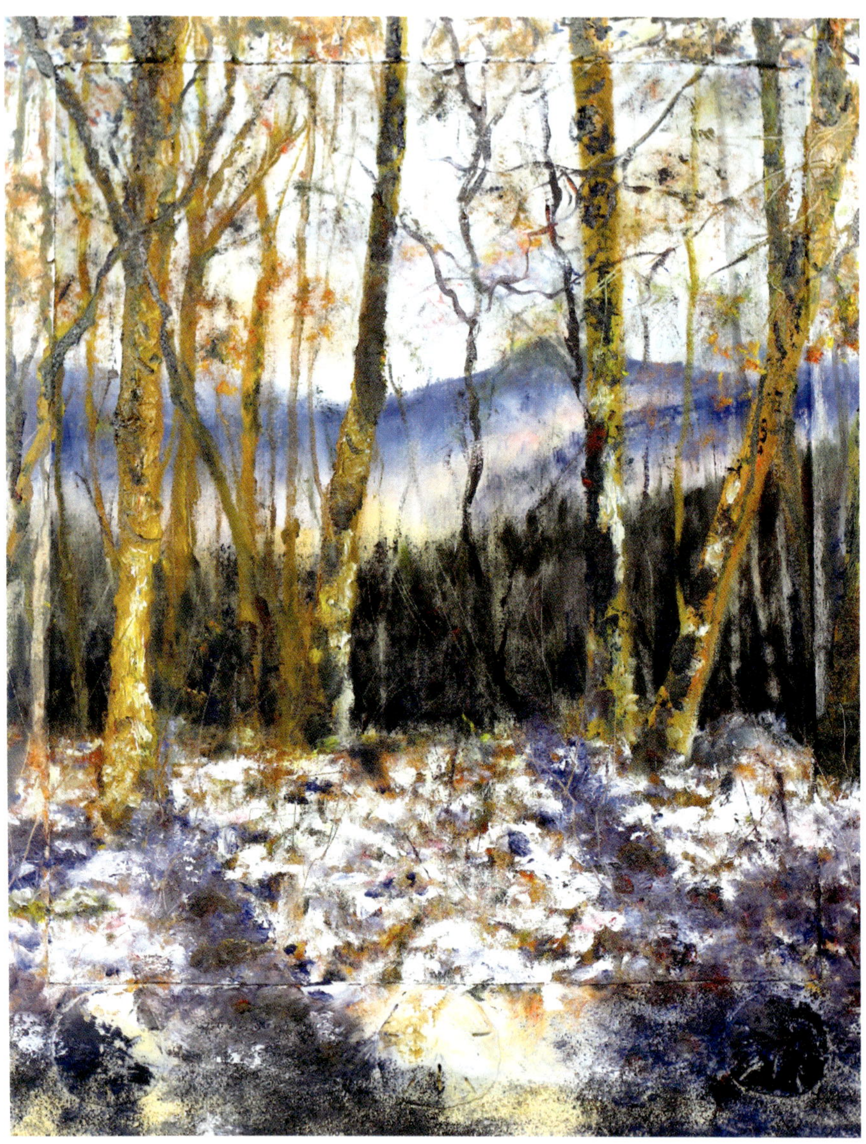

Took a Long Time to Get Back Here. National geologic surveys of the Great Smokies tell us that sedimentary rocks were formed 450 to 540 million years ago as part of a shallow marine continental margin. Limestone rocks in the Smokies can contain fossils. This leads me to why this painting contains sand dollars that I found on a barrier island in the Gulf of Mexico. I doubt there are fossils of sand dollars here in the Smokies, but it's a pleasant thought, and so these three are a part of this painting of trees along the high ridge of our property.

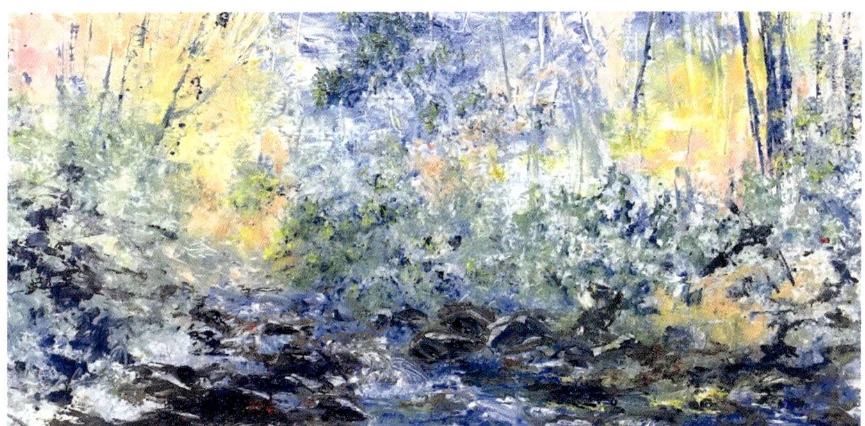

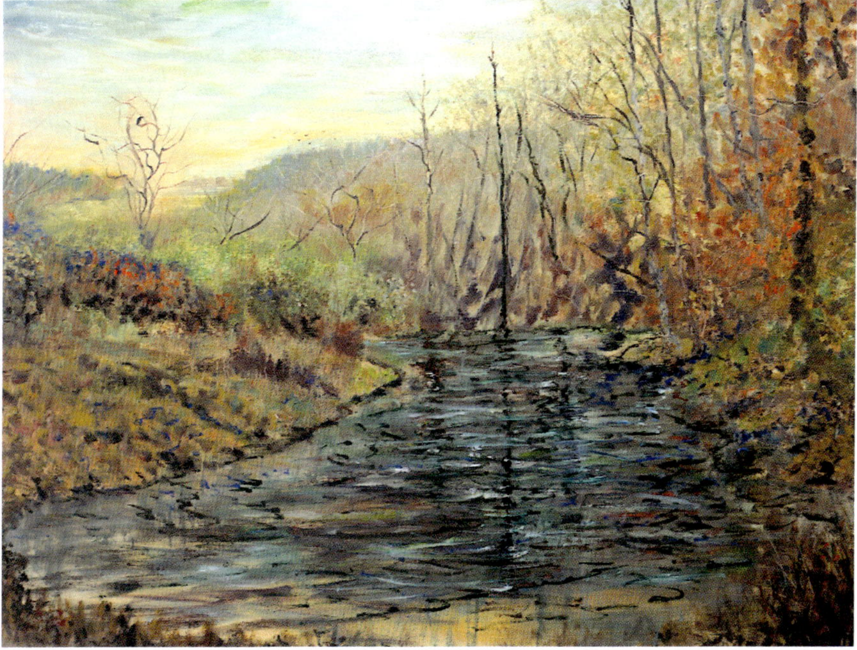

TOP *Kephart Prong*. Kephart Prong Trail crosses the Oconoluftee River beside U.S. 441 through the Smokies, from Oconoluftee Visitor Center to Sugarlands near Gatlinburg, Tennessee. I think it a wonderful area to visit and a rather challenging, but interesting, hike from the trailhead to Kephart Prong shelter.

BOTTOM *The Slough at Kituwah*. The Cherokees revere Kituwah as the motherland of the Cherokee Nation. The lands are very peaceful, situated as they are along or near the Tuckaseigee River. It feels like a spiritual place, and we all respect that and feel the spirit of the ancient Cherokees. The slough in my painting changes every time we visit, but it is always a wonderful place to bird. Sometimes it is aloud with birdsong. I also love the vegetation found in the area—it, and the water, seems filled with an energy that is different from rapidly flowing creeks or branches.

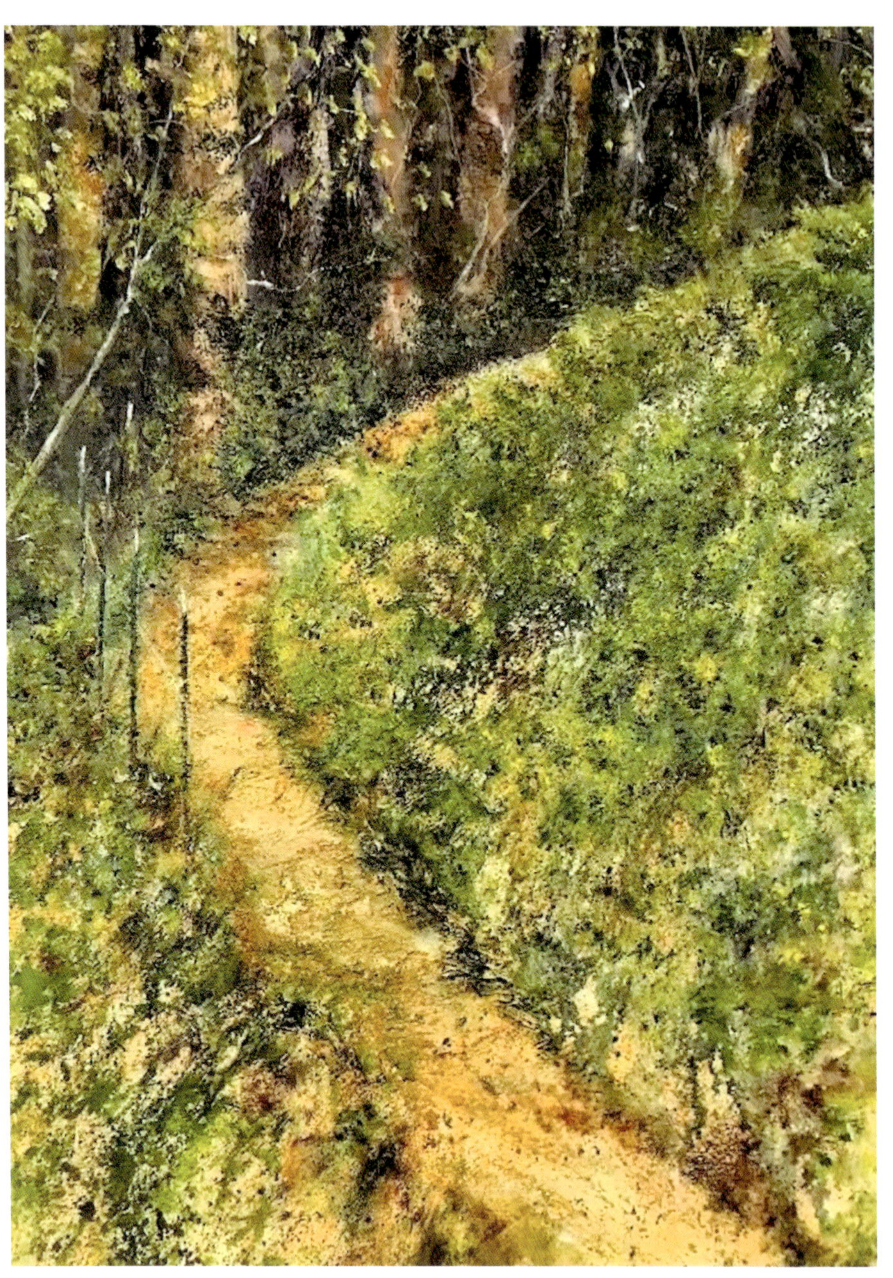

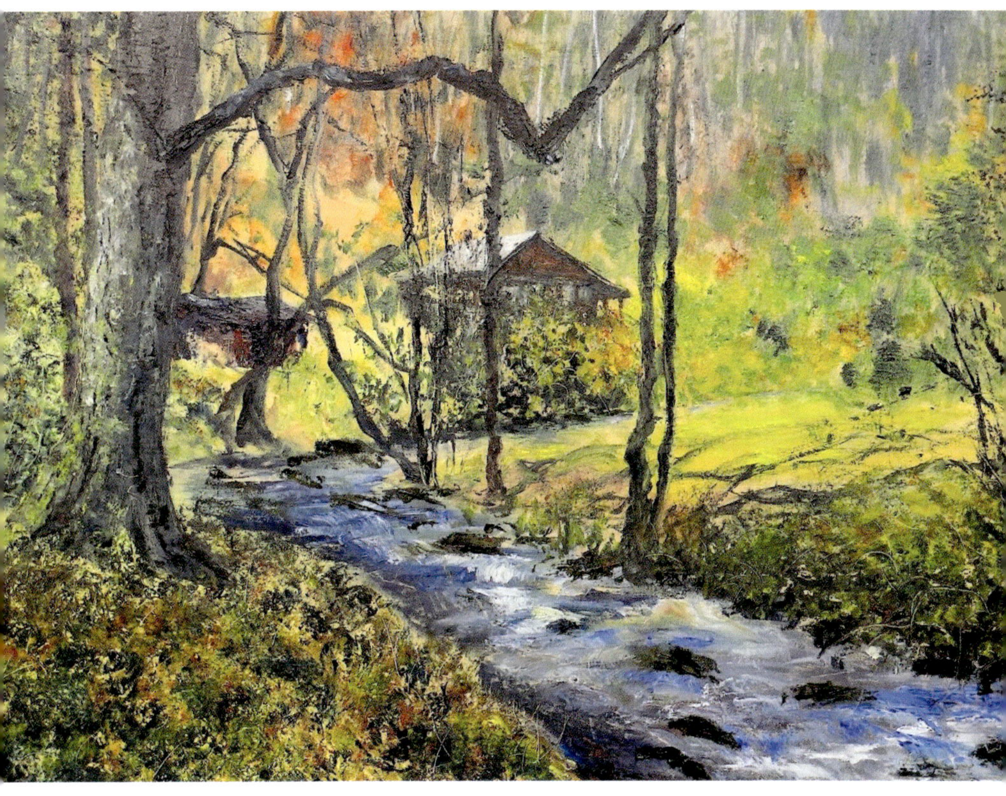

OPPOSITE *Sunshine and Shadow*. This is the narrow path to the reservoir, which catches spring water and serves as our water supply. The overflow helps feed Lands Creek and the Tuckaseigee River. George spread some of his good friend Fred Houk's ashes alongside the branch, and thus this path, which is visible from our dining area.

ABOVE *Beyond the Basswood Tree*. The large basswood growing on the bank of the creek near our house marks a special memory. When George and I for the first time followed the old wagon road from the river, it led to a path beside the creek. When we got to the tree, we saw the shack where we lived for about twenty years. The tree remains sort of a cornerstone of the turn our lives took.

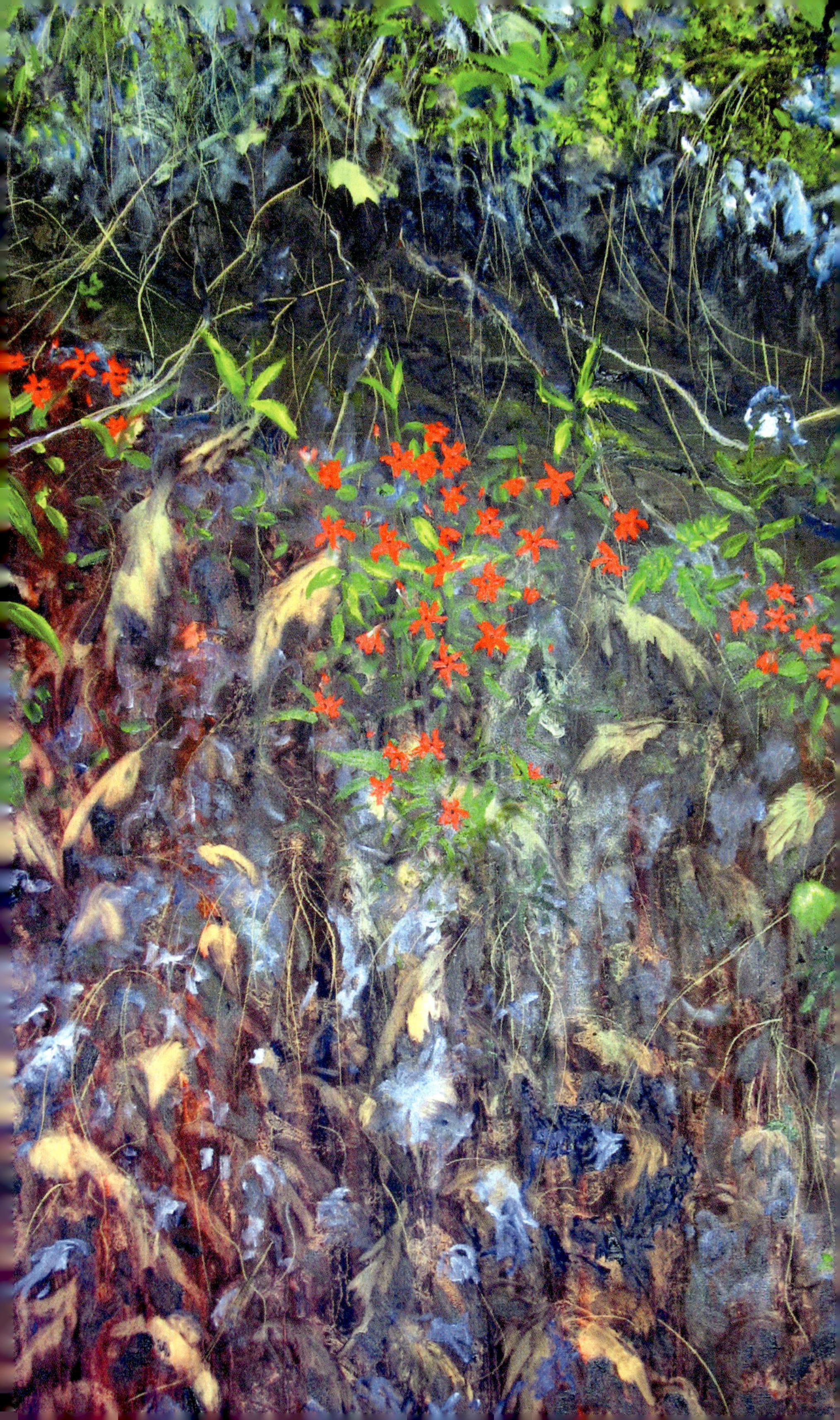

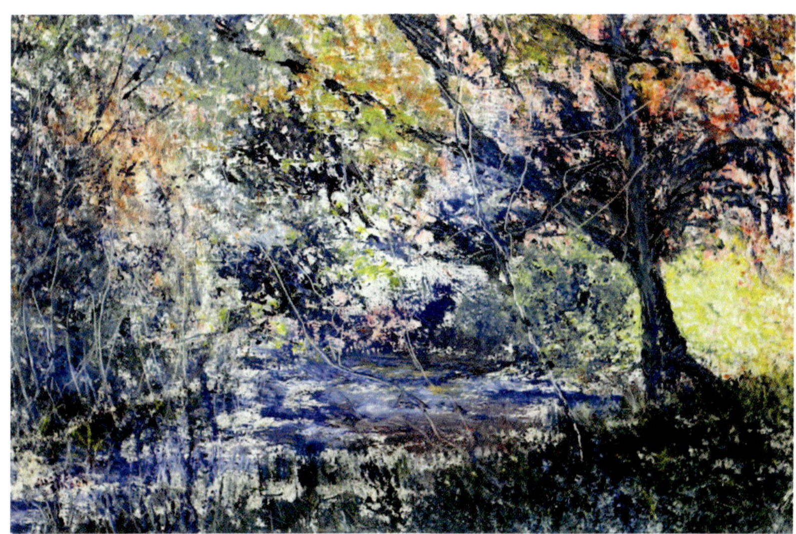

OPPOSITE *The Warbler's Song.* And I sing with him that at this moment, in this place, everything is perfect!

ABOVE *Spring Comes to the Valley.* In early spring, the vegetation around the creek quickly changes. The forsythia bush, caught in intense sunlight, lights up the bank as the creek makes its turn into the park and to the Tuckaseigee River.

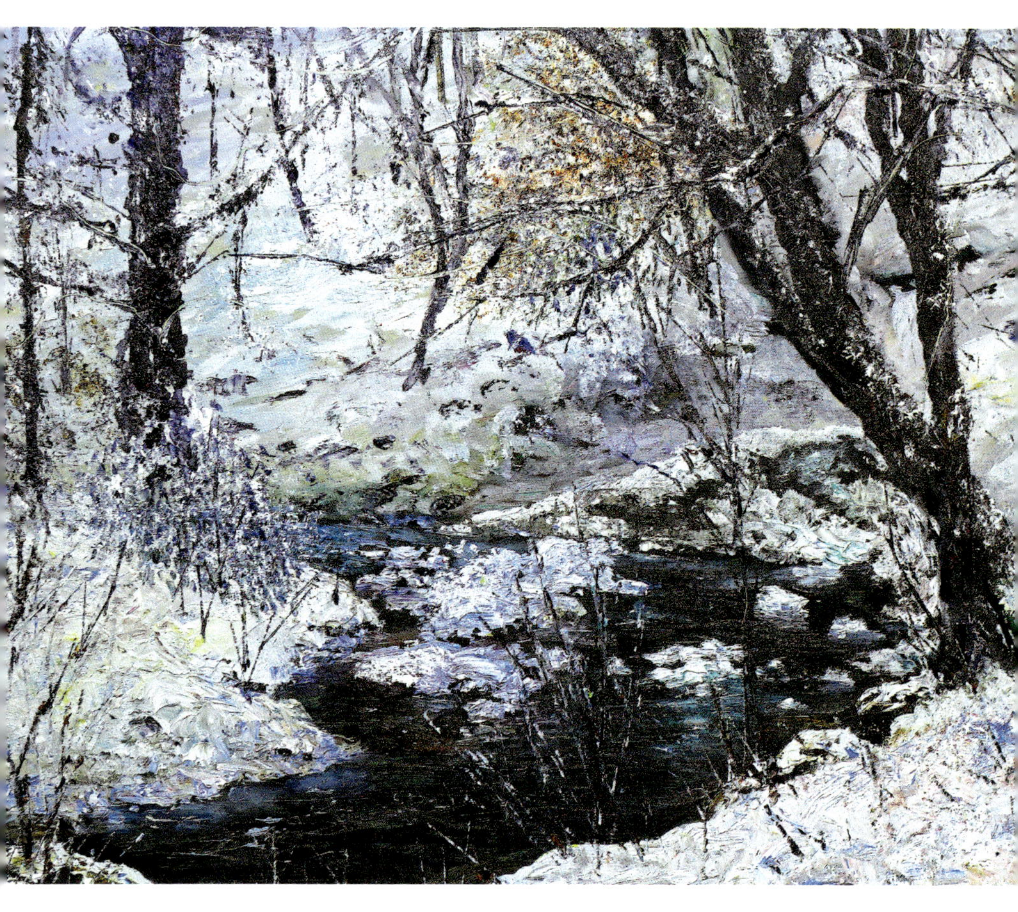

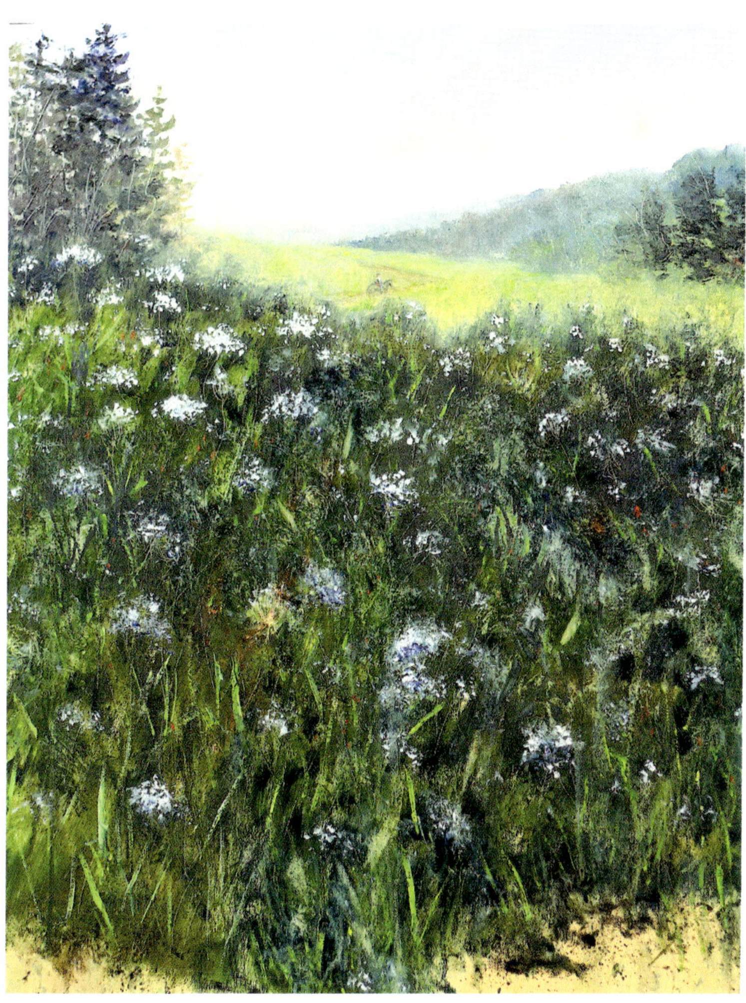

OPPOSITE *Stones in the Creekbed.* The title of this painting is a line from a haiku George wrote that I have always loved. This is, again, the turn the creek makes in its journey to the river and, eventually, the Gulf of Mexico.

ABOVE *Those Halcyon Days.* I tried to keep the horse and rider dreamy to enhance the feeling of those wine-and-roses days, whatever they might have been to each of us. The field of Queen Anne's lace, an ordinary roadside and waste-area flower, yet which so many of us love, is the real focus.

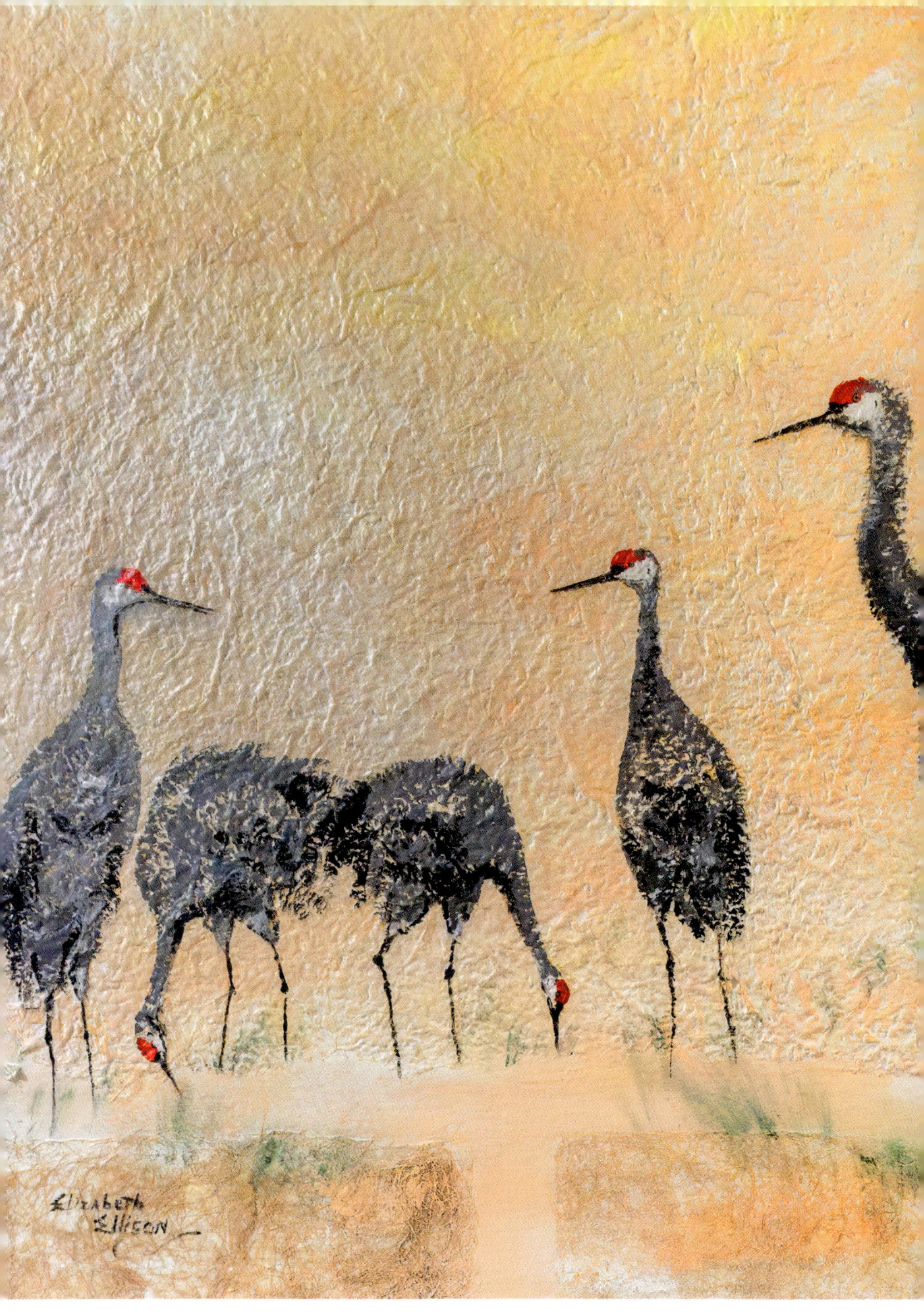

Sandhill Cranes. On occasion, sandhill cranes put in an appearance in Western North Carolina. This canvas incorporates handmade paper.

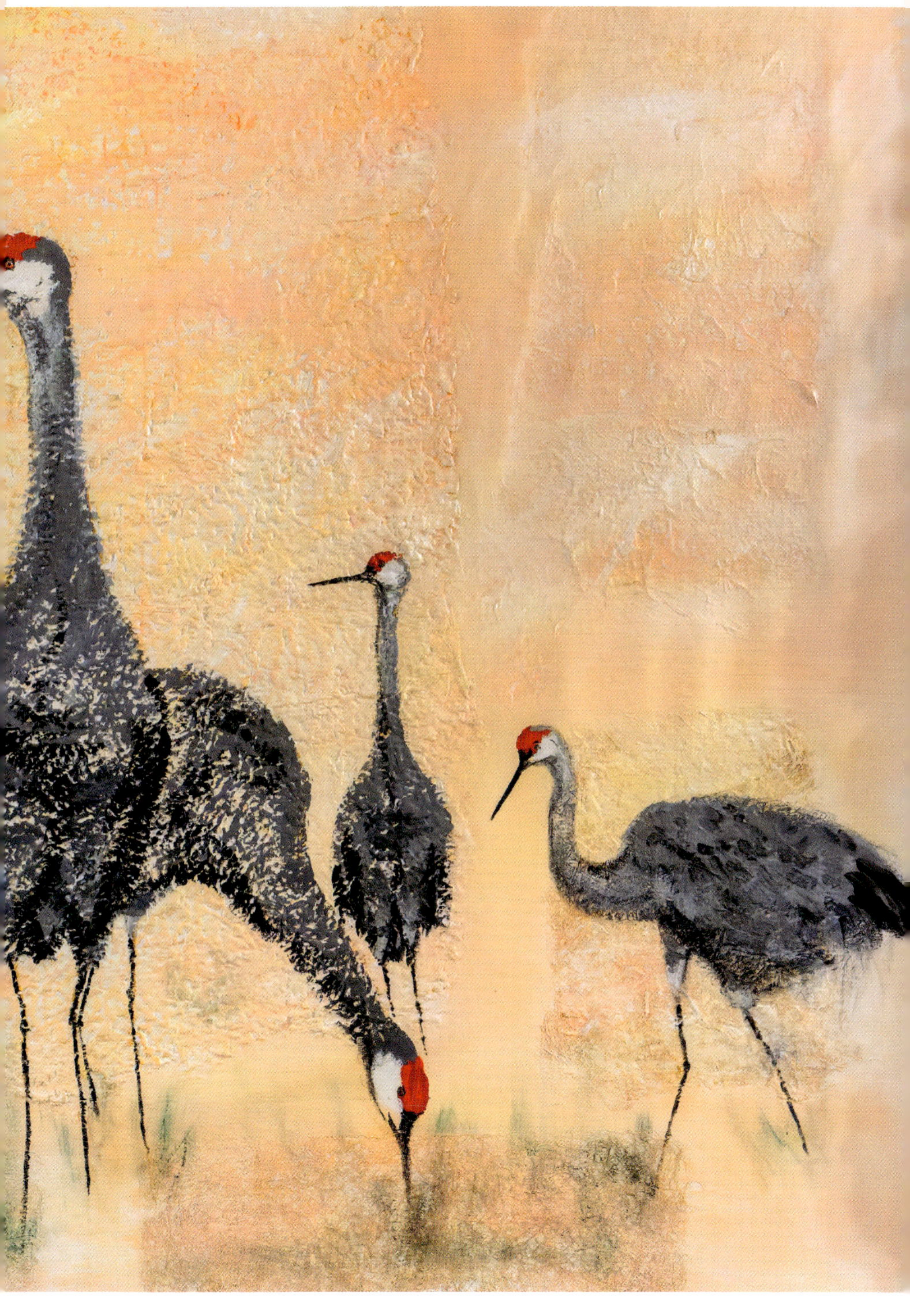

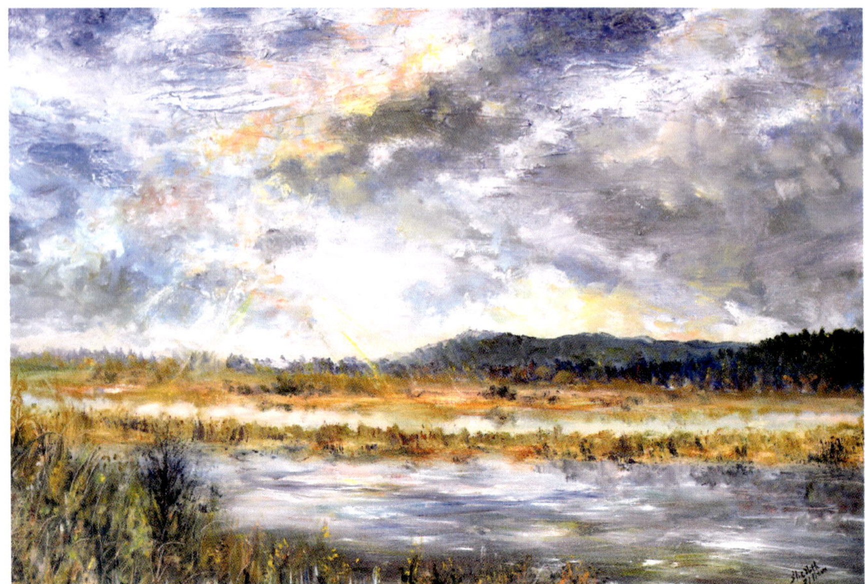

The Shining Water. The wetland areas near the headwaters of Nantahala River inspired this canvas. It is based on a memory of that area after torrential rains.

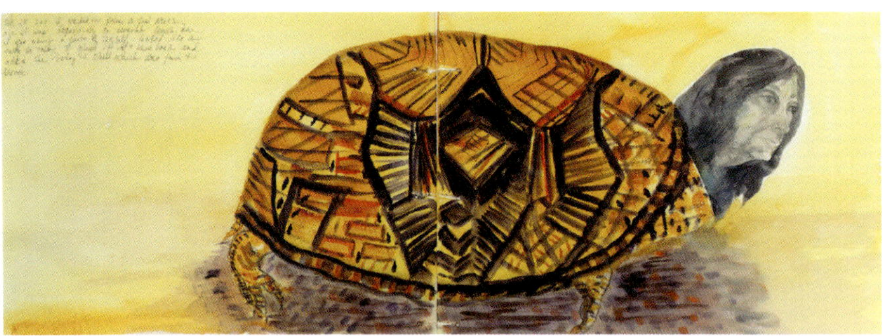

Herself as a Turtle. Wouldn't it be nice to carry your shell on your back, into which you could withdraw whenever things seem unsafe or out of control? And what fun to release yourself once again, to continue on your slow and thoughtful journey. This is a page from one of my journals—it serves as a self-portrait.

ACKNOWLEDGEMENTS

We wish to thank Ann Smith, family friend and skilled editor, for compiling George's poetry after his death. None of this would have been possible without her help. We also thank Janet McCue, who cherished George as we did and who wrote the introduction to this book.

Additionally, for their advice, editing support, encouragement and inspiration, we thank Frances Figart, Monica and George Brown, Monty and Diana Clampitt, Lydia Aydlett and Ashley Hornsby Welch and her employees with the 43rd Prosecutorial District, as well as colleagues at the *Asheville Citizen-Times*, the *Franklin Press*, the *Smoky Mountain News* and the *Sylva Herald*.

Special thanks are owed to Arcadia Publishing/The History Press for its publishing excellence, particularly Banks Smither and Ryan Finn.

ABOUT THE AUTHORS

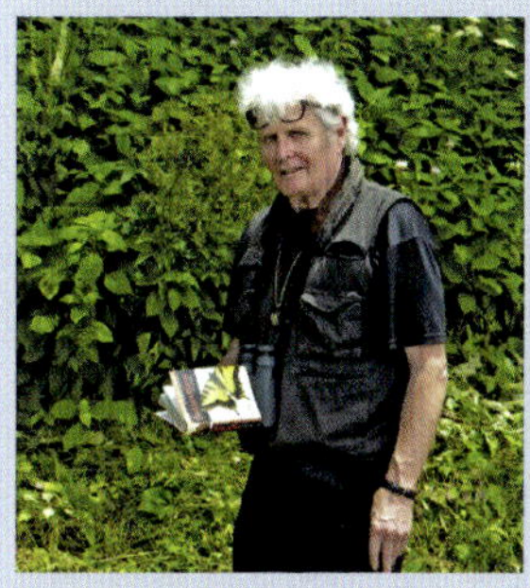

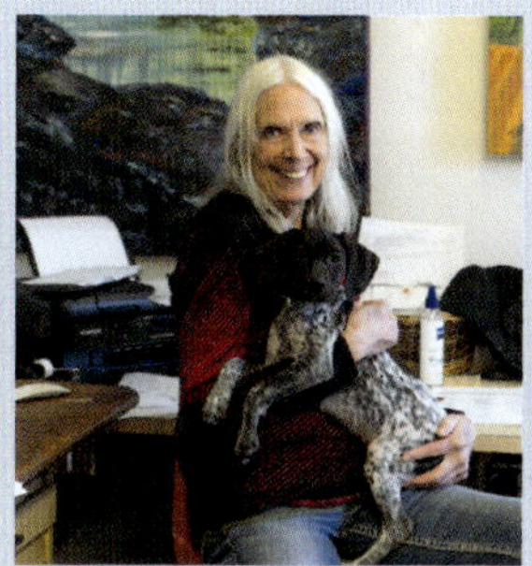

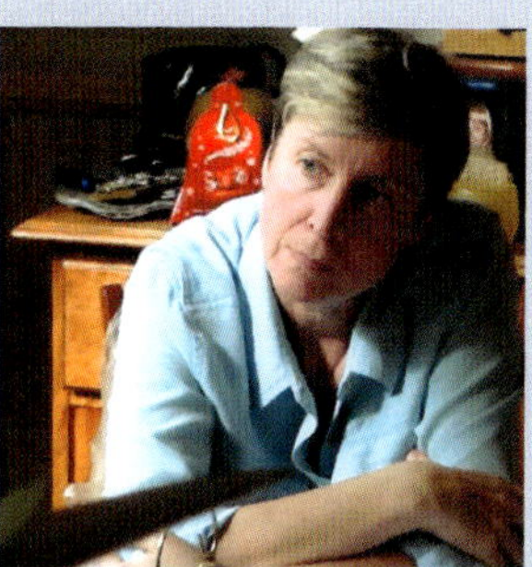

George Ellison was an iconic writer of Western North Carolina and lived directly adjacent to the Great Smoky Mountains National Park and near Qualla Boundary, home to the Eastern Band of Cherokee Indians. His columns appeared in the *Asheville Citizen-Times, Chinquapin: The Newsletter of the Southern Appalachian* and the *Smoky Mountain News*. He was the author of *High Vistas: An Anthology of Nature Writing from Western North Carolina and the Great Smoky Mountains*; *Mountain Passages: National and Cultural History of Western North Carolina and the Great Smoky Mountains; Permanent Camp: Poems, Narratives and Renderings from the Smokies*; and *Literary Excursions of the Southern Highlands: Essays on Natural History*, as well as coauthor of *Back of Beyond: A Horace Kephart Biography*.

Elizabeth Ellison is a professional artist who resides in Western North Carolina. She has been owner/operator of Elizabeth Ellison Gallery in Bryson City since 1986, and her work is widely collected in the United States and other countries. She works in oil and other mediums and often incorporates her handmade plant fiber paper into her paintings. Her work is singular and strongly expresses her immersion in the natural world.

Quintin Ellison is a writer and photographer who enjoys documenting the people and places of Western North Carolina. She grew up in Bryson City and now lives in Sylva. Quintin worked in newspapers for twenty-eight years as a reporter, editor and manager. She has written articles and taken photographs for tourism groups, nonprofits and magazines in North Carolina and beyond. In addition to street photography, Quintin is an avid wildlife photographer.

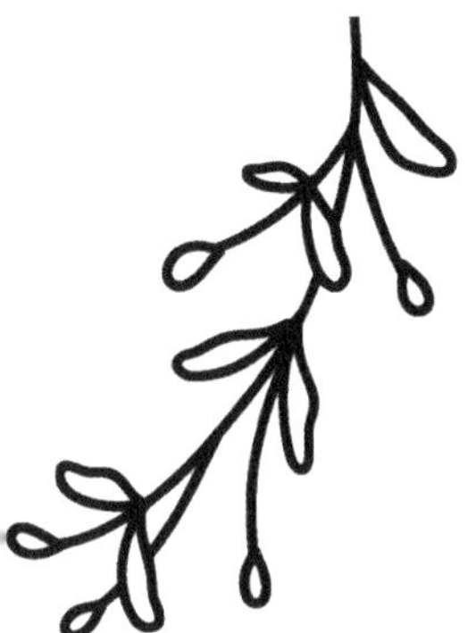

Visit us at

www.historypress.com

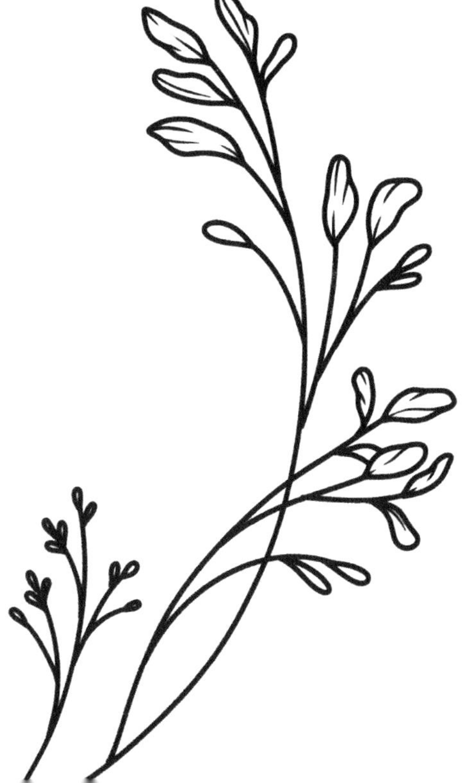